Healthy Intelligent Training

Healthy Intelligent Training

The Proven Principles of Arthur Lydiard

Dr. Keith Livingstone

Meyer & Meyer Sport

British Library Cataloguing in Publication Data
A catalogue record for this book is available from the British Library

Keith Livingstone – Healthy Intelligent Training
Maidenhead: Meyer & Meyer Sport (UK) Ltd., 2009
ISBN: 978-1-84126-311-3

© 2009 by Meyer & Meyer Sport (UK) Ltd.
2nd, extended Edition 2010
Auckland, Beirut, Budapest, Cairo, Cape Town, Dubai, Graz, Indianapolis,
Maidenhead, Melbourne, Olten, Singapore, Tehran, Toronto
Member of the World
Sports Publishers' Association (WSPA)
www.w-s-p-a.org

Printed and bound by: B.O.S.S Druck und Medien GmbH, Germany
ISBN: 978-1-84126-311-3
E-Mail: info@m-m-sports.com
www.m-m-sports.com

Contents

Acknowledgements

This book started as a Powerpoint presentation and 20-page summary sheet for local coaches in Victoria, in late 2005. As athletes and coaches asked more and more questions it became evident that more was needed, and so the book idea was born.

There are many people to thank, and I hope I miss no one. Firstly, my thanks go to my beautiful wife Joanne and her patient parents Graeme and Junette Phillips for all their support. This book could not have been done without them. My mother Valerie McCabe has encouraged me all along and taken great interest in the book's progress. Dr. John Hinwood and Dennis Jones have been a great support during a challenging year while the book came to fruition. Gavin and Allison Richards at MBE Bendigo helped us print the initial drafts for proofreading.

My brother Colin, who has been a tower of strength during the last year, contributed the superb cartoons for this book. Colin was an accomplished runner who has coached local athlete Tim Davies from 17th in Wales to 5th in the world mountain running championships, as well as to 3 victories in the annual race on Mt. Snowdon. Colin's gifted wife Diana Mills took some of the photos in the book. Next, I'd like to thank

Barry Magee, Lorraine Moller, Nobby Hashizume, Vern Walker and Rod and John Dixon for their input, as well as Arch Jelley, Chris Pilone, Nic Bideau, Robbie Johnston, and the flying professor, Roger Robinson.

Vern Walker corrected my historical and typographical mistakes with an eagle eye and teaming up with Barry Magee, provided an enormous amount of information about training directly under Arthur Lydiard. I grilled Barry and Vern about every possible detail I could think of, and they responded admirably.

Gary Moller and Gavin Harris provided detailed information for the early drafts, and long-time Auckland middle-distance coach Don MacFarquhar, who also trained under Lydiard, gave me some in-depth background about Peter Snell's training.

In Australia, I was greatly encouraged by Australia's "Mr Running," Trevor Vincent, known to everyone as "TV." Pat Clohessy, who ran with the Lydiard squad in Europe in 1961, gave me insight into how he so successfully applied the Lydiard principles with his runners over many years. His phrase "freedom running" should become enshrined in running literature.

Thanks to my great friend and coaching colleague, John Meagher, and all the boys in the "H.I.T. SQUAD" who allow us to coach them. We hope you have a lot of fun and friendship as you achieve your potential.

Thanks also go to Dr. Ron Brinkert, exercise physiologist and coach, who introduced John and me to the benefits of VO_2 max training over 20 years ago.

Thanks to Geelong coach Neil MacDonald for your wonderful photos and detailed information, and thanks to Melbourne coach Kevin Prendergast for allowing me to use some of your material.

From the USA, I was greatly encouraged by the upbeat Dr. David E. Martin, exercise physiologist, who insisted I submit this manuscript to Meyer and Meyer and "go for gold." Coach Greg McMillan was also very encouraging and gave me useful input for the flow of the book. Dr. Jack Daniels generously allowed me to draw on his concepts early on, and Pete Pfitzinger was very encouraging. These last two running authors, along with Dr. Tim Noakes, I regard as among the best in the business. Thanks to Meyer and Meyer for taking this book on, too!

Finally, I'd like to thank Garth Gilmour, Arthur Lydiard's long-time friend and confidant, who authored many of the early classics that inspired me and thousands of others to get out and run. Without all Garth's early work with Arthur, there'd be nothing published to draw on.

Keith Livingstone

Foreword by Barry Magee

As one of Arthur Lydiard's original boys, it is indeed a privilege and an honor to be associated with Keith Livingstone's H.I.T book. The Master Coach's world-changing principles of training are still applied with great success in the modern era by the greatest athletes in the world. Now this book explains why these principles have always worked so well, as we are taken through the science of each phase in a very easy-to-understand manner.

I had 12 years of direct coaching under The Master, and trained and raced with fellow Lydiard Olympians Halberg, Snell, Baillie, Puckett, and Julian, to name just a few. We were each transformed by Arthur's revolutionary new training methods into world-class athletes. It was indeed a thrilling and exciting time to run.

Murray Halberg and I were the first two athletes to do the full track schedule that Arthur had spent years developing and which proved so successful for the next 30 years. Male and female Kiwi runners shocked the world time after time with amazing performances from the middle distances to the marathon. The athletics world could not understand how so many world champion athletes could come from a country with less than 3 million people. Eventually the principles were used all over the world.

In the mid 1960s I myself began coaching the Lydiard way with immediate success. In the years that followed, I coached a young man named Keith Livingstone and perhaps from that association has come this book. Before he died, Arthur Lydiard had left me with his personal approval as the one man who fully embraced and understood his coaching principles. Over recent years I have often been asked when I was going to write a book to explain more about Lydiard's training methods that could either enlarge or simplify the system by presenting it in a new way to the modern-day coaches and athletes of the world.

Well, lo and behold, Keith Livingstone has done a superb job and in my mind, a much better one than I could have done, with extra information to help coaches and athletes to fill in some of the cracks and to give us more understanding of how and why this brilliant system works. H.I.T. does exactly that! Coaches around the world would have to be very foolish if they do not read and use this book to the maximum.

In my opinion, Lydiard holds all the *Keys* to running success. H.I.T. shares many of the KEYS that have been lost, forgotten or misunderstood. I totally recommend Dr Keith Livingstone's book to anyone who is looking for the complete training system to complement what Lydiard has left us.

Barry Magee
1960 Olympic Marathon Bronze Medalist
1961 World Cup 10,000m champion

Foreword by Lorraine Moller

Like Keith Livingstone, I grew up on Lydiard. For young Kiwi runners, it was unquestionably The Way. One who had the good fortune to be the recipient of Lydiard's influence remained a convert for life, not from some faddish following or blind devotion but because his system made complete and utter sense and showed consistent results. Countless Lydiard-trained runners like me enjoyed a range of abilities from middle-distance track to marathon, significant athletic longevity, and the attainment of personal dreams.

Lydiard himself never expected athletes to accept his way without question; he often said that if your coach cannot explain to you the reason for doing a workout then you need a new coach. That is because "Lydiardism" is a system based on sound principles, and each element of the training is a logical and necessary step up the pyramid to excellence: stamina, strength, lactic acid tolerance and racing speed are all building blocks one upon the other, and understanding their inter-relationship is essential to sound coaching. Each phase of training is based on correct sequencing and timing, and the synergetic effect created is more than the sum of its parts: physiologically and mentally the athlete is fully prepared to break his or her limits on the day that counts.

Each cycle of training builds upon the next so that one can reasonably expect personal best performances year after year.

In our fast-paced culture we have been conditioned by many influences, especially media to look for quick fixes and the short-term pay-off. Lydiardism offers neither of these. Like most things of value in life, this system is based on long-term commitment and the pursuit of the highest in athletic achievement. No method has withstood the test of time and had more success attributed to it in the athletic world.

H.I.T. captures the genius of Lydiard and delivers it to athletes and coaches in a comprehensive and complete form. Keith Livingstone, a long-time aficionado of Arthur Lydiard, has produced the definitive work on Lydiard training since Lydiard himself, and brilliantly conveys the art and science that has built champions of all abilities and events with clarity, humour and historical reverence. The Lydiard Foundation has proudly adopted this book as its official text for all Lydiard coaching courses.

Lorraine Moller
1992 Olympic Marathon Bronze Medalist
Co-founder of Lydiard Foundation

About the Author

Keith Livingstone is a former New Zealand athlete who has worked as a chiropractor in Australia for 20 years. He has "coached quietly" for over 20 years and can claim to have successfully coached a current Olympic triathlon gold medal coach and a World Masters Games treble champion. With coaching colleague John Meagher, he has helped guide Australia's strongest middle distance and cross-country high school squad to a number of Australian titles.

Born in Kenya in 1958, with a twin brother, Colin, the boys emigrated with their family to Owairaka, Auckland in 1965, and grew up within a few hundred meters of Arthur Lydiard's home. They lived in Owairaka Avenue, went to Owairaka Primary School, and ran for Owairaka Athletic & Harrier Club, founded by Lydiard. Both brothers later represented Auckland in national competition.

Keith was coached for 5 years by the family grocer – Olympic marathon medalist Barry Magee, one of Lydiard's very first pupils, starting at 17. He won an Auckland Under-18 3000m title in record time in bare feet in his first championship, after a summer of enthusiastic self-coached 100-mile weeks.

Keith worked as a copywriter for Radio New Zealand for 5 years and then moved to Melbourne, Australia to study chiropractic for 6 years. For over ten years, Keith consistently ran with the best athletes in New Zealand and Australia, in very strong eras where each country could boast Olympic or world champions. He claimed a number of decisive wins and titles in senior track, cross-country and road competition.

As a chiropractic student at RMIT University, Keith had access to some of the best facilities in Australia in sports science, biomechanics, anatomy and physiology. He ran with the powerhouse Glenhuntly Athletics Club in Melbourne, and was a key member

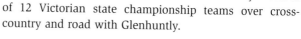

of 12 Victorian state championship teams over cross-country and road with Glenhuntly.

His best track times (which he was never happy with) include 3000m in 8:06, 5000m in 14:04, and 10,000m in 29:19. His road times include a 44:37 for 15 km, and several 10km road times near 29 minutes.

Keith was named "Victorian chiropractor of the year" in 1999 and was on the board of the Australian Spinal Research Foundation for 5 years. He has been married to Joanne for 17 years, and they have 5 children.

Introduction

Years ago, I became a serious runner. It was no accident. It was inevitable.

I grew up in a little suburb one could "toss a blanket over." The Auckland suburb of Owairaka was the home of Arthur Lydiard, New Zealand's great Olympic running coach. It was also the home of a motley band of neighbourhood kids who Lydiard shaped into a fearsome squad that smashed world records, won Olympic titles, and changed the face of world athletics forever. The basis of his conditioning system was a formidable weekly run of 22 miles that started and finished in Owairaka. This circuit, the 'Waiatarua,' climbed high onto the ridges of the Waitakere Ranges overlooking Auckland from the west. Lydiard once said that every school and suburb had kids who could be world champions, if trained correctly. We all believed him.

For impressionable kids with a bit of talent and desire, the possibility of a world-class career in athletics was real. The neighborhood was dotted with world luminaries on the athletics stage, all home-grown. Later, New Zealand had a renaissance of world champions in middle-distance and distance athletics. So did Finland. The common link was the remarkable Arthur Lydiard and his principles.

Sadly, the golden days of athletic domination have long passed for New Zealand and Australia. Arthur Lydiard's principles have been shelved by a whole generation of athletes and coaches who seem to have forgotten the benefits of intelligent endurance work followed by systematic speed development.

The torch has been passed to third-world countries in Africa, whose athletes follow systems that bear much similarity to those of the original "Flying Kiwis." There are signs of resurgence though. One of the few male non-Africans to break the African stranglehold over middle or distance track races in the last 18 years at world championship level has been Australian Craig Mottram. World-class at every event from 1500m to 10,000m, he has shown that anything is possible with his blend of extensive year-round endurance training. Early in 2006 in New Zealand, Mottram was shaded by the brilliant Kiwi runner Nick Willis in a 3.52 mile. Afterwards, he and his coach Nic Bideau met privately with some of the great "Flying Kiwis" of the past, including Sir Murray Halberg and Dick Quax. They asked to see some of his training diaries.

"It looks just like the way we used to train!" exclaimed Dick Quax.
"If it ain't broke, why fix it?" retorted Bideau.

So that's what this book is about. Applying the principles pioneered by Lydiard over 50 years ago, in a modern context, with the hindsight of current physiology.
And, most importantly, you'll have a lot of fun doing it!

Unfortunately we can't give you Lydiard's uncommon insight and genius as well… but why not develop your own? Arthur would probably be very pleased if you did.

Keith Livingstone

Arthur (right) with Nike founder and Oregon coach Bill Bowerman (left) and Lydiard Foundation co-founder Nobby Hashizume.

Prelude

Growing Up with Lydiard

As twin boys of six, my brother Colin and I landed in Auckland, New Zealand, after emigrating with our mother from Nairobi, Kenya, where we had been born.

This was January 1965. Our father had to remain in Kenya for quite some time; the political situation had become quite unstable.

Our mother, an experienced secondary school-teacher, secured a good teaching position at Auckland Girls' Grammar School. This was before the days of equal pay for women. The only decent place my mum could afford was a small flat at 92 Owairaka Avenue, in the suburb of Mt. Albert, Auckland. We were promptly enrolled at Owairaka Primary School. Owairaka Primary School was a little school with its own concrete swimming pool, and several older weatherboard classrooms, with a modern block built in the early '60s.

On the east side of the road were all the pricey houses on the slopes of Mt. Albert. The dividing line was Richardson Road. Owairaka Primary was on the west side. Around it on three sides were all the "State houses." Just below the school grounds on the west side was a little park that none of us ventured into; it had State houses backing onto it from three sides, and you'd get a hiding from any one of several gangs who lived down there if you ever went into it. The only safe time was sometimes in summer when they had a version of Little Athletics. The park was called Murray Halberg Park.

Owairaka, meaning "place of Wairaka," was the Maori name for Mt. Albert. Wairaka was a Maori queen. The hill and its environs were the center of our new little universe, and we'd often be up the "mountain" poking around the pa (village) sites. "Wairaka's tunnel," an ancient lava cave escape route to neighboring Mt. Roskill, had its entrance from the downstairs garage of a house in Mt. Royal Ave. We'd visit there when the owners weren't home. It was a typical carefree "Kiwi" childhood for the time.

The Stoddard Road shops were about 400m from the school. There was a small Four Square grocer's belonging to a guy named Barry Magee. We bought our groceries there. He had been a very good runner we were told, and on one occasion he had all his medals in the window. (Barry Magee was one of Arthur Lydiard's first serious pupils; he was bronze medalist in the 1960 Olympic marathon, and he was ranked first in the world in 10,000m in 1961).

We were just little kids, of course, and the world of sport and athletics meant very little to us. Our little Irish neighbour, Mrs. Vesey, who had four children of her own, would dose us up on cod-liver oil after school so that we would grow up "big and strong like Peter Snell." We heard that this guy was the best runner in the world and would keep our eyes peeled for someone who obviously looked a bit like Superman.

All little boys need a place to explore and have high adventure in. For us, this place was "the creek," complete with brambles, rusting car bodies, old supermarket trolleys, surprised ducks, frogs and tadpoles. A veritable Disney-land. This creek and green strip also ran straight beside Lydiard's place, although it was considerably more civilized there, with concrete walls. His home, as the crow flies, was only about 300m from our home in Owairaka Avenue, but across the other side of the creek. We'd often play down there amidst fennel and ferns, oblivious to who lived a few meters away.

After a while we became aware of another guy who was becoming famous for beating the No. 7 trolley bus into the center of town in the mornings; his name was Jeff Julian, and he'd won some big marathon races, including the Fukuoka marathon in Japan. Every day he'd run to and from his work at the Bank of New Zealand in Queen Street, and the bus with all its stops had no hope of matching him over the 6-mile journey.

My mum got another teaching job at Manurewa High School on the other side of Auckland. A boy there was a very good runner who'd won all the schoolboy races. His name was John Walker, and his picture was in the school magazine she brought home. He looked very lanky, with a short haircut.

One day our friend Gavin showed us where Peter Snell lived. It was a very nice-looking house in Allendale Road, on the "rich" side of Mt. Albert. Two stories. We knocked on the door but no one answered.

As the '60s rolled by, we got used to the sights of wiry runners padding past us each year in the Owairaka Marathon, or training in big packs along the roads. We'd hand out sponges from buckets or point a hose if they wanted. One guy with a barrel chest, who looked more like a tough boxer, had his framed picture in a local library. His name was Bill Baillie. One day we saw him run past our house, just like in the picture! He was the best road runner in the world, and a world-record-holder for 20,000m and one hour.

We didn't know who this Murray Halberg guy was who had the park named after him. We weren't sure about him at all because the park wasn't anywhere to hang around in. Apparently he grew up around there: in Hargest Terrace, which backs onto the park. He must have been pretty tough, anyhow, whoever he was. A little plaque on the building at the park said he was an Empire and Olympic champion and world-record-holder in running. Someone said he had a store in Balmoral or Sandringham, on the other side of the hill.

I went to Wesley Intermediate School when I was 11. This was situated beside a continuation of the same same belt of State housing that my last school was near, and the same creek that ran beside Lydiard's home. Barry Magee's daughter Diane was in my class. Her dad was still running in races and winning around Auckland, as were Jeff Julian and Bill Baillie.

The Lovelock Track, named after the 1936 Olympic 1500m champion, was over the fence from our school, in parkland beside the creek.

The track was asphalt and black rubber. This was the headquarters of the world-famous Owairaka Athletic and Harrier Club, which Arthur Lydiard, the best running coach in the world, had founded. His house was on Wainwright Avenue, a hidden dogleg around a few corners from the club. It was a State house like the rest.

Kevin Ryan, one of New Zealand's toughest distance runners of the 1970s, lived a few streets away, and his parents-in-law had a house backing onto the track. Kevin was coached by Barry Magee. Dick Quax, who was emerging as one of New Zealand's world champions, lived up the hill somewhere near Summit Drive. In 1970, Quax pushed Kip Keino all the way in the Commonwealth Games 1500m in Edinburgh.

Quax was coached by John Davies, who had been Olympic 1500m bronze medalist in 1964, and Davies had been coached by Lydiard.

Secondary School came and we went to Sacred Heart College on the other side of Auckland; a Catholic day and boarding school. It was a rugby, cricket and music school, famous for producing All Black captains and a group of young rock musicians called Split Enz.

Our first year there was 1972. Each night after getting off the train we would trudge with our heavy bags from Mt. Albert station, up Allendale Road, past Peter Snell's old place, then up over the hill itself and down again.

That first year we read of Quax being a favorite for the Munich 5,000m. Then Quax was out with stress fractures. A young guy from the South Island surprised everybody by getting bronze in the 1500m. His name was Rod Dixon. The guy who won the 1500m in Munich, Pekka Vasala of Finland, was trained under the Lydiard principles, as was his compatriot Lasse Viren, who won the 5000m and 10000m. Lydiard had earlier spent about 18 months in Finland, coaching the coaches.

Even though we had no particular interest in running yet, it was not unlike growing up in Melbourne and not being aware of AFL football or growing up in Chicago and not being aware of basketball.

1974 came, and with it the amazing Christchurch Commonwealth Games. We watched on TV like the rest of sports-mad New Zealand. Dick Quax missed the Games due to injury. Dick Tayler, coached by Lydiard and Alastair McMurran, won the 10,000m in a fantastic time with a huge kick. New Zealand went wild. John Walker medaled in the 800m and 1500m, nipping under the world record in chasing down Filbert Bayi. Rod Dixon was fourth in 3:33, a phenomenal time itself. Jack Foster got silver with a 2:11 marathon- at age 42! A young girl named Lorraine Moller ran 2:03 to get fifth in the 800m. She was coached by Dick Quax's coach, John Davies.

This was the start of the second golden era in New Zealand. Tiny New Zealand with its three million people could match any nation on earth. The men's and women's teams dominated World Cross Country championships in the mid '70s; the "Big Three," Walker, Dixon and Quax, guaranteed filled stadiums anywhere in Europe. It was a very heady time to grow up for an impressionable teenager just starting to discover some athletic ability.

My brother went to Mt. Albert Grammar School for the art programme in 1974, when we were 15. Peter Snell had gone there and played rugby and tennis, and in the early 1930's Arthur Lydiard went to the same school. My brother started running and getting into the school athletic team. This was funny because he'd never been interested in sport at all until the Commonwealth Games.

In 1975, Rod Dixon was ranked world number one in 5000m, two years after ranking first in 1500m. In 1976, John Walker won Olympic Gold over 1500m. Quax secured the 5000m Olympic silver while Dixon was out-lunged for bronze by the German Klaus-Peter Hildenbrand. Both were beaten by the relentless Finn Lasse Viren, while he defended his Olympic double. Quax achieved the 5000m world record the next year.

The best team ever to leave NZ. Left to right. Alison Deed, Dianne Zorn, Euan Robertson, Lorraine Moller, Heather Thomson, Anne Garrett, John Walker, Bryan Rose, Kevin Ryan, and John Sheddan.

NZ World Cross Country Champions, Morocco, 1975
The men's team was superb despite absence of Rod Dixon. Mile champion Walker finished 4th.

John Walker's coach, Arch Jelley, lived over the hill in Mt. Albert, on Asquith Avenue, a mile up the road from the famous Western Springs Stadium where Snell and Australia's great Ron Clarke had run world records a decade earlier. Arch Jelley was with Owairaka Athletic Club. His son Martin ran for Owairaka Athletic Club, and was very talented.

Around this time we became more aware of Kevin Ryan, who was going to win the 1976 Olympic marathon as far as we were concerned. He lived near the Lovelock Track, and was coached by Barry Magee.

Kevin Ryan was tall and very strong and ran over 100 miles a week, and was the New Zealand cross country, marathon, and road champion. He'd already won marathons overseas. Lydiard's Wainwright Avenue house was only a short jog away from Kevin's place. Lydiard wasn't there now; he was overseas a lot of the time and we didn't know where his new house was really. The new occupants used to leave a plastic jug upside down over the tap on the lawn for Waiatarua runners, in deference to its heritage.

Kevin Ryan used to run his "official" Waiatarua run around the famous Lydiard course, only counting the stretch from and to Lydiard's house. It was a big 22 mile loop. Others used to run the "Waiatarua" course, but of course they would start in slightly different places, and even though the middle 90% was exactly the same, it was never "official."

Waiataruas HAD to be run from Lydiard's old place to do the job. "Gotta do the work" was Kevin's motto.

I was boarding at Sacred Heart College now, and sometimes on weekends my brother would drag me out for a run around Mt. Albert and it felt like a lung-burning sprint the whole way. He'd become pretty tough just from running at school.

On long weekends and school holidays, we'd often go hiking around the West Coast of Auckland. We'd camp out and cover large distances, carrying all our gear. Eventually our vista would grow to include the Coromandel Peninsula, Mt. Ruapehu, the Bay of Islands, and Waiheke Island. Mum was probably glad to get us out of the house.

The next year, 1975, my brother came back to Sacred Heart, and we were both boarders. We decided to win the School Athletic Championships at every distance above 400m. Colin coached me because he had run for over a year. We ran a five mile hilly course around the school each night after school for several weeks, and sometimes we would surge lamp-post to lamp-post. At first it was very hard, but gradually I caught on.

The school 800m came and we tore off like bats out of hell. Only one other guy could hang on as we died on our stakes, and he snuck past on the line. Colin out-kicked me with his thumping speed. 'Stretch' Arbuckle, the guy who beat us, won the Auckland Inter-Schools 400m title a few weeks later. Heavens knows what we all ran our first lap in.

Colin had a "rock and roll" head on a super-athlete's body and could often thrash me in training, even when I was winning championship races at senior level. In later years, he much preferred running with his dogs to racing, but he still represented Auckland as a junior and senior athlete and ran around 50 minutes for 10 miles. He said he got far more fun out of chasing his dogs for hours in wild steep country than wasting a Saturday waiting for a race.

"We" won the 1500 and the 3,000 in new school records; Colin would ride close shotgun, seeing off any pretenders. In the school cross country we took off and there were several minutes of daylight before the third finisher. We'd run a couple of times a week and play soccer in the school team; sometimes we'd front up at Wesley Harriers and run the pack runs. This was Barry Magee's winter club.

The next year Colin went off to art school in Dunedin, hundreds of miles away in the South Island. I stayed on for 7th form. During the summer before he went away we decided that we should train properly, and that, according to the Peter Snell book in the school library, meant 100 miles a week was required. Fine.

We both had summer jobs at the Chief Post Office in Auckland, sorting the Christmas mail. We rigged up a system where we'd run to and from work, carrying daywear, and shower at the post office. I still have my diary from then; being 17 years old, in my new Adidas Malmo basketball shoes with gum-rubber soles, I clocked up my first 100 mile week after several 80s and 90s, and then kept going.

It was mostly twice a day at first, but very quickly I came on with the long runs, often by myself. We'd worked out where the Waiatarua course went by reading the Snell and Halberg books and talking to guys. Our friend Gavin once asked a kid at school who lived next door to Snell if he could ask Snell to draw a map of Waiatarua. Snell obliged, with a scrawled note saying "Good luck!"

One day in January 1976 I showed up at the Lovelock Track for Owairaka's Wednesday night club race, and asked to join so that I could run in the Auckland Championships. One guy asked me if I had done any training and scoffed when I answered truthfully. I duly won the Auckland Under-18 3,000m title in 8:54, by 11 seconds, in bare feet and a borrowed singlet. It was an Auckland record. A big tall guy in an Owairaka uniform kept yelling at me not to turn around so much as I lost several feet each time. It was Kevin Ryan.

Shortly before the Olympics that year, poor Kevin sliced through his thigh with a skill saw, ruining his final preparation for the Games. He subsequently ran 2:11 for the marathon on several occasions and was a top-five finisher in Boston.

Later Kevin moved to Boston and trained with the great Bill Rodgers, as well as coaching Pete Pfitzinger, who would go on to become a two-time U.S. Olympian in the marathon, surprisingly defeating world number one Alberto Salazar in the process. Pete is now an exercise physiologist, coach, and highly published writer, living in Auckland.

So that year was my first year as a distance runner, and by the end of it I'd acquired Barry Magee as a coach and won several more titles in track or cross-country.

I was finally introduced one weekend to the great Arthur Lydiard, who now and again would run workshops for coaches and athletes under his employment with the concrete manufacturer Winstone's.

Lydiard gave a talk at our club running weekend in the Motu Moana Scout Camp on May 16, 1976. We were a varied bunch of ages and abilities. No current superstars were present. Barry

Magee briefly introduced us, and Arthur, who was about 59 at the time, peeled off his tracksuit after his talk and said he'd join us for our run. All I wrote in my diary was "Arthur Lydiard came and ran Waiatarua with us."

Arthur did the Waiatarua circuit that day under three hours with no trouble. He was a very fit, nuggety little guy, but he seemed chatty and friendly enough. The bunch thinned considerably over the business end up the big climbs, but Lydiard was fine in the thick of things. I was probably in awe so I didn't speak to him much, but I did listen in as he dispensed advice to the group. He spoke quickly, in staccato bursts.

When we had finished, Barry told Arthur that I was his new pupil, and Arthur nodded approvingly, telling me that stamina was king and to do everything Barry told me. It took five years to become a champion and 10 years to become a world champion. He'd probably seen kids like me a hundred times before, and he reminded me of the gruff movie star Brian Keith. Then after a cup of tea and some biscuits he was off!

Over the next five years I got to regularly run over 100 miles a week on the Lydiard program, and lived in Auckland, Christchurch and Wellington in my job with Radio New Zealand. I got to represent each province in national championships and won senior races and titles over road, track, and cross country in Wellington, as well as some good races in Australia. I got to know or meet lots of good and great runners, but frustratingly, never fulfilled what I thought was possible.

Athletics was my life, and all I wanted to do was one day run in an Olympic 10,000m or a World Cross Country championship. With the Lydiard culture and program it seemed like a logical conclusion at the time.

"My athletes didn't have to deal with pain! We enjoyed ourselves!"

Arthur Lydiard

It wasn't to be. A bad (non-running!) injury in 1979 led me to ask Lorraine Moller for advice. She said "try a chiropractor." I did, and now I am one! I left New Zealand in 1982 to study in Melbourne but continued my running as much as I could.

I rang Lorraine in Colorado after Lydiard died. She helped arrange his last tour. She told me that in Boulder and in Texas he'd spoken to packed rooms with standing ovations. It doesn't get better than that at 86.

On what was to be his last talk, an American coach repeatedly asked Arthur how his athletes dealt with the pain of training. Arthur didn't seem to understand the question, whichever way it was put.

In the end he responded with an indignant reply: "My athletes didn't have to deal with pain! We enjoyed ourselves!"

October 2007. The author with Barry Magee, Lorraine Moller, and Allison Roe. Two Olympic marathon medalists, and one former world marathon record-holder.

How to Use This Book

This book is written for serious, competitive athletes who wish to reach their potential over middle distance races and longer. The sole purpose of this book is to furnish a good understanding of the major energy systems of the body and apply this understanding to your athletics. If we succeed in that, the mission will be accomplished.

We have avoided deeply exploring such topics as biomechanics and injury prevention for good reasons. Some books on athletics training try to be "all things to all people," and we feel they suffer as a result. So this book is simple.

The whole book rests on a good understanding of the "Training Pyramid" and the energy systems and muscle fiber physiology as explained in Part Two.

Each level of the training pyramid depends upon successive blocks of work having been performed thoroughly, and if this work can't be done because of other priorities and demands, then the program fails.

"As to methods there may be a million and then some, but principles are few. The man who grasps principles can successfully select his own methods. The man who tries methods, ignoring principles, is sure to have trouble."

Ralph Waldo Emerson

There are many systems of conditioning for middle distance and distance running, and many athletes and coaches have been successful with approaches that appear to vary greatly.

So use this book as a *guide*, and see where you can use the *principles*. Every individual situation for athlete and coach is different.

Make Training Specific

So if the major thrust of this book is in developing the aerobic foundation to its highest possible level in the time available before serious competition starts, the secondary thrust is working out which of the anaerobic energy systems you're training, as *specifically* as possible for your current ability. It is totally possible to run anaerobically at a level way beyond your level of development, with disastrous results. If you understand these concepts alone and apply them, then reading the book will be worthwhile.

At each level of the training pyramid, there will be specific types of workouts described that are designed to achieve the major goal of each phase leading to peak performance. The examples given are just that; examples, and especially when developing race-specific speeds and working the anaerobic energy systems at the business end of a season, there are endless variables possible.

It is important to realize that *the* important thing is the aerobic base, and without it, the anaerobic training falls over, and results become unpredictable.

"I'm not a great believer in sports psychology. At the highest level, the training programme is everything. It has to be the right training, and it has to be the right timing."

Olympic Gold Medal
Triathlon coach Chris Pilone

Lydiard would add to this that the *balance* of the program was extremely important. With hawk-like vigilance, he could balance a program so that the different energy systems required for maximal performance were all fully trained, rested and "ready" on the big race day.

As a general principle with younger athletes especially, once this work is continued into the race-specific preparation phase, only one or two "intense" sessions a week are generally required. A great deal of the remaining training time can be geared to totally non-specific work, namely slow recovery jogging that enables any acidosis in the working muscle to be flushed back into the general circulation, allowing the whole system to be "taken back to neutral."

The Great Secret

This is the great "secret" of aerobic training that has been largely ignored by current middle distance coaches. Whatever you do that is very intense has to be balanced out with a reasonable volume of easy work. The harder you go, the more the volume of easier work required, and the easier the better. Total rest won't do it. Easy aerobic activity will. That's the secret. We'll leave the physiologists and PhD theorists to tell us why, but if more athletes and coaches did just this there'd be far more certainty in racing.

As I write this, while coaching two good male athletes through a track season, we noticed several competitive athletes drop away, over only a fortnight, from personal-best 800m times of close to 1:50 for 800m, to times 4 to 6 seconds slower in good races.

What happened there? Here's my guess. Our young athlete, full of testosterone and great natural ability, has popped a PB off a haphazard blend of hard and fast repetitions and aerobic runs. The athlete and coach, euphoric at getting so close to a very respectable "sub 1:50," decide to "really do some hard training" to nail the one minute, forty something that's around the corner. And nail the training, they do.

It only takes ONE poorly thought out, too-hard session, to drive *six inch nails* into one's own coffin. As Australian exercise physiologist and super-coach Dick Telford has stated, a "cloud of fatigue" ensues. Any confidence gained goes out the window, to be replaced by anxiety. Not good. If only the athlete had jogged slowly around the park for most of his runs, and done a *little* specific pace work in between races to maintain development; *then* we'd see another PB!

But that's too simple, isn't it?

The Tortoise and the Hare

Every year in Australia, New Zealand, the UK, and the USA, super-talented and motivated junior athletes pop up who really do have "the goods" to become world champions. Two or three years later their immense potential has not been realized and frustrations set in as no improvement in times has been made, or times oscillate between unpredictable seasonal highs and lows. The reason? Their early racing came off what naturally developed aerobic capacity was already there, but no significant aerobic training has been done since.

Unfortunately, an attitude has snuck into modern athletics that endurance running will "slow" athletes down and that it's not "specific" to the speeds of competition. Such criticisms are absolutely justified … in the short term. But if you read this book, you'll see that they have no basis in the real world of international success. Look at any African or European world champion in middle distance and distance events, scratch behind the glossy magazine articles, and you'll find a significant component of endurance-based work in the preparatory season, without exception.

In his autobiography, Haile Gebrselassie mentions competing in a marathon at age 15, finishing with blisters in 2 hours 48 or so on the rough high roads of Addis Ababa. We can't complain about his speed or range, as he ran 3:32 for 1500m indoors a few years ago and was the fastest finisher in the business over his hallmark distances.

In the "Lydiard era," professional athletics and year-round competition were decades over the horizon. Winter seasons could be used for preparing the aerobic systems because the race distances were all "aerobic," while the summer could be used for sharpening the "anaerobic" systems. Important provincial or national titles were at a fixed time of year that never really varied, and the only important international competitions were the four-yearly Olympic or Commonwealth Games.

All that having been said, once you've read this book, you can take your knowledge and apply it sensibly, and if you have to manage athletes through a maze of varying competitions through the year, at least you'll be able to ensure some level of progression and consistency.

As mentioned earlier, the obvious answer for athlete and coach is to choose the big aims for any competitive season, and tailor a program backwards from the major races, treating any competitions along the way as purely "training information." This requires a great deal of confidence and control because as Arthur Lydiard would often say, "when everyone else is running first, you'll be running last, but you'll be running first when it's important."

Here's an instance where Arthur was "wrong": a well-prepared athlete will be running solidly, not last, early in the season, but when it's important, he or she will be running very well. However, you get the point.

Melbourne athlete, teacher and coach John Meagher has successfully guided his team of schoolboys year after year to Victorian and national titles over track and cross-country. Some have now become successful senior competitors with a continuing love for the sport. His squad, the "H.I.T. Squad," features in segments of this book, and in one chapter we show how the young squad puts the principles together.

John, in his 40s, has personally used these principles to win three World Masters Games running titles and a national age group triathlon event in record time. He's won medals in world age-group duathlon, and an outright second-place in the Melbourne Marathon at 41.

Years ago, John trained with great athletes such as Nourredine Morceli in the American College system, as well as spending weeks in Kenya's Rift Valley with the boys of St. Patrick's College, Iten, where he helped build a dormitory. He has "seen it all." Together, we have refined our interpretation of the Lydiard principles so that we can fine-tune them to the individual athlete.

John has personally trained schoolboys to times as good as 1:52 for 800 meters and 3:50 for 1500 meters, on year-round aerobic principles. One of his squad, now on an American track scholarship, ran 49.6 for 400m and 78s for 600m in training, as well as 1:51.9 for 800m. This same athlete, at 18, has so far kept up a regular hilly 90-minute run on weekends, and with another couple of years of aerobic development should run a very decent 800m. Another member of John's squad, Daniel, now 22, won the Victorian state men's 1500m title in 2007.

While exceptional youngsters can emerge who run faster than these athletes, at least we can say that there is still room for a great deal of improvement as these young athletes mature into their simple programs. Their anaerobic energy systems haven't been burnt to bits, and the aerobic work has been fun and varied.

These young athletes, if they have the desire and commitment to compete at senior level, at least have an ingrained way of doing things that will ensure they approach their potential over the coming years.

Efficient or Effective?

In terms of short-term results, there are many ways of approaching a season that are more *efficient* than Lydiard's. There's no question about that whatsoever. If you're healthy and reasonably fit, then the types of training advocated by popular running magazines will ensure rapid progression in the short term because they sharpen whatever innate aerobic development is already there and maximise current anaerobic potential.

In terms of an athletic lifetime, and achieving one's fullest potential, Lydiard-based systems are the most *effective*.

What's the difference?

Which parachute would you prefer to jump with? The parachute packed by the person who prepared 100 parachutes in an hour, or the parachute from the slower, more methodical person who could absolutely guarantee that every one of his parachutes would open?

You are effective when the value of what you get done is significantly higher than the cost of getting it done.

An example of **efficient training** is a weekly blend that incorporates long steady running, anaerobic threshold running, short bursts of VO_2 max training, several runs at very slow aerobic recovery levels, and perhaps a short sharp session of leg-speed drills. That sort of training can ensure an athlete races up to his or her current capabilities throughout the year. But it doesn't increase the total capability because the faster work tends to "sand down" or counteract the aerobic work. This is all explored in different ways throughout the book. At some stage, the total aerobic capacity has to be increased methodically.

Effective training is thorough, and leaves no stone unturned, and is done with the attitude that doing a job correctly is an end in itself. For the athlete who wants to see just how far he or she can go, there's a trade-off to be made. Regular short-term results or long-term glory? Neither is "right"; sometimes a talented athlete pursuing a life-time vocation has to choose a path that goes right down the middle, and good luck to him or her.

Marathon Endurance for Middle Distance Speed

Lorraine Moller is a four-time Olympian in the marathon and was a medalist at 37 years of age. She followed Lydiard's system throughout her career, and she was world-class at every distance from 800m to the marathon.

Lorraine said that one of her biggest frustrations in dealing with groups of coaches and athletes these days was their inability to grasp the simplicity of endurance training for middle distance speed. "Their eyes glaze over and they look at the floor. They'll grumble and say "Lydiard training! That's all outdated!"

Lorraine's fellow Kiwi, Dick Quax, himself an Olympic 5000m medalist and world record-holder, apparently received the same response when he talked to coaches and athletes.

According to Barry Magee, one of Lydiard's original Olympic medalists, Lydiard himself had this to say about why modern coaches and athletes can't comprehend his proven system: **"It's too damned simple!"**

As far as the Lydiard system being "outdated," here is something for today's coaches and athletes to ponder. The time of 1.44.3 for 800m was run on a **grass** track by 22-year Peter Snell in February 1962. It's *still* the fastest 800m ever run by a New Zealander or Australian. What could he have done on today's fast tracks, with today's pace-making and professionalism?

(We'll forget his 100% success rate of 5 gold medals out of 5 attempts in Olympic or Commonwealth competition for now.)

Modern coaches can also note well that the performances of Snell and his compatriots came from men who generally worked full-time and ran their long runs in glorified tennis shoes. No sports medicine, podiatry, exercise physiology labs, heart rate monitors, corporate sponsorships, sports psychology, government grants, designer drugs, performance nutrition or anything as we know them today. Zilch. Zippo. Nothing.

These amateur enthusiasts were coached by a milkman! A very clever, well-read and pragmatic milkman, mind you, but a man who also had to support his family while coaching world champions. Without assistance.

It's probably safe to assume that Lydiard's theories can still apply today.

Snell, now with a PhD in exercise physiology, in recent years said that with his current knowledge base he would have changed very little of his preparation apart from dropping some periods of jogging at speeds that were "too slow."

"Keep Things as Simple as Possible... but Not Simpler"

Albert Einstein

Although the basic premise of the Lydiard principle is of great simplicity, there are key distinctions in its application. This is what Lydiard had to say about his system shortly before he died, and it's a great overview of the true nature of his philosophy.

"If you want to be a successful runner, you have to consider everything. It's no good just thinking about endurance and not to develop fine speed. Likewise – it's no good training for speed, or anaerobic capacity with lots of interval type of training when you haven't developed your aerobic capacity to maximum. You have to take a long view and train on all aspects of development through a systematic program. It's a lot of hard work for five, six or seven years. There's no secret formula. There's no shortcut to the top."

Referring to his original method, Lydiard said it this way:

"My original training schedule required six months to complete. It started with a two-month long aerobic build-up, followed by a month of hill resistance. Then you'd move on to a three-month period of track training."

That's pretty simple isn't it? On the surface, it looks very similar to the schedule followed by New Zealand's latest middle distance superstar, track cyclist Sarah Ulmer, gold medalist in the Women's 3000m Pursuit at the 2004 Athens Olympics.

Ulmer not only lowered the world record by several seconds in the heats and semi-finals at Athens; in the final, she pulverized it yet again.

How did she do it? Many coaches have analyzed the last months of her schedule and concluded that the intensity of her track training far exceeded anything seen before in women's endurance sprint conditioning. Correct. The next step was to assume that it was this mode of training that got her there and therefore portends the way of the future. Partly correct.

Sarah Ulmer's preparation for Athens came off several months of intense anaerobic preparation and speed development, following a month of progressive resistance training (low cadence and high resistance on an indoor cycle), following several months of endurance cycling of up to 800 kilometers a week. Sound familiar? It's as near to the principles of the Lydiard system as one can go on a bike.

Before Athens came a dozen years of endurance-based preparation, and a slow and steady progression in times and results. Just like Peter Snell so many years before, Ulmer was able to handle very high intensity workloads *because* of her endurance background. A classic case of the more one does, the more one can do.

In A Nutshell ...

The Lydiard system can be viewed as a "training pyramid." The vast bulk of the pyramid represents aerobic training. The tip of the pyramid represents anaerobic training. The higher the foundation of the pyramid before anaerobic metabolism starts, the higher the ultimate level of performance.

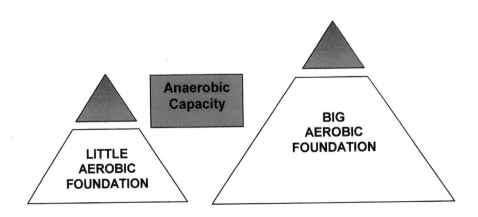

Part 1
The Training Pyramid

For the purposes of this book, I've described Arthur Lydiard's work as progressively moving up a pyramid of training intensities, until the most intense work is done before the most important competition. This is now known as periodization.

Different energy systems in the body take differing times to grow to their fullest capacity. The slowest to develop to full capacity is the aerobic energy system, which can be constantly improved for many years.

Possibly the fastest to develop is the glycolytic anaerobic energy system, otherwise known as the lactic acid system, which can reach its highest capacity in a number of weeks if a suitable aerobic foundation has been laid.

The alactic anaerobic energy system, which contributes less and less to overall performance as distance increases, can be developed very quickly too. However, while alactic capacity at the chemical level in the cells can be pushed up to its maximum quickly, the neuro-muscular coordination to run fast is a skill that has to be learned over time. This is well-explained in a later chapter.

The efficient movement patterns learned with fast alactic running can contribute to efficiency at all speeds. So although the overall energy contribution of the alactic system is minimal for the duration of a middle distance or distance race, alactic training is very important because of its effect on efficiency and economy, and also because many races come down to a sprint at the end.

This type of work can be done safely on a year-round basis, especially on easy days, and doing so will not harm the aerobic systems.

So it can be seen that the training pyramid concentrates on different energy systems at different times, in a balanced way that ensures all of them come up to the maximal capacity possible at just the right time. Imagine a master chef timing his preparation of ingredients over a large stove and you get the idea. If just one ingredient is on the stove too early or too late, and at the wrong temperature, the whole meal may need to be thrown out.

One type of work leads progressively into another. It must be remembered that aerobic work of an easy or extremely easy nature can be continued in reasonable volume right into the race phase with great success.

In fact, if intense work is being done at the top of the training pyramid, it must be assumed that it is being buffered by ample very low intensity running sessions that are very aerobic in nature. This balances the system and allows the body to cope with the mounting acidosis that hard training and racing invokes, and come back for more intense training again.

Key Points

- Only one or two key sessions each week would concentrate on the respective energy system or pace being developed. Other sessions of the day and week would be restorative and aerobic, especially the further up the pyramid we get.

- Middle distance high-intensity training is buffered by ample easy aerobic running until the system "neutralizes" again and is ready for more. Easy days are generally run the day before and after a high intensity session. Sometimes two or three easy days might be necessary. Application of the principles will vary according to the individual and the coaching overview.

- Distance Preparation (5k-10k) would have far less emphasis on the top of the pyramid, and the most intense efforts would generally be at VO_2 max level.

- If high-intensity efforts are run too frequently, harm is done to the developing aerobic systems at the enzymatic and cellular levels. The individual tolerance will vary, but many good runners respond to and improve with one such session a week.

Physiology of the Lydiard Training Pyramid

Please read this chapter very carefully, because it is foundational to the rest of the book. Below is an illustration of the key energy systems and training phases we will be referring to throughout the text.

Read the definitions that follow this page before we proceed with the rest of the book.

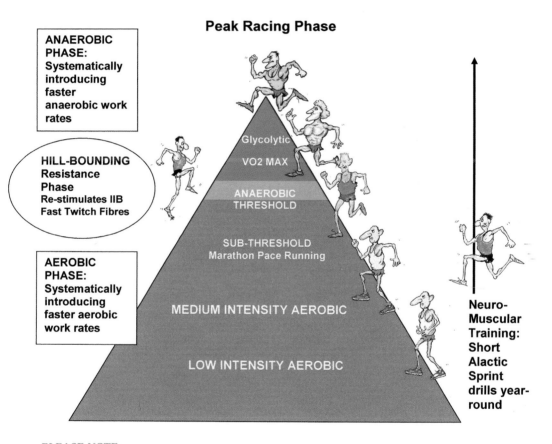

PLEASE NOTE:

This is the correct and logical sequencing of the energy systems and intensity levels as we approach a peak racing phase for middle distance. The phases each represent a specific energy system, a specific range of muscle fiber types, and a specific type of training that will best develop these. Leg-speed drills can be continually used, year-round, and although technically they are anaerobic, the work bouts are so short and recoveries so long that acidosis isn't created to any degree.

Physiology of the "You Can't Run Fast if You Don't Train Fast" Pyramid: Too Much, Too Often

You will see that by continually pushing during training, that not only does the aerobic part of the pyramid never get to its highest possible levels in the available time, but "Yo-Yo" results are more likely, and *systemic acidosis* results, leaving the athlete open to illness and injury. It is impossible to get the best anaerobic training results because the cellular mechanisms for balanced chemistry and repair are compromised. We never ever get to our potential. We may approach it quickly in our first year or so of training like this, but then as the aerobic base declines, as it will, we will never really improve.

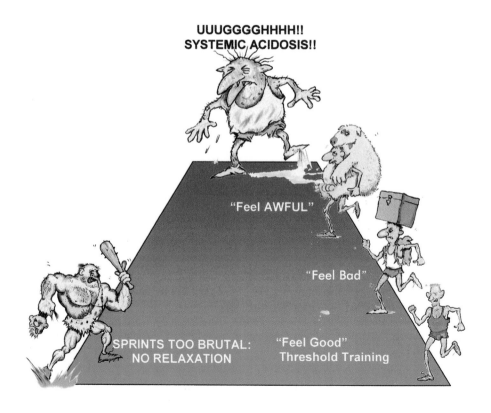

Running Physiology Terms

Exercise physiology is still an infant science. We don't deal in areas of black and white when dealing with the variations in genetics that will surface in any population, and we probably never will. We deal in broad principles, likelihoods, and tendencies. Particularly when discussing the energy systems, we are dealing with a spectrum of grey shades. Nothing is absolutely black or white, but some things are very dark grey and some things are very light grey. For instance, at any given exercise intensity, ALL of the energy systems will be active, but some are extremely active, some play a supportive role, and some are nearly silent. What follows, in practical terms, is all we need to know for now.

AEROBIC RUNNING: Exercise with oxygen. Running that is at an effort level and heart rate where the oxygen breathed in is more than enough to supply the demands of the exercise. In practical terms, this sort of running can be maintained for many minutes or hours in a fit athlete. At slow rates, body fats (fatty acids) are used more as fuel. At faster aerobic speeds, more carbohydrates are used. Fat fuels are abundant in the body, whereas carbohydrate stores are far more limited.

ANAEROBIC RUNNING: Running that is at a higher effort level where the blood supply and oxygen delivery are insufficient to meet all of the demands of the exercise. Fuel is used without oxygen, but acidic by-products build up that eventually stop the exercise. This can happen very rapidly with high-intensity running or can build up gradually with very strong running over much longer distances.

ANAEROBIC THRESHOLD: **The zone or "grey area" where the oxygen delivery to the working muscles is only just enough to meet the energy demands.** Above this level, the muscles are unable to easily disperse acidic waste products, and work rate is forced to slow again. Below this level, the working muscles can still function efficiently in the presence of oxygen.

This is the pace a well-trained endurance athlete can race at for between 50 and 60 minutes; whether of average or world-class ability, threshold can only be maintained for about this time range.

ACIDOSIS suppresses normal nerve function and muscle contraction, so if a high rate of work is continued, eventually the exercise is forced to stop. This creates an "oxygen debt" that has to be paid back with rapid breathing once exercise has stopped.

All running above or faster than the "anaerobic threshold" pace is considered anaerobic.

ISOCAPNIC BUFFERING ZONE: Fancy name for prolonged running just a heart beat or two above your anaerobic threshold.

Enzymes, Acids and Chemistry

Enzymes are substances that greatly speed up the rate of chemical reactions, sometimes to the order of several hundred thousand times.

OXIDATIVE or AEROBIC ENZYMES: Oxidative enzymes produced in the energy factories of the muscle cells (mitochondria) greatly increase the ability of the muscle to extract oxygen from the blood, and energy from fats and sugars. They exist in very high levels in trained slow twitch muscles, and in high levels in some endurance-trained fast twitch muscles.

GLYCOLYTIC ENZYMES: These enzymes extract energy rapidly from glycogen stored in muscle cells, in the absence of oxygen. This process of anaerobic energy extraction is known as glycolysis. Glycolytic enzymes are highly concentrated in fast twitch (Type II) muscle fibers, which are the primary source of anaerobic energy for short, high-intensity work bouts.

LACTIC ACID OR LACTATE: As mentioned earlier, this is an energy-rich substance produced by exercising muscles in the absence of oxygen. The production of lactate accompanies a sharp rise in hydrogen ions, and it is these that create the acid environment that causes muscular work to cease. It is a reasonably harmless or inert substance. Once blamed for post-exercise muscle soreness (now called DOMS or delayed onset of muscle soreness), the culprit has now been deemed as micro-trauma to the muscle fibers, and the attendant inflammation.

Muscles

MOTOR UNITS

These are groups of muscle fibers, usually all of the same type (i.e., slow twitch, fast twitch), supplied by a single incoming nerve axon (like an electric cable). If sufficient electrical charge is delivered by the nerve, every fiber in the motor unit will contract at once. If not enough, the motor unit doesn't fire at all.

'ALL OR NONE' PRINCIPLE

The principle of "firing" a motor unit is very similar to that of "firing" a spark plug in a car engine. When enough voltage and current is delivered (threshold summation) by the lead to the spark plug, it fires. If the current is below the level required (sub-threshold summation), the spark flug fails to fire. The electrical current (electromotive force) that fires motor units is generated by the brain, and delivered by the nervous system.

So we can see that muscle fiber recruitment and coordination is very much a brain function, and just as in regular electronics, large voltages and currents are best delivered by large insulated cables, and small voltages and currents by small insulated cables.

THE SIZE PRINCIPLE

Within a contracting muscle, motor units usually fire off according to the size principle, which means that they usually fire off in the order of smallest motor unit to largest, smallest nerve axon to largest.

The smallest motor units are usually made up of slow twitch fibers with small nerve axons, and the biggest of fast twitch fibers with big nerve axons.

Slow Twitch Type I	Fast Twitch Type IIA	Fast Twitch Type IIB
Fires 1st until all fatigued	Fires 2nd to maintain tension	Fires last only if forced to
Small incoming nerve axons	Big incoming nerve axons	Massive incoming nerve axons

Usually, the huge and powerful fast twitch fibers are not easily trained (i.e., recruited first) unless there is either a massive load to lift (hard to do when running), *or* if the size principle is *reversed* (possible with a certain type of simple exercise), or if all the slow twitch and IIA fibers are taken progressively to exhaustion by prolonged endurance exercise, thereby forcing the massive IIB fibers to be recruited to maintain tension (very long runs).

This leaves us with three options to train and increase the cross-sectional area of our most powerful muscle fibers.

1. Lifting very heavy loads above 85% of our maximum.

2. Reversing the size principle with a simple type of exercise

3. Running for long enough to exhaust the slow twitch fibers and the intermediary IIA glycolytic fibers

Options 2 & 3 have always been part of the Lydiard principles for over 55 years. For now we will briefly look at Option 2, before re-examining it in detail in the Hill Exercise section later. Option 1 is discussed in the Strength Training Section in Part 9.

Reversing the Size Principle

The *size principle* can be reversed by a sudden lengthening (eccentric) stretch of a (concentrically) contracting muscle, as in *plyometric* exercise, or *skipping*, or *hill-springing*. This is why Lydiard's hill exercises were so effective: we now know that he was using a principle in physiology that has only recently been demonstrated by research.

Selective Muscle Fiber Recruitment

For small loads, only some of the slow twitch fibers are required, and therefore the brain and nervous system selectively choose which slow twitch fibers to "fire." In fact, the car engine analogy is very useful here. Recent advances in engine design have mimicked nature by allowing large engines to selectively fire fewer or more cylinders according to requirements. This is exemplified by Honda's variable cylinder management or VCM device.

MUSCLE FIBERS

The previously named muscle fibers are the three main types that we need to know about.

Two are contrasting sub-types of the fast twitch variety.

Slow twitch fibers (Type I, also called ST) are fatigue-resistant, generally highly aerobic, and have a very rich blood supply. They are redder in colour due to the presence of myoglobin, the equivalent of hemoglobin in red blood cells. The slow twitch muscle cells have very high concentrations of *mitochondria*; furnace-like structures that can use carbohydrates or fats to produce high yields of energy. Slow twitch muscle fibers can have very high levels of oxidative enzymes, and although they can't contract as explosively as fast twitch fibers, they can generate equal tension given equal cross-sectional area. In other words, they can move just as much weight, but not as quickly. Their motor units are smaller than those of the big fast twitch fibers, and so more muscle fibers will be present given an equal cross-sectional area.

Although called "slow twitch," they're more actually described as "slower twitch," as they can "twitch" at 10-20 times per second, compared to fast twitch fibers, which can twitch 30-70 times a second. They can contribute a lot of force production at very high aerobic speeds and combine with IIA fibers in producing force at glycolytic speeds approaching those of 800m running. They can continuously contract for up to two hours or more at lower loads. At low load levels, slow twitch muscle fibers can fire off asynchronously; meaning differing fibers will come into play across a muscle according to local fatigue levels and fuel levels. Fast twitch fibers fire off synchronously in an all-or-none pattern directed by their large incoming nerve axons.

The ultimate slow twitch muscle is the heart muscle, which never rests during our whole life. Of course, it looks completely different under the microscope than the slow twitch muscle in your limbs because it needs to expand and contract outward and inward, like a balloon, but physiologically the requirements are the same.

The sports genetics cheats of the future might give themselves away when they stand at starting lines with their legs rhythmically expanding and contracting.

Fast twitch fibers (Type II, or FT) as a group are more explosive, bigger, and are generally anaerobic in nature if no endurance training has been applied. They can contract quickly, but fatigue quickly because they lack the richness of vascular supply, myoglobin, oxidative enzymes, and mitochondria of the slow twitch fibers. They are whiter in color because they store starchy glycogen as fuel. Hence they used to be called "white muscle" fibers.

Type IIB, or FT-B fibers are the biggest and most explosive fibers. They will tend to use creatine phosphate as a primary fuel in short-term anaerobic (or alactic) work bouts lasting less than 10 seconds, and they will have the biggest motor units. They can also burn glycogen. With endurance training some FT-B fibers can acquire aerobic qualities and become FT-A fibers.

Type IIA or FT-A (Fast Twitch Aerobic fibers) are intermediary fibers that have aerobic and anaerobic characteristics. They can access fats and carbohydrates from the bloodstream as well as locally stored glycogen and creatine phosphate, and have a reasonably rich blood supply. There is evidence that endurance training changes some FT-B fibers into FT-A fibers. They come most into play after the powerful FT-B fibers have temporarily run out of creatine phosphate and are activated most in glycolytic (long-term anaerobic) work bouts lasting between 13 seconds and 90 seconds.

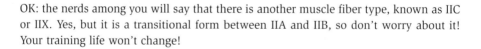

Fiber type ratios are genetically ordained, but studies with identical twins show that these ratios can be changed somewhat with specific training. Slow twitch fibers can't acquire fast twitch characteristics, but some fast twitch fibers can certainly acquire fatigue-resistant slow twitch characteristics with extensive endurance training.

OK: the nerds among you will say that there is another muscle fiber type, known as IIC or IIX. Yes, but it is a transitional form between IIA and IIB, so don't worry about it! Your training life won't change!

If we wish to make things absolutely simple, we can assume that the three fiber types relate strongly to three main energy systems: Type I = Aerobic, Type IIA = Glycolytic (Lactic) anaerobic, and Type IIB = Alactic anaerobic.

Characteristics of the Three Main Muscle Fiber Types

Property	Type I (ST)	Type IIA (FT-A)	Type IIB (FT-B)
Contraction time	"Slow"	Fast	Very fast
Size of motor axon	Small	Large	Very large
Resistance to fatigue	High	Intermediate	Low
Activity used for	Aerobic	Glycolytic anaerobic	Alactic short sprints
Force production	Low	High	Very high
Mitochondrial density	High	High	Low
Capillary density	High	Intermediate	Low
Oxidative capacity	High	High	Low
Glycolytic capacity	Low	High	Very high
Major storage fuel	Triglycerides	Glycogen, CP, some triglycerides	Creatine phosphate, glycogen
Myoglobin Content	High	Medium	Very low
Enzyme Types	Oxidative	Oxidative & glycolytic	Glycolytic & alactic

Table above is from Karp, J. R. "Motor unit recruitment strategy in muscle during eccentric contractions." Unpublished master's thesis. The University of Calgary, 1997.

How does VO2 Max fit into the muscle types and their energy systems?

VO$_2$ Max, like Anaerobic Threshold, or sub-Threshold running, represents a level of *intensity*. Each level of *intensity* will use a combination of muscle types and energy systems as they're phased in or out.

Intensity LEVEL	Muscle Fiber Contribution		Systems Most Trained	
Alactic	LOTS!	SOME	Alactic	+ + + + +
			Lactic / Glycolytic	+
			Aerobic	+
Glycolytic	LOTS!	SOME	Alactic	+ + +
			Lactic / Glycolytic	+ + + + +
			Aerobic	+
VO$_2$ Max	LOTS!	LOTS!	Alactic	+
			Lactic / Glycolytic	+ + +
			Aerobic	+ + + + +
Anaerobic Threshold	LOTS!	A FEW!	Alactic	+
			Lactic / Glycolytic	+ + +
			Aerobic	+ + + + +
Aerobic	SOME!	A few IIA fibers will contribute initially, and contribute more as slow twitch fibers tire.	Alactic	+
			Lactic / Glycolytic	+
			Aerobic	+ + +

Heart Rate and Training Zones "Simplified"

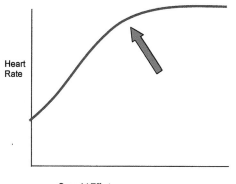

1   As running speed increases, heart rate rises proportionally to a certain point

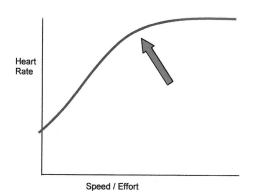

2   This is called the Deflection Point

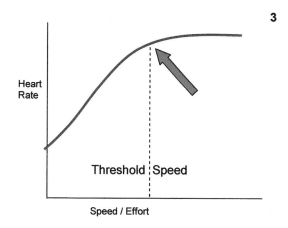

3   The speed run at the deflection point is called Threshold Speed

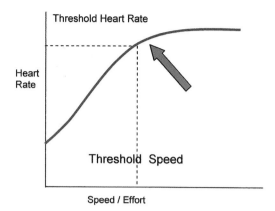

4   The heart rate at the deflection point is called the Threshold Heart Rate

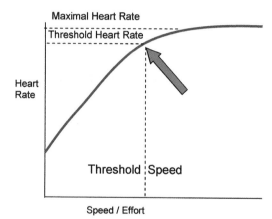

5   The heart rate levels off after this till it reaches maximum

6   Any work after the deflection point is called **maximal work.**

This is also called **ANAEROBIC Work**, meaning performed without oxygen.

Any work before the deflection point is called sub-maximal work.

This is also called AEROBIC work, or ENDURANCE work.

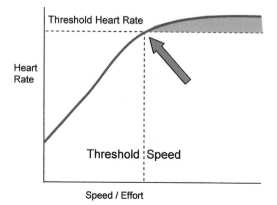

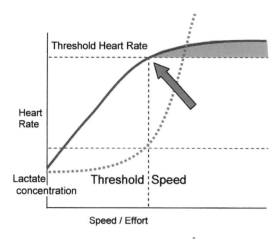

7 At the same time as heart rate rises, LACTATE rises slowly, UNTIL threshold speed is reached. Then it increases exponentially. Threshold occurs at a lactate concentrate of approximately 4 mmol/ litre, though individuals may vary greatly from this average figure.

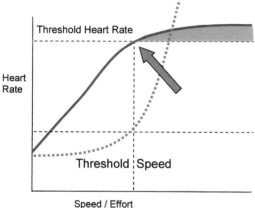

8 If work continues at a high rate, ACIDOSIS will slow the athlete down until exercise is stopped.

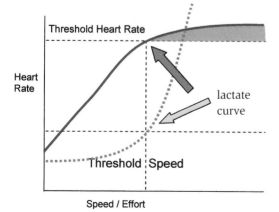

9 This curve is known as the LACTATE CURVE

Note that the deflection point of the heart rate is at Threshold Speed. This point is also the Deflection point for the lactate curve.

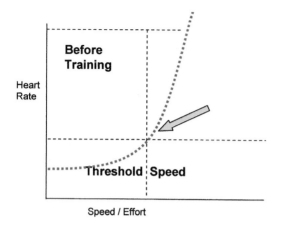

10 Good training will move the deflection point and lactate curve to the right: the athlete will run faster at aerobic speeds

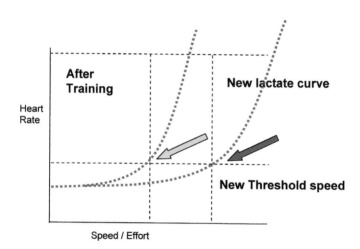

BUT WAIT! THERE'S MORE!

How the Cardiovascular System Changes

With endurance training, the maximal heart rate doesn't increase, but the total work capacity of the heart does. The heart muscle is the ultimate slow twitch muscle, because it *never* stops (while alive, anyhow!).

The heart muscle uses whatever fuels it can to keep on pumping, and unlike linear slow twitch muscle fibers in all the skeletal muscles, the starfish-shaped fibers overlap each other in all directions. This gives the muscle the ability to expand and contract, like Spandex or Lycra.

Prolonged endurance training over time will result in an increased work capacity for several reasons:

1. The heart develops a massive circulatory bed throughout its muscular walls, as do the leg muscles.
2. The muscle walls of all the pumping chambers of the heart become bigger and more powerful
3. The effective volume of the chambers, especially the left ventricle, increases significantly, sometimes within weeks.
4. Under all workloads, more blood can be pumped with more force and a lower heart rate.
5. The resting pulse will therefore decrease significantly, even though the maximal heart rate will be very unlikely to increase.
6. The result will be an increased work capacity, (named the *heart rate reserve*) and at each successive effort level, the heart rate will be lower than before.

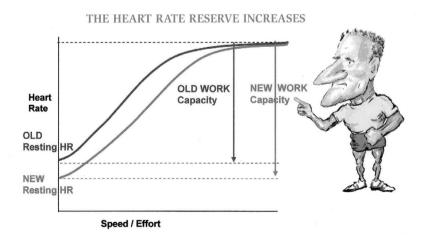

THE HEART RATE RESERVE INCREASES

Training by Heart Rate

Heart rate monitors are very useful, but by no means should they be relied upon to dictate training and racing. You should learn to listen to your body. The best use of heart rate monitors is with people who tend to push their longer runs at too high an intensity. A lot of runners buy heart rate monitors but don't really know how to use them.

Here, in a nutshell, is a quick guide to establishing your training zones without having to get them established in a lab.

The keys are your resting heart rate and your maximal heart rate. Forget the (220-Your Age) formula; that should have disappeared with the dinosaurs!

Your resting heart rate will decrease over time with good aerobic training, but your maximal is far less influenced by training. Nevertheless, the ability of the heart to pump blood will usually increase a great deal, because the size of the left ventricle (the stroke volume) increases with training, and there will be a greater heart rate reserve or work capacity.

Establishing Maximal Heart Rate

Your maximal heart rate is genetically determined and doesn't appear to be increased by training. When you first start endurance work, it is possible that your nervous system will make your heart beat like a jack hammer in response to the new demands of supplying large areas of muscle with blood. As the leg muscles and cardiac muscles capillarize and adapt, the heart's stroke volume will also increase, and a high heart rate is no longer necessary. Your maximal heart rate should be established when you're quite fit already, as should your resting rate.

Maximal heart rate is best discovered by an already fit and rested athlete after several minutes of high intensity running. Try running hard, straight up a steep hill for at least 3 minutes, after a thorough warm-up. Record the pulse every 15 seconds or so, and wherever you max out is about right.

If you're carbed up, glycogen-loaded, and rested, you'll achieve a better heart rate than if you're tired. The heart is a muscle too, and it likes high energy fuel. It will also only respond to the demands made on it by the nervous system, and if the legs are tired then there's not the need for as much cardiac action. In fact, tired legs and glycogen depletion will lower your VO_2 max capability across the board.

Establishing VO_2 Max Heart Rate

Your VO_2 max heart rate is within just a beat or two of your maximal heart rate. It often is just below maximum because at maximum the heart becomes relatively inefficient at filling and emptying.

Establishing Anaerobic Threshold Heart Rate

Your anaerobic threshold rate is the one you need to quantify more and stay well under for most of your endurance training. This is often around 85% of your maximum heart rate, but some athletes can hammer along at above 90% very well.

Your average heart rate recorded during a 50-60 minute road race will suffice for a threshold reading, but you can time-trial at your 15k road racing pace (for a reasonably performed athlete) and by about 20 minutes your threshold levels should even out.

Establishing Your Resting Heart Rate

Your resting heart rate is best averaged from your waking up heart rate; take it three mornings in a row, before you get up and about, and that average will do for a start.

The most useful endurance workloads are done between 60%-80% of your heart rate reserve (HRR). The HRR represents the number of truly available heart beats between rest and maximum.

Establishing Your Heart Rate Reserve

To work out this figure, use the following formula:

HRR = (max HR-resting HR).

For someone with a maximum HR of 195, and a resting HR of 45, the HRR will be 150.

The lowest useful aerobic zone in this example, for gently increasing total capacity, will be [60% x (150)] + [resting HR], or (90 + 45), or 135 beats/minute.

Any lower than this is really only for aerobic recovery or restoration of normal blood pH; the really useful aerobic zones start around 60% of HRR, which coincide with a lactate concentration of about 2mmol/litre. This is also known as the *aerobic threshold*.

Establishing Your Training Intensities

Work out your rates for 65%, 70%, 75%, 80%, 85%, 90%, etc. These then can be entered into your diary and you can see what zones you venture into when you're running over varying terrain, (the HR will go up on up-hills, and decrease on descents) and set an alarm at an upper limit if the purpose of your run is basic aerobic bread and butter endurance.

% HRR	HR
60%	135
65%	143
70%	150
75%	158
80%	165
85%	173
90%	180
95%	188
100%	195

The table on the left shows the pulse rate expected at each intensity in the previous example. The best heart rate for the weekly or bi-weekly "$^3/_4$ effort" run would be between 75% and 80% of maximum HRR: in this case it's an HR between 158 and 165, which is a full 6 beats lower than a typical threshold zone, which would hover around an HR of 173. In the case of this "marathon intensity" run, you can see that the "$^3/_4$ effort" is equivalent to 75% of maximum HRR. The diagram below illustrates this concept further.

As you get fitter aerobically, your comfortable cruising speeds will come down, and, for any given heart rate, more distance can be covered. A good test of condition, then, is what distances you can cover at extremely low heart rates as well as high. Four-time Olympic champion Lasse Viren and his coach measured these adaptations constantly. They would even cover distances with a heart rate as low as 80 beats/ minute.

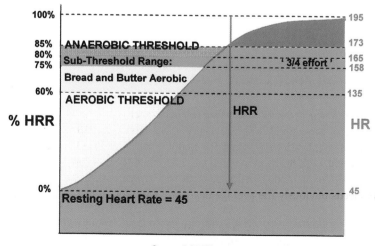

Just thinking about going for a run will achieve this heart rate for a lot of people.

Coach Nic Bideau often gets his athletes to do workouts at very controlled heart rates well below threshold, at rates that approximate potential marathon pace or slower.

He likes to get them to run for a set time with the heart rate in a tight range. Sometimes he'll set several ranges that gradually climb or descend in a workout. He suggests that the most useful conditioning ranges are found around marathon pace or slower, rather than at maximal work rates.

The vast majority of athletes have a threshold level around 85% of heart rate reserve or less. Robert De Castella and other marathon stars were probably well over this, but for practical aerobic endurance training purposes, we will be very safe if we assume that we should generally stay below this zone as much as possible when building the aerobic endurance base, and now and again approach it, but with easy days before and after.

Once you know your zones, it's a matter of getting used to "controlling" training efforts so that the athlete knows exactly what a set heart rate range feels like. Then it's a matter of planning these different aerobic zones into regular endurance training, so that the athlete gets used to going up and down the different intensity levels.

Heart Rate Monitor Tricks

Once over the threshold, and heading towards the maximal heart rate, the heart as a pump can become relatively inefficient. No longer is there a nearly linear relationship between blood pumped and distance covered.

So at any truly aerobic heart rate, at a given level of fitness, and in similar moderate conditions, it will take an athlete a certain number of beats to cover a specific distance. This ratio can be easily calculated with an ordinary heart rate monitor that records average heart rate for an elapsed time.

For instance, if a good athlete covers 10km in a high-aerobic 35 minutes at an average heart rate of 155, that would mean he has covered 10,000m in (35 x 155) heart beats. That would result in 5425 heart beats per 10,000m, or (10,000/5425) meters per heart beat. This would be 1.84 meters per beat. The same athlete could expect to cover 10,000m at 40 minutes and 45 minutes with the same ratio... so at the slower sub-threshold speeds obviously the average heart rate will drop to maintain the ratio.

So if we assume that our athlete is going to take close to 5425 heart beats to cover 10,000m on a known course, we can more or less predict what he should average for different aerobic times over the course.

If he takes 40 minutes, then the 5425 heart beats will be divided over 40 minutes for an expected HR average of just over 135, and at 45 minutes, it will plunge further to just over 120, till eventually it will approach the resting rate.

The exact ratio will vary according to individual biomechanics and will improve over time with the development of aerobic capacity and leg-strength, but within any short-term training block these changes won't be so apparent with someone who has trained for a few years.

This sort of record-keeping is at its most useful when determining when it's safe to do a hard session again. Systemic acidosis will elevate resting heart rate, and glycogen depletion with muscular tiredness will lower stride distance.

The athlete simply has to go for a very easy morning run over a known course and determine the ratio. If it is back to normal, he is running efficiently again. If it is not, he should look at easier aerobic recovery until ready.

The set course should be largely unchanging (i.e. road) and doesn't have to be accurately measured. So long as the same set course is used for such tests, the ratio over that course is all that matters. Olympic triathlon coach Chris Pilone will discuss the effects of overtraining in a later chapter.

NB: Some of the latest HRM's have an in-built heart-rate variability sensor. This detects variation between beats, which may also signify elevated stress levels systemically.

Nic Bideau on Heart Rate

The heart rate progression is something I like to use either at altitude or when athletes are in good racing shape on the track. At altitude, the athletes often find it hard to go fast enough to get their HR up, as compared to sea level but once it's up it can very quickly become difficult to control – usually because they've been working too hard to get it up to normal AT levels in the first place. So it is more of a control mechanism to gradually build from: starting from what is probably marathon race pace effort, to half marathon pace and eventually to around 10 mile race pace effort.

When athletes are in great racing shape I find they have no problem running fast and getting their HR up high very quickly – but while the effort to get HR up at this high speed may seem easy in the first 5 mins. This is due to an increased efficiency at high speeds but this eventually becomes more difficult than they imagined it would according to how they felt in the first 5 mins to maintain and HR starts racing so again it's a control thing just to ensure they are running aerobically for most of this work rather than too anaerobically.

Another thing I do is sometimes throw in a 1 min float, which just lets their HR drop down before they get rolling again. An example of this may be 5x8 min with 1 min float breaks for a 45 min AT pace run.

I believe that there is still a good deal of conditioning effect achieved when running slower than most people do in threshold pace runs, say at marathon race pace, and I find more often people who think they are running with what should be blood lactate content of around 3.5 – 4.5mmol* are probably more likely running 20 min time trials at 10k race pace with the last 10 min of such work producing way too much lactate and this just doesn't have the same effect.

(*This approximates anaerobic threshold in many people, although it can vary.)

I don't always stick to HR – another method I use once they are racing is 85% of 5k race pace – when Mottram is in 13 min shape he often does 10 laps at the beginning and at the end of his workouts at 3 min/km pace – he finds this reproduces a similar effort to when he just goes off HR early in his training prep.

(Since 5000m race pace is about 109% of threshold speed for well-trained runners, then [85% of 109%] will equate to Mottram's 10 lap steady state pace; this works out to be 92.5% of threshold, or just below marathon pace, which is 95-96% of threshold pace on average.)

Mottram rarely trains much above this level of effort, except in a specific sharpening phase.

Cardiac Drift

Cardiac Drift occurs mostly on hot days, during longer runs. A constant paced effort might be accompanied by a steady increase in heart rate throughout the latter part of the run. This is a combination of dehydration and glycogen depletion: the blood plasma volume can decrease significantly due to sweat loss, and this reduced volume is still expected to be kept at a constant pressure when pumped to the rest of the body. Therefore the pump (heart) has to work harder.

Sessions aimed at particular heart rate zones or training intensities should probably be done in temperate conditions and be of medium duration.

If cardiac drift is rapid, you are dehydrating and need to slow down and drink, and perhaps thinking about doing the session on another day.

Training Terms

There are many differing terminologies in running. We've standardized ours as follows:

Steady Stuff

Aerobic Runs

These can range from absolutely slow and easy "recovery" runs, to runs approaching higher intensities below anaerobic threshold training, and at low intensities their main use is to "restore" the system. Extended long runs at low intensity can be enormously useful for an athlete who is having erratic training and racing form. It's very wise to mix in different blends and intensities of "aerobic strata" in a training regime.

Sub-Threshold Runs

Also called marathon-pace runs, these are slightly slower but a lot more comfortable than threshold. **These can give nearly all the benefits of threshold training, without the danger of "going over the top" of the anaerobic threshold.** Sub-threshold runs can be longer than tempo runs, with a similar warm-up and cool-down, but if too long can also use up significant carbohydrate stores that have to be replenished. Lydiard would introduce these into the buildup or base phase gradually, so that one or two "strong" runs of about an hour at marathon race pace were run each week.

These runs will be described in detail later.

Threshold Runs

Also known as tempo runs. These are run as near to the anaerobic threshold as possible. This is often described as "comfortably hard," and is very close to the maximum pace a well-conditioned runner can race at for an hour. The most efficient threshold runs last about 20 minutes and can be slotted into medium-length runs of about an hour in total, after a good aerobic warm-up and with a good aerobic cool-down period.

Threshold running is very effective once good aerobic conditioning has been established, but it uses lots of muscle glycogen (stored carbohydrates). **It's arguable whether athletes without a large aerobic base will benefit much in the long term from such work.**

This work shouldn't be done too often, because it can have a cumulatively tiring effect similar to racing. Short runs of a few minutes at threshold or sub-threshold pace have been found very useful when preparing for faster-paced work in training sessions and even in warming up for important races.

How Lactic Acid Builds Up Exponentially Above Threshold Speed

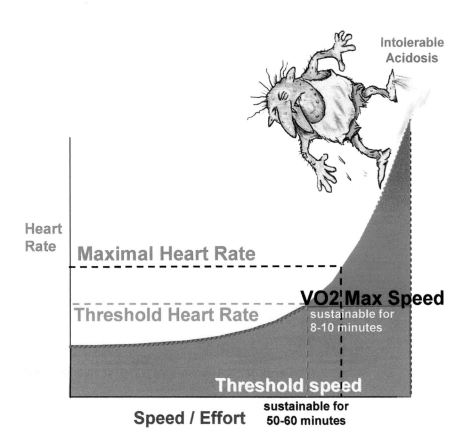

Relating Racing Speeds to Threshold Running Speed

This is based on data from world records and appears accurate for well-trained club athletes as well. You will see that despite the heart rate reaching near maximum at or near VO$_2$ Max, it is possible to keep running faster and faster until acidosis forces the exercise to stop or slow.

Distance	42.2k	21.1k	15k	10k	5k	3k	2000m	1500m	800m
% Threshold Speed	95%	99%	101%	104%	109%	113%	119%	122%	133%

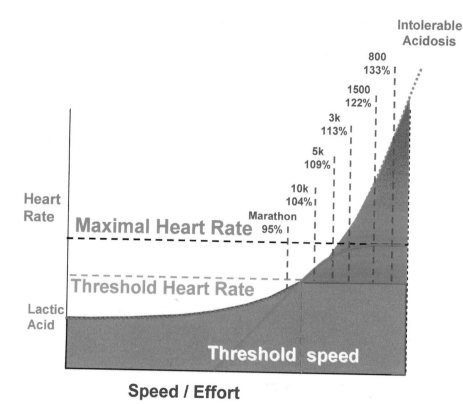

(concept from: Janssen, P. *Training Lactate Pulse Rate*, 1987)

Relating Racing Speeds to VO_2 Max Running Speed

Distance	42.2k	21.1k	15k	10k	5k	3k	2000m	1500m	800m
% VO_2 max	84%	88%	89%	92%	96%	100%	105%	108%	118%
Time Run	2hr 30	70 min	50 min	30 min	15 min	8 min	5 min	4 min	2 min

These speeds are accurate for good club level or better male middle distance runners. For significantly slower athletes, it is best to go by maximum distance achievable in a certain time. For instance, VO_2 Max speed can be held for 8-10 minutes at the best, by either a well-trained slower athlete or a world champion. Threshold speed can be held for 50-60 minutes in a well-trained athlete, regardless of ability.

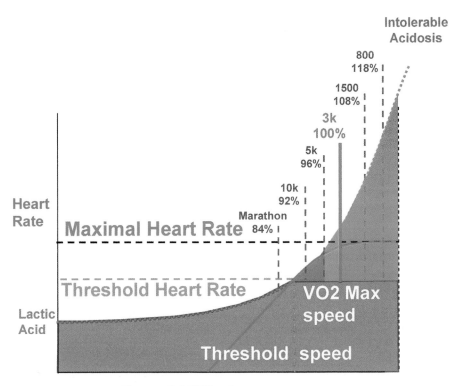

Fast Stuff

VO$_2$ Max Intervals

For the sake of this book those are work bouts run at **VO$_2$ max pace**, with a recovery generally equal to or shorter than the duration of the work bout. They are essentially anaerobic in their effect. **These challenge the Type I slow twitch fibers to their maximum, and probably recruit a good number of IIA glycolytic fast twitch fibers as well.**

VO$_2$ max intervals are very effective when performed for 2-5 minutes, with equal or shorter time recoveries. 5000m pace (95% VO$_2$ max pace) is very safe and effective, yielding all the benefits without the dangers of 100% VO$_2$ pace work (3000m pace). There is simply no real need to go any faster to extract all the benefits of this particular type of training. Any faster and we are training the glycolytic systems, with all the acidosis that invokes. **These runs develop *anaerobic capacity*, by being at an intensity the body can cumulatively hold for some minutes.**

Glycolytic (Lactic) Repetitions

These are work bouts that are considerably faster and shorter, with a much-needed recovery that is far longer than the work bout. They are run at a glycolytic anaerobic pace, which is usually specific to 1500m or 800m pace. They are very anaerobic in their effect. They should never be run in an aerobic base period. **These stimulate the IIA glycolytic fast twitch fibers the most.**

These runs develop *anaerobic power* very well, especially if long or complete recovery is taken.

Leg-Speed Drills

These are very short work bouts, generally less than 10 seconds in duration, that use the alactic anaerobic system, meaning that very little acidosis is possible. They are very safe to do year-round, especially with a good walk or jog recovery of over 30 seconds. These increase power, muscular efficiency, and speed. They are best done when well-rested, near the start of a training session, before moving onto other work. These challenge the IIB fast twitch fibers the most.

Types of Anaerobic Exercises

1. Alactic Exercise

Very short, explosive bursts of exercise lasting only a few seconds. The main fuel for this exercise is a substance called creatine phosphate, stored in the local muscle. The high-energy phosphate can be rapidly restored with a short recovery walk or jog without ever triggering the sluggish lactic acid system, thus avoiding the "acidosis" that halts any longer bursts of intense running. Lactate will only start to accumulate at a high rate after 10-13 seconds of intense exercise. Alactic running is ideal to develop the brain-muscle pathways and coordination associated with sprint speeds, while still building and maintaining aerobic condition.

2. Glycolytic (or Lactic) Exercise

Uses carbohydrate (starchy sugars, such as muscle glycogen) without oxygen to produce rapid energy for longer-term anaerobic work bouts lasting over 13 seconds, but a by-product is **lactic acid** or **lactate**, which can be used as a very energy-rich short-term fuel. The acidosis that stops muscles contracting is really produced by hydrogen ions released at the same time as lactate from the muscles. Lactate eventually is broken down and dispersed back to the liver where it is re-made into sugars.

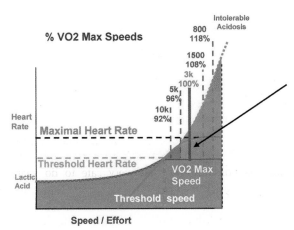

Glycolytic (Lactate Tolerance) Exercise starts to occur here, above VO2 max speed, where lactate increases exponentially. It is best trained at 400m-600m race pace, or the fastest pace that can be maintained between 45 and 90 seconds, with complete recovery. The heart rate will often reach maximal during recovery, as it reacts to the muscular demands for oxygen. It usually won't reach maximum in a short work bout unless prior repetitions have been done.

3. VO₂ Max Exercise

Technically, VO₂ max is the term used to describe the maximal possible level of oxygen uptake when we exercise at sea level. Absolute VO₂ max is measured as total volume of oxygen consumed regardless of body size. Relative VO₂ max is measured in litres of oxygen consumed per kilogram of body weight. This is expressed in mls/kg/minute.

Many people think that somehow VO₂ max represents the upper level of aerobic capacity and is therefore "aerobic" training. Uh-uh. Nope.

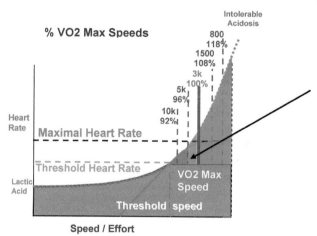

VO2 Max Exercise occurs here, between 3k and 5k pace, before the point where lactate increases exponentially. You can see that VO2 max work is maximal, anaerobic work, well above the anaerobic threshold.

This is most safely trained at 5000m speed or best 15 minute pace (96% VO2 max). Later as one gets fitter it can be trained at 3000m (100% VO2 max) or best 8 minute pace.

At VO₂ Max, your heart rate is near its maximum, and at this maximal work rate, huge amounts of oxygen are consumed. However, the amount of oxygen consumed is nowhere near enough to meet the demands of the muscles, and the work rate can only be maintained for several minutes at most in a fit athlete. The working muscle cells are being asked to do two things at once: extract whatever oxygen they still can from an increasingly acidic bloodstream and extract anaerobic energy by glycolysis.

So even though this level of work represents the highest level of oxygen consumption possible, we must remember that the work intensity is *anaerobic* and mounting acidosis in the working muscles will force the exercise to stop at the maximal rate.

More on VO₂ Max

Brief periods of training at this pace can be very beneficial in elevating race potential over middle distances, but the changes in maximal oxygen consumption are mainly in body chemistry and muscle cell chemistry. Maximal oxygen can be extracted because of greatly increased concentrations of oxidative enzymes and buffering agents in the working muscle.

Brief periods of training at maximal rates can naturally train the top end of cardiopulmonary capacity as well (to get efficient at these work rates, the body has to be exposed to them), but capillary development and blood supply to the working muscle are best developed with prolonged endurance work at a much lower level.

Blood supply to the muscle cell isn't efficiently increased by VO_2 max efforts because the very high work rate invokes acidosis that chemically suppresses normal aerobic functions and can inflame or rupture the muscle cell wall. VO_2 max pace is very close to the pace one can hold for 8 minutes. For good athletes, current 3000m pace is 100% VO_2 max pace, and current 5000m pace is 96% VO_2 max pace.

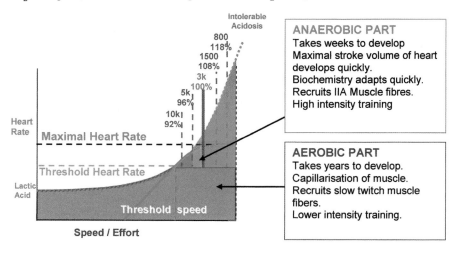

There Are Two Parts to VO₂ Max Development

The first and most important part is the aerobic base below the anaerobic threshold. Time spent running aerobically has been shown to be the biggest stimulus to the aerobic development of the body. Time spent exercising at lower intensities will encourage the safe development of the cardiovascular delivery systems of the body and the proliferation of mitochondria, which together constitute more or less the pure aerobic contribution to VO_2 max via the slow twitch muscle fibers being extended to their fullest capacity.

The second portion, where maximal oxygen is consumed, is of course, terribly anaerobic. This portion is the cellular chemistry contribution, where the biggest stimulus is really time spent at VO_2 max (or, more safely, 95% Max – 5000m race pace for a good athlete). The safest and best stimulus for this is several 2-5 minute bursts of exercise at 5000m pace, with equal or shorter recovery, progressing over several weeks to 3000m pace intervals.

Physiologists may or may not agree with this breakdown of VO_2 max but, for all practical purposes, it works. It provides a rational reason why different studies give different answers to the "best" way to raise VO_2 max.

The answer is there isn't a "best" way to elevate VO_2 Max.

It depends on which contribution to VO_2 max we're talking about: the pure aerobic or the anaerobic.

Any short-term scientific study done over only a few weeks automatically excludes the key requirement of sub-threshold aerobic development: time.

There is a clear two-fold progression, with the development of "pure" aerobic pathways at low intensities the first priority, (stimulating the type I slow twitch fibers, mitochondrial activity, capillarisation, and oxidative enzymes) followed by higher intensity exercise that is really well above the anaerobic threshold and stimulates the cell chemistry to buffer acidosis and extract energy anaerobically.

Part 2
"Complex" Training Systems

Many modern approaches incorporate work at different energy levels of the training pyramid on a regular basis; perhaps every week. Does this mean they're "no good" or ineffective?

No. By paying attention to key basics, and ensuring that ample recovery and steady state aerobic running is completed each week, it certainly is possible for an athlete to race and train well year-round, and progress constantly. The "complex" system of training developed and refined in Australia by Pat Clohessy, Chris Wardlaw, Rob De Castella and Steve Moneghetti is an example.

Earlier, Ron Clarke, who broke 16 world records, ran using a similar system. Clarke wrote years ago that he "didn't believe in peaking," and he implied that if one trained constantly, improving aerobic efficiency, then one's peak was always at the current aerobic level reached. This was inferred by many Lydiard advocates as a criticism of Arthur's methods, but on reflection, it is a confirmation. There is no better example of an athlete prepared to constantly raise his aerobic training tempos, year after year, with the direct result of increased performance, than Ron Clarke. My only comment here would be that we never did see what Ron Clarke could have done had he put a specific anaerobic topping on his awesome aerobic base.

Funnily enough, Michael Johnson, world record-holder over 200m and 400m, has also been quoted recently as saying he "doesn't believe in peaking." Well, whether he believes in it or not, I don't know what else to call the largest-ever improvement on the world 200m record ever on an Olympic day that counts. (His stupendous 19.32s improved on his own recent 19.66, which in turn broke the 17-year old world record of 19.72 set by Pietro Mennea of Italy). Anyhow, Michael and I will have to agree to disagree on this one.

The "Australian system" is a weekly "template" including different types of running and different aerobic and anaerobic tempos on different days. Like any "template," it can be fiddled with slightly and fine-tuned as the athlete learns his or her reactions to the weekly work. An advantage can be that the athlete always knows generally what to do each week, and also the racing muscles and energy systems are never far away from race conditioning. The disadvantage in many of these "complex" systems is that athletes can overdo the anaerobic work at the cost of their aerobic systems and that true race-specific speed development for middle distance is never done.

It isn't periodised training leading to a seasonal peak, but it is extremely effective conditioning that could easily lead into a specific middle distance race preparation with outstanding results. The keystone of this system is the regular long running, but interspersed through the week are short bursts of faster running that are well-buffered by very easy aerobic running. The percentage of faster running is extremely small, but pivotal.

This training was the conditioning basis for 3:31.96 1500m runner Simon Doyle, who was ranked by *Track and Field News* as No. 2 over 1500m worldwide for two years running in the early 1990s. Doyle's time is still the Australian 1500m record. Coach Pat Clohessy told me that after a disappointing 1990 Commonwealth Games where he finished 4th in the 1500m with 3:35.70, Doyle wished to move up to 5000m. Clohessy got him to train with Shaun Creighton, who was later the Australian 10,000m record-holder, and they were well matched over hill-circuits and 15-mile runs. The result of this increased endurance work was a big breakthrough over 1500m and 800m, as well as an Australian 3000m record.

Pat Clohessy pointed out that in earlier years Doyle had done "tremendous amounts of hard repetition work," and this combined very well with a new relaxed approach to long "freedom runs" through the Stromlo Forest without a watch. Frequently Doyle and Creighton would do "surge work" of up to 10-15 minutes over the varying circuits in the forest, and other times do "quick hills" of about 180m on forest trails.

In our "H.I.T. System" adaptation of the Lydiard method, we have also followed a weekly template system that can be easily adapted year-round. The main things we include on a year-round basis are a focus on maintaining and developing leg speed, which can be done very successfully while increasing aerobic capacity, and always a long weekly run. This is all explained in Part 5, where we share how we train our squad on this basis, with consistently good results.

Perhaps my only criticism of the "Australian" system is in its poor interpretation by many athletes and coaches, rather than the system itself. Athletes never seem to regularly go to some parkland in spikes and work on pure leg speed and turnover, with ample recovery, before commencing other work, for instance. However, Rob De Castella was an exception. He would put on his track spikes to do leg-speed work before any of his "sprint / float" sessions (400 fast/200 float).

One session, usually done over parkland or trails, is named after Steve Moneghetti. The "Mona fartlek" consists of bursts of faster effort over successively shorter time intervals (i.e., 20min. 2x90s, 4x60s, 4x30s, and 4x15s with equal 'float' recoveries). This sort of workout will never develop all of the middle-distance capacities efficiently because true leg speed running requires a rested state before we do the fast work … not minutes of preceding fast tempo work and legs full of acidosis!

Therefore it's a VO$_2$ max workout, not a race-specific glycolytic workout for middle-distance runners, and definitely not a leg speed workout, although the popular running magazines will tell you it is a "speed workout." Not in my book. However, if Joe Runner were to do a specific leg speed workout with plenty of recovery before moving to a Mona fartlek, then he'd be able to absorb both types of training and his nervous system would be able to adapt and make sense of it.

Other proponents of year-round "complex" systems include such successful distance runners as Frank Shorter and Arturio Barrios.

Shorter's notorious interval sessions were of extremely high quality, with short recoveries. He must have had a huge anaerobic capacity which he needed to train constantly to reach his potential. He would alternate intense days with days where young teenagers could jog with him for miles. There is a tale of a young athlete who joined Shorter on one of his easy days and was amazed at how easily he could keep up with the superstar. Shorter then invited the youngster along for a track workout the next day, and apparently the kid lasted just a couple of laps! For Frank Shorter, with a 7:51 3000m time and marathon endurance, track intervals with short recoveries around 61-62 seconds are only VO$_2$ max pace or very slightly faster. For an untrained kid, they will be intolerable.

Sometimes individual athletes emerge with a very unusual blend of muscle fiber types that loudly dictate their responses to training.

De Castella's hard efforts were short and sweet sessions. However, both De Castella and Shorter stressed very, very easy long running on recovery days.

Another athlete who achieved the highest levels was Irish runner John Treacey, who was notorious for the slowness of his long runs. Fellow Irish athletes refused to train with him because of the boredom, according to Chris Pilone. However, it didn't stop Treacey from becoming world cross-country champion in 1979.

So if you're going to train this way, err on the side of caution after hard effort days, and you'll be in very good company.

Start with the End in Mind

The Lydiard program starts with the end in mind. In this way, it is no different from any other planning exercise.

If the end in mind is superlative performance at the very limit of our trainable capacities, then we have to ask ourselves what the most fundamental requirements are. In planning terminology, we have to supply abundant fuel and get rid of wastes quickly.

Obviously, when we're running at our physiological limits for several minutes, fuel delivery has to be as highly developed as possible and waste removal has to be equally well-developed.

Imagine a huge city like New York that was expected to just "grow" without some form of infrastructure or planning. By the time a population of a few thousand was established, reliable infrastructure would be expected to ensure a supply of water, food, and consumables, and infrastructure would also be expected to quickly get rid of wastes. Without such infrastructure, a city like New York would have stayed the size of a small trading village. The potential of that village to grow to its fullest functional potential would have been limited without proper planning and long-term vision.

Clearly for a huge city to function well, the infrastructure of supply and removal has to be huge and well-planned. The trillions of cells in the human body have the same requirements.

Now if we continue the car/engine analogy, imagine a high-performance racing motor that had small fuel inlets and small waste extractors. No matter how much horsepower this engine could develop in short bursts, its capacity would be severely limited.

Evidently the engine would run much better for much longer if the fuel and air intakes were ample to meet demand, and if burned fuel wastes were removed as soon as they were produced.

We can look to nature for the best possible analogy of what I am trying to describe here. Nearly all of the 1200 known bamboo species are notorious for extremely rapid growth. One species, Bambusa oldhamii, is known to grow up to four feet a day, often reaching 90 feet in just 60 days, with no further growth until the next spring. But what is not commonly known is that the seedlings can stay underground for 5 years or so before even a shoot appears. Despite prolific watering, weeding, and soil preparation over 5 years, nothing appears, *on the surface*. But underground, the plant (a supergrass) has developed a magnificent root system that extends far and wide, preparing all systems for the massive spurt that eventually occurs. Does this growth occur in just 60 days, or in 5 years and 60 days? It is during the latter. The 5 years of unseen growth just makes it all possible.

So for the ultimate high-performance athlete, the first thing to plan is the fuel supply and waste removal infrastructure because this takes the longest to develop and is the limiting factor for all high-intensity exercise. To understand this more, we have to go right down to the cellular level.

Unless there is ample attention paid to the progressive development of the circulatory system at the microscopic level a long-term improvement in performance is hindered.

Why? Because eventually a point will be reached where there is inefficient supply of nutrients and inefficient removal of wastes.

This is the point where the energy demands on the muscle exceed the ability of the circulation to supply it with fuel and oxygen, or where the body cannot quickly flush acidic wastes away from the working cells. This ends in a pooling of substances that inhibit normal nerve and muscle function, and can attack the cell wall and cytoplasm (cell contents) as well.

To counteract this we have to develop the circulation at the tiniest level: where the skeletal muscle cells uptake oxygen and glucose and offload waste products: carbon dioxide, lactates, and other intermediary by-products.

The energy production in the cells is done by workhorses called the mitochondria. These turn fuel and oxygen into the energy required for forceful muscle contractions.

In a very fit endurance-trained athlete, the skeletal muscle cells and mitochondria are supplied by many tiny blood vessels called capillaries.

Mitochondria are the "energy furnaces" of the human muscle cell. They gobble up fatty acids and sugars within the cell, and are prolific in the red slow twitch fibers. Fast twitch fibers that have responded to endurance training will have some mitochondrial development in the cell. These IIA fibers can alternate between aerobic and anaerobic energy systems.

The slow twitch fibers are rich in myoglobin, the muscle's equivalent of hemoglobin, the iron-rich protein that enables oxygen to be carried in the red blood cells. Mitochondria are richly endowed with the enzymes necessary to extract oxygen from the blood, and also with the enzymes that can break large molecules of glycogen and globules of fatty acids down into simple fuels.

Mitochondria and myoglobin are noticeably absent in the super-powerful IIB fast twitch fibers.

The DNA that runs our mitochondria is inherited only on the female X-chromosome; in fact there is strong genetic evidence in the mitochondria that all humans descend from a common human female ancestor in the distant past. As with all scientific conjecture, there is debate on this, but a point of agreement is that there are only about 7 basic mutations from a common maternal ancestral DNA in all modern Europeans, and the European DNA is only a step removed from that of our East African and North African brothers and sisters.

So, athletes, at the end of the day, you inherit a large portion of your sheer endurance capacity at the cellular level from your Mum!

Whatever the science is, it makes basic good sense to choose your maternal line wisely. British coach Colin Livingstone agrees. "Choose good hardy peasant stock in your maternal line. Preferably women who could work all day in the fields, from sun-up to sun-down, then get home and cook for their men folk."

Livingstone has carefully scrutinized his family line and found an unbroken line of females extending into antiquity. (Not surprisingly, many of their male partners didn't live as long.)

There you go; you now know all of the practical exercise physiology concepts we need for this book. Now you can stun athletes and coaches alike by nonchalantly dropping phrases like "glycolytic acidosis" into training conversation. Wouldn't that be fun?

If you really need more, go to the "For the Nerds" section in Part 11.

Part 3, which comes next, ties your new knowledge together, within the framework of the Lydiard System, so that as well as stunning people with your vocabulary you can stun them with results. That's a lot better!

Part 3
The Lydiard System Explained

First Things First – Your Training Diary

If you're serious about your athletics, you'll keep a daily training diary. It doesn't need to be complicated: the simpler the better.

I know of some decent national-level athletes who don't bother, but they pay when it comes time to sort out a training pattern or when the coach needs to find out where the athlete has gone off the path. If you don't measure things and write them down, you usually can't manage them! Imagine any business that didn't record daily transactions: it wouldn't be going anywhere fast!

Kiwi running superstar Rod Dixon was coached for years by his brother John. John insisted that Rod keep an ordered diary of all his training. Sometimes when Rod was in Europe and having troubles adjusting his program, all he had to do was ring John in New Zealand and read out his sessions from his diary.

"John would be onto things in a flash! He could sort things out for me very quickly, and I was on the other side of the world!" says Rod.

At the end of a season, John would sit down and re-examine Rod's training diary to look for patterns and results that were below par. This information was invaluable for planning the next season.

Lydiard was the same: he would examine his athletes' diaries regularly for the same reasons.

I know of some athletes who keep all their training data on a computer: this is OK for complex heart rate analysis, but what happens when the computer dies or the program gets superceded?

For day-to-day stuff a cheap, ordinary year calendar diary is sufficient for Olympians and club athletes alike. I have over twenty years' worth in a little box under my bed. The best type of diary is a simple business diary, with one week to the open double page. These diaries usually have a little year planner in the front – perfect for the business of entering important race dates and counting back.

All you have to do is run a ruler about 5 cm in from the right margin of each page. The top part of the margin is where you enter the sessions your coach has planned for the day. The bottom part is where you enter the total distance covered for the day. The larger area to the left is where you write in all the meaty stuff of exactly what you did. That's all you need. You can also enter morning heart rate, how you're feeling, etc: this is best kept in one specific part of your diary entries every day.

At the end of the week, you can enter your total miles run, and any other data, in the top right part of the right-side page and transfer this information to the year planner at the front for at-a-glance totals.

We've found diaries very useful with our athletes, especially if things go awry at the peak end of the season. We can quickly go back to when they felt they were running very well and see just what type of session done recently they responded to.

One of our runners had recorded a 3:46 1500m time (his PB) off a weekly Tuesday session that went along the following lines:
1. short warm-up followed by several fast relaxed strides over 60m:
2. 10 minutes of threshold running on parkland
3. after several easy minutes, 3 x 800m @ 3000m pace, 2 minutes recovery
4. easy half-hour aerobic recovery

We had done that sort of work for several weeks in our VO_2 max phase, and he had raced well over 800m and 1500m early season, even pushing his 1:52.0 PB at 800m. The more intense sessions of the week are nearly always done Tuesday in our adaptation of the Lydiard system, so it's pretty easy to spot how changes in training can affect the athlete because we keep most parts of the training week quite constant year-round.

When we upped the intensity of his Tuesday work to glycolytic work at 1500m pace, his form became erratic. So we know now that Daniel responds best to 3000m pace intervals, and that he needs barely an injection of faster work, with racing, to reach his potential each season.

By the same process, we have worked out that his training partner "Chubba" responds very well to 800m races run 2 days apart and fast glycolytic work. His training diaries from last year and this year show that he ran a PB 1500m each time he had done this in regular racing in the previous week. In fact, he ran a winning 800m PB this season of 1:52.0, less than two days after getting a tired 5th in another 800m in 1:55.0.

Both athletes are very closely matched from 800m to 3000m on the track, but for them to race to their best for the remainder of the season they will have to concentrate on different types of work.

At the business end of a season, different variations will work best for individual athletes, but you won't be able to find these individual patterns unless you keep excellent records. So keep a diary!

The Lydiard Endurance Base in Detail

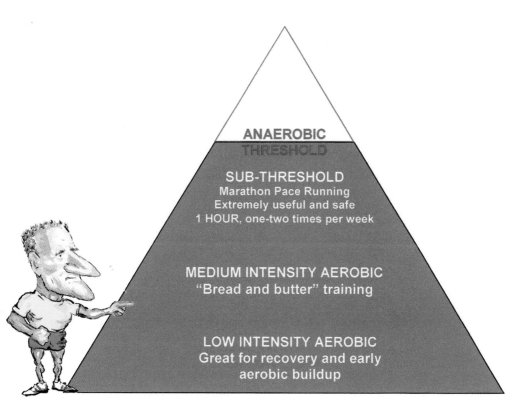

This is the base of the training pyramid: the foundation of all that comes later, and will therefore be covered in some detail. The biggest misconception for modern athletes and coaches is that this period emphasizes "long slow distance." Wrong. Wrong. Wrong.

That is a myth that emerged with the philosophy of enjoyable running for the masses in the 1970s. It has its place for sure, especially in recovery running, but it is miles away from the most effective type of endurance training required to perform at world-class levels.

It may also have emerged because Lydiard espoused long slow running for people at risk of heart disease. The Auckland Joggers' Club and the Honolulu Marathon Clinic used this sort of slow running very successfully with people who'd suffered cardiac events.

So, in the interest of keeping things as simple as possible, but not simpler... here's a quote from Arthur Lydiard in a Chicago interview when he was 85:

"LSD (long slow distance) has its place. Long slow distance of three, four or five hours certainly will enhance your capillary development well because you are engaging the exercise for a very, very long period of time. But the point is it takes longer to obtain the same result as if you were to do your aerobic training at higher aerobic speed.

We had to obtain the best possible result in the limited time that we had and the best way to develop aerobic capacity was to train at higher aerobic speed. My runners did a very hilly 22-mile course, with one hill of three miles, somewhere around 2:10 and 2:15*. We used to do our Monday 10-mile run in about 55 minutes. They were all aerobic running, but we weren't mucking around at all."

* Barry Magee says that these times were achieved by the elite athletes such as Snell and himself, towards the end of the endurance phase: not every week. At the start of the endurance phase, the aim was to get around the whole 22-mile course in good condition. Most good distance runners would aim to cover the course in around 2 hrs 30 mins to 2 hrs 40 mins.

There's a Time and Place for Everything

Lydiard was very clear that each phase of training had a particular purpose and a time-frame in which to achieve the intended results. He didn't like to introduce new things until a phase had been largely completed and the body was ready for the next step.

When the next step or phase was introduced, the previous development would be maintained while the new work was concentrated on. For instance, during hill-work, a weekly long run and some easy recovery runs would maintain the fine aerobic development, but the focus was the hill-work.

The body would be ready for the next step when the law of diminishing returns took effect. For instance, there was no use introducing the hill-strengthening phase until the strong aerobic runs done during the "buildup" ceased to show much improvement. Improvement would be constant and powerful for a number of weeks but would usually trail off between 8 and 10 weeks, depending upon the prior development of the athlete. A new athlete could stay in this phase for months on end and still continue to improve; however, at some stage, the body would need faster work to get the very best results.

This didn't mean that more aerobic improvement wouldn't occur: in practical terms it was a matter of prioritizing the type of work that would get the athlete into the best possible condition to race well in the time that was available. Eight weeks of aerobic buildup may get an athlete's aerobic capacity to within a whisker of its current potential, whereas double that amount of time might yield little more change. To some, this tiny bit of extra potential was worth spending months and years to acquire if it meant a tenth of a second at the business end of an Olympic final.

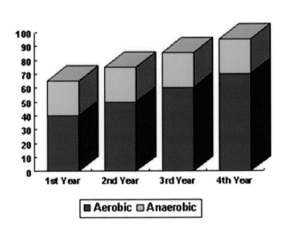

Athletes like the great Finn Lasse Viren, coached by Lydiard's protégé Rolf Haikkola, would spend years on the endurance phase, and use most domestic and international competitions between Olympics as "development races" or measures of condition. Viren's execution of his training plan was perhaps the epitome of Arthur Lydiard's concepts: Viren was prepared to run several extra thousand kilometers in training at controlled aerobic speeds in

Finnish winters and forego gold at competitions as important as the European championships (he won bronze), in order to win the ultimate prize, which he did with "double doubles" over 5000m and 10000m at the 1972 and 1976 Olympics.

The endurance phase was all about strong aerobic running. At no stage in a "buildup" would an athlete deliberately undertake sustained work above the anaerobic threshold. Lydiard considered this to be totally counter-productive and harmful to the development of the aerobic systems. In fact he was very emphatic about this. Lydiard had his athletes undertake a high volume of work, with a portion approaching the anaerobic threshold, but never deliberately exceeding it during the endurance phase. His runs each week were of varying distances, with varying "effort levels," each one developing different levels of the aerobic strata and all with the intent of raising the ability to run at speed aerobically.

There was a very simple reason for not running every run at a pace that pushed the anaerobic threshold; this pace would be the equivalent of running the mileage of 4 marathons at race pace, each week, or faster. This would be very tiring and would hammer the glycogen reserves and recovery ability of the body. Longer runs at lower aerobic speeds could actually speed recovery from faster efforts.

Having said all this, athletes such as Snell definitely "mixed" some of their phases of training on occasions. This was especially important when trying to fit in short racing tours with the demands of long term planning for major competitions. They could do this because there was a substantial aerobic base and training maturity that was already developed, and the "balancing act" could still yield satisfactory short-term results.

However, it wasn't the ideal structure of training Lydiard aspired to, and in the "real world" that Lydiard's first pupils lived in, training had to be efficient and very time-effective. They did whatever got the best results possible, which meant never skipping the aerobic phase, but hill resistance and anaerobic phases could certainly be compressed, with excellent results, especially if the aerobic work had been excellent.

Flexibility and Individuality

On discussing this with Barry Magee, it is also very clear that some other myths have to be exposed here. No two athletes are alike. This is screamingly obvious. We differ as much on the inside as we do on the outside. Even the Kenyan highlanders as an interrelated group, exhibit startling individual differences in responses to training.

We have to understand that you and I have different blends of muscle fibers that give us different capacities to respond to the different types of training. We have different nervous systems and different perceptions of discomfort and pain and differing types of intelligence. We have different cardiovascular capacities.

Despite all these differences, the rule is still to develop the aerobic systems to their utmost first.

While many writers associate Lydiard's system with rigidity and inflexibility, in practice the opposite was true. Lydiard was intuitive, as all great coaches are, when dealing with his athletes personally. Like a good horse trainer, he could tell very quickly if a program was not working for an athlete and would change a schedule around very quickly if need be. The principles behind the training never changed, but the intensity and duration of workouts could be fine-tuned to the individual.

Magee once presented himself to Lydiard during a buildup, still carrying a little "condition" despite having trained over 100 miles a week for months. Magee was a natural endurance runner who could coast at high aerobic speeds all day. Lydiard immediately made him train with Ray Puckett, a notoriously hard racer and trainer, for several weeks. The weight came off.

Don MacFarquhar, a well-known Auckland coach who trained with Snell, recounts that Lydiard had "many different schedules for different ages and stages of development. His 100-mile a week preparations were really only for the exceptionally talented or serious athletes."

MacFarquhar also recounts how Arthur's standard response to any new training method or suggestion was "No! It won't work" until he'd had time to think about it and trial the suggestion. MacFarquhar noticed that Snell was "ploughing" the ground with his raw power when he sprinted, rather than flowing over it. Snell was already an Olympic 800m champion, so new suggestions to Lydiard on training were not advisable.

Nevertheless, MacFarquhar suggested to Lydiard that Snell should work on his technique regularly under the instruction of a top sprint coach. Lydiard duly thought this over and realized that Don was absolutely correct, and initiated regular Monday night technique drills under the tutelage of 400m champion and sprint coach Colin Cameron. This work was started after Christmas each summer for the next few years, at the time when the endurance buildup had been completed.

Lydiard had already intuitively coached his champions to Olympic medals and world records when he was finally introduced to the physiology of what he was doing after a European tour in the early 1960s.

MacFarquhar relates how the whole squad was called together when Arthur had returned, and he explained concepts such as "anaerobic" and "aerobic" exercise.

He "lost" his squad almost at the outset. Bill Baillie, later a 6th placer in the Olympic 5000m and a world record-holder for 20,000m and 30,000m (still the New Zealand 20,000m track record-holder, since 1964!), chirped up saying "You mean fast stuff and slow stuff, coach?" Olympic champion Halberg was even more to the point: "Coach, does all this change anything we're doing in training?" "No, not at all," said Lydiard. "Good. So we can cut the B.S. and get on with it!" replied Halberg.

Lydiard was also never overly concerned with counting mileage *except* for the period of the endurance phase or "buildup" as we knew it. As this phase was the foundation, no shortcuts were possible, and aerobic volume was the key. However, although the exact amount was individual and negotiable; the principle wasn't.

Lydiard once wrote, "No one can say exactly what the limits are for the individual; it's a question of each runner adjusting to running and doing what he or she likes, on the basic understanding that the more they run aerobically, the better the prospects for development are going to be."

As far as the endurance base is concerned, the principle of individuality has to be applied with common sense. I remember a very talented athlete who had run 50 seconds flat for 400m at 17 years of age with very little specific training. He had designs on 800m running. As he could also cover 200m in close to 22 seconds and win his school cross-country on soccer training, he was obviously a special talent. In terms of muscle fibers, he had a great number of IIB and IIA fibers, and a small "tank" of type I slow twitch fibers that he developed enough to win a school endurance race, but that was about it.

However, he was a hopeless sight as he struggled on long runs and fared much better later on when he cut back and ran sustained 12 mile (20k) efforts over big hills at close to his best aerobic speeds. For him, that was enough to achieve the goal of long runs initially, and in later years he could have progressed to the truly longer runs. For various reasons he didn't persevere, so we'll never know what might have been.

Peter Snell was possibly a similar physical type, and a far more determined character, so he managed to persevere through the early endurance years enough to turn his IIB fast twitch capacity to IIA fast twitch oxidative capacity, and we all know what became of Peter.

Lorraine Moller, who was trained on Lydiard principles since her early teens, was able to run 56 seconds for 400m at the age of 15, beating much older women. Her coach nurtured her initially on 50 aerobic miles a week under Lydiard's instructions, and she thrived and increased distances from year to year. Before she was out of her teens, she'd placed 5th in the Commonwealth Games 800m final, and later, 5th in the world cross-country championships.

After moving to marathon training in 1979, she won Commonwealth medals over 1500 and 3000m in 1982, as well as breaking the New Zealand women's 1500m record in 1985. In between these track performances she was 5th in the inaugural Olympic women's marathon.

The great Dick Quax, who coached Lorraine Moller to her Barcelona Olympics marathon medal, says this about individuality: "Every runner is unique. I have never coached two runners who have reacted in the same way to training. There is no recipe for success – only sound physiological principles, which must be adhered to." It's a case of horses for courses, but everyone benefits from correct endurance training.

It will take an athlete and coach a couple of years at least to learn the likely reactions to different types of work for that individual. Often we don't even know "what's in there" until muscle fibers get well-trained. It can be very surprising, and one may find that the athlete is suited to a totally different distance range than he or she initially found success with.

An athlete I coach who had great success as a schoolboy distance runner recently commenced his track racing and was asked on the spur of the moment to run in a 4 x 400m relay for his club. Earlier in the month he had won a couple of 800m races with short sprints in the straight, competing against state-level competitors, on a diet of weekly long VO_2 max intervals, with nothing faster than 64s 400m pace. After running a disappointing 1500m race and feeling "tired" from working all day before in a bottle store, he ran 49.6 for the relay leg. We hadn't even trained this energy system or those paces yet at all, so he may have a very big tank of glycolytic IIA muscle fibers just waiting to be trained.

Train, Don't Strain

The purpose of this phase was to systematically build the aerobic capacity to the highest level possible before commencing faster work. The biggest stimulus to the development of aerobic capacity is often *uninterrupted time spent* at higher aerobic or sub-threshold levels: especially with regard to the development of the very fine blood vessels in the running muscles (the capillary beds) and the muscular walls of the heart itself.

While it's an established fact these days that repeated intense exercise bouts well over the level of the anaerobic threshold can stimulate "growth factors" in capillaries supplying skeletal muscle, (as long as sufficient recovery time is allowed between intense exercise bouts) it's also an established fact that the prolonged "acidosis" and muscle trauma that accompanies such exercise can be detrimental.

More recovery time is required that could otherwise have been spent doing productive aerobic training, without such "down time." Even mild acidosis has been shown to disrupt the body's aerobic and anaerobic energy systems, the nervous system, and the function of cells. Training too intensely is like playing with fire. Aerobic training is safe and predictable. There is certainly a place for more intense work, later, when the time is right.

Lydiard found that most healthy competitive adult distance runners could handle a volume of around 10-12 hours of steady to strong aerobic running a week, and still improve significantly. This effectively would result in a figure around 100 miles per week for a good runner, and became a good yardstick to aim for.

Originally Lydiard's schedules were written for male runners aspiring to national and international competition. He completely changed his schedules to time-based formulae when one dear elderly lady runnerat a YMCA talk informed him that she had been following his schedules religiously and had completed 102 miles the previous week, but it took her rather a long time (20 hours!).

Lydiard noted that if an athlete was able to add slower easier recovery running in secondary sessions, according to his or her ability to maintain the workload, that even finer results could be attained.

The trick was to do as much strong aerobic running as possible while improving week by week but not so much that general fatigue would result. Lydiard found that the best way to balance the weekly schedule was by varying the distances and efforts so that the athlete was always able to *absorb* the training and come back for more. The axiom here was *Train, don't strain*.

Absorb Your Training

If we use another analogy here, getting base miles in can be compared to studying. There is only so much one can absorb effectively. Have you ever spent unproductive hours studying for an exam when you were already too tired to absorb the information? There is only so much that can be absorbed, and beyond that point, it's a complete waste of time. So find what your level of "absorption" is and don't go over it. This is your "set-point," and though it may shift over time, don't rush it. Just because your body can do something when it's tired doesn't mean that you're getting an optimal result. Do enough to get the result and have the wisdom to leave it right there.

There is no point in setting a record week of mileage if you get sore knees and ankles, a sore throat, and lose the next three weeks from minor problems. When I was on the Lydiard program, at about age 20-22 I could do endless weeks of 125 miles a week at 6 minutes a mile average (for my evening runs). This was made up of morning or lunchtime jogs of about 5 miles, Monday-Friday, and longer runs Tuesday, Thursday, Saturday, and Sunday. A few times I bumped it up to over 135 miles a week, and my joints felt stiff, so I didn't do more. I never got an injury, a cold, or flu in my best year of training, which totaled 5400 miles, including a full summer. That year I had a very enjoyable job with regimented hours.

I had plenty of colds, flu infections, and injuries in other years when I had disrupted work and study schedules, and tried to keep old levels of training up in altered circumstances.

Rome Wasn't Built in a Day

Control of efforts was a key Lydiard principle. One would start the endurance phase at a lower level of performance and gradually raise it by deliberately scheduled "effort runs" that over weeks would increase the aerobic capacity and shift the anaerobic threshold. At no stage was "racing" of training desired or encouraged: the "acidosis" created by running too hard early in the schedule would slow progress and possibly send the athlete into a pit of fatigue.

Patience was everything. Start at one achievable level and chip away steadily week by week, and by week 8 to 12, definite changes would have occurred.

The resting heart rate would be lower, the left ventricle would have a larger capacity, the blood plasma volume would have increased, and the Heart Rate Reserve (the difference between the resting heart rate and the maximal heart rate) would usually increase. The running muscles would greatly increase their capillarization, their mitochondrial density, and their levels of oxidative enzymes. The maximal oxygen uptake and the anaerobic threshold would be pushed up as high as possible in the given time, without being pulled down by anaerobic running.

The body would utilize more fats as fuel, sparing carbohydrates, and excess body fat would drop away, leaving the runner as a lean, mean, running machine.

Effort Runs

Certain days were designated as higher aerobic effort days. For instance, on Mondays and Fridays, 10 mile (16 kilometer) "steady state" efforts were to be run at a good effort, which at the start of the "buildup" might mean runs of 65 minutes on Monday and 62 minutes on Friday for Magee. By the end of 8 weeks, these steady state runs were covered in a natural progression at 58 minutes and 55 minutes respectively. Nowadays we'd call these runs sub-threshold tempo runs, or marathon-pace medium distance runs.

On those days that didn't have a longer run, it was very common to supplement with a very easy morning run of half an hour to an hour. Some athletes ran twice a day on every day except Sunday, with excellent results.

Great New Zealand athletes, such as Quax and Rod Dixon, also employed similar runs, and both confirmed with Barry Magee in recent years that they would end up covering these "keystone" runs at closer to 52 minutes by the end of the build up phase because they were capable of faster high-aerobic efforts. **This was solid training, not racing, and definitely not a threshold run.**

Lydiard devised an "effort" system that would accurately describe the level of effort required for any scheduled run. He expressed levels of perceived exertion by simple fractions. A steady long run or general aerobic run could be described as 1/4 effort:

a hard time trial during final race preparations would be 7/8 effort. A strong run for an hour at 3/4 effort during the aerobic base would be equivalent to a run just below the anaerobic threshold, or marathon pace.

Many North American and European runners who purport to train on the Lydiard system mistakenly run their effort runs a little too hard.

The idea is always to push up an energy system from below

The safest and most effective pace to push up the aerobic ceiling, and therefore the anaerobic threshold with it, and therefore increase the time we can hold our VO_2 max at, is under threshold: strong "3/4 effort" runs of about an hour, at about 90-95% of anaerobic threshold speed- or, really, "marathon pace," are the best.

"Marathon training" does not only apply to distances run – it also very much refers to aerobic effort levels run.

The chart here shows the heart rate zone that relates to "marathon-pace" effort runs for a well-conditioned athlete with a resting pulse of 45 and a maximal heart rate of 195 beats/minute.

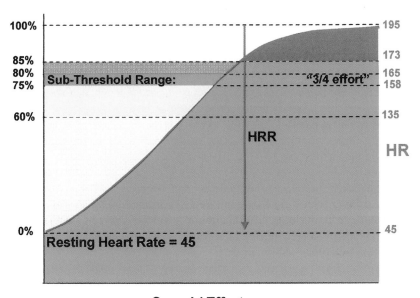

"Learn About Your Body"

The athlete has to closely monitor his or her responses to the schedule. These days many athletes use heart rate monitors to do similar things, but the beauty of the Lydiard system was that the athlete had to listen to what the body was saying at every stage. (Lorraine Moller describes the Lydiard system as "response-driven" and "intuitive": qualities she says are imperative to develop for the loneliness of racing).

Here is what Lydiard wrote in 1978.

"Always bear in mind that the wise only train according to their age, physical condition, and their capacity to exercise. They learn quickly about themselves and train by that knowledge, increasing volume and intensity of work only when they feel their condition is improving. If you try to train and race fast too soon, without proper consideration of the various aspects involved in training, you are doomed to disappointment. You must clearly understand what you are attempting and what effects your exercise will have. And you must work within that understanding."

A typical week's schedule for this phase (for elite athletes) would have Monday and Friday as the stronger effort runs for about an hour, with Tuesday and Thursday reserved for significantly longer runs at an easier effort, and Wednesday for a fartlek workout of about an hour.

Maintain Speed and Technique

This latter workout could be run on a golf course or on the road, and would involve a number of short sharp sprints and inclines interspersed with ample aerobic recovery. This work would maintain a stimulus to the fast twitch fibers and maintain good biomechanics at speed, while not crossing into the unwanted longer anaerobic zones that brought on acidosis.

One of the things that Lydiard intuitively understood long before most exercise physiologists and distance coaches was that fast efforts of less than 10 seconds were too short to trigger the sluggish lactic acid system, and depended on another short-term energy system that could be quickly replenished within a short aerobic recovery.

We now know that this work used the alactic energy system, which depended on intra-muscular creatine phosphate, the explosive short-term fuel utilized most by the very powerful type IIb fast twitch fibers.

Consistency with Variety

The weekly schedule of the "build up" phase would look something like this: it was full of variety, and would stimulate different layers of the aerobic energy systems every week. Lydiard was well aware that constantly varying levels of effort and duration in the aerobic throughout the aerobic phase accomplished far more than constant steady running alone.

Monday	10 miles/16km @ 3/4 effort
Tuesday	15 miles (24km) @ 1/4 effort
Wednesday	1 hour fartlek (app. 10 miles) on golf course or road
Thursday	18 miles (29 km) @ 1/4 effort
Friday	10 miles/16km @ 3/4 effort
Saturday	15 miles @ 1/4 effort
Sunday	22 miles @ 1/4 effort (mountainous hill road course)

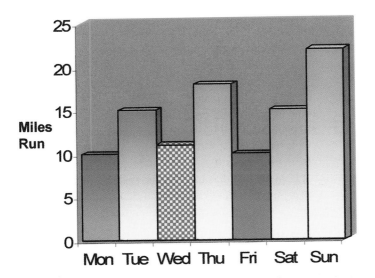

You can see that run duration varied, as well as intensity. To break things up and retain a speed element, fartlek running was done on Wednesdays.

Ron Clarke's Melbourne training group, which included Commonwealth steeplechase champion Trevor Vincent, and 10,000m runner Tony Cook, would often do some of their "bread and butter" runs around Caulfield Racecourse. Lydiard's runners would do the same sort of thing around Avondale Racecourse.

Vern Walker, trained by Lydiard, was a very good Auckland runner who, on several occasions, beat his more famous Olympian running partners over cross-country, road and track in the early 1960s. He theorizes that race-course running had two main benefits. The longer grass gave recovery from the inevitable pounding accrued by long road runs, and at the same time a certain amount of extra leg-lift was required with each stride to push off. This was a form of low-level resistance work that strengthened the hip flexors.

"When you hit the road again to run home after an hour or so of race-course running, you felt light as a feather," notes Walker.

These days, many athletes use heart rate monitors to make sure that they stay in designated aerobic zones. Of course, heart rate monitors weren't around in the early Lydiard days, so athletes really had to learn to "listen" to everything their bodies were telling them.

We have discussed the use of heart rate monitors in an earlier chapter, but it is possible to reach an extremely high level without one. I imagine Lydiard would have found them very useful, but he'd rather his athletes became intuitive and self-reliant, and not depend totally on a little machine to tell them what their own bodies were doing.

Experienced track runners would spend 8 weeks in this phase before moving to their hill resistance and faster work: road runners and marathoners would spend 10 weeks. If there was enough time, working back from the important competition, a longer period would be spent on the aerobic buildup.

Eminent athletes like Dick Quax spent as long as 12 to 16 weeks in the aerobic buildup; they needed this to power them through very long and arduous European seasons, where the early parts of the tour could be used as final conditioning. And as mentioned before, the Finns were prepared to spend many months on this phase each year.

Lydiard was adamant until he died that the base building period should remain aerobic. Here's what he said a week before he died, to the editor of *Running Times,* in reply to a query about weekly intervals during aerobic conditioning:

"First thing: No. No. Never do anaerobic work in conditioning. Never. Ever. That's one of the first things: You don't do it. Don't even try. Don't even run fast to the finish. That's the one thing you've got to learn."

"For how long?" I asked.

"At least 12 weeks. . . . The whole program takes six months."

(Of course it is impossible to run a long hilly course without at least approaching or exceeding the anaerobic threshold, but the point of keeping the exercise mostly aerobic is well understood.)

Clearly, this system could therefore be implemented twice in one year, once for the winter cross country and road season, and once for the summer track season. These days, international athletes and even junior athletes have to adapt the principles to accommodate the year-round availability of races. This is even more reason for coaches and athletes to be very clear on their target races, and plan their seasons meticulously. Barry Magee says that under his 10 years with Lydiard, it was always 8 weeks of conditioning before track and cross-country, and later on, 10 weeks before a marathon. Lydiard could give longer endurance phases to people brand new to his system, or he could be including the 4 weeks of hill training as largely aerobic work. The repeated short efforts in hill bounding, with recoveries, and short sprints and strides, never really crossed over into the acidosis created by the lactic acid system, and it was very common for people to come off this phase in the best shape of their lives.

The Long Run: How it Increases Anaerobic Potential!

Weekends had the long 22 mile (35km) run, which included the notorious 5km hill ascent, followed by another 15 kilometers or so of undulating running on the ridge of the mountains overlooking Auckland, before a long gradual descent and undulating to flat finish.

The main aim of this run was to put constant pressure on the cardiovascular and aerobic systems and exhaust the glycogen stores in the fast twitch muscle fibers, although in the 1950s and 1960s, neither Lydiard, nor physiologists, knew all that. If one's legs felt "tired and heavy" in the closing stages, then that was "mission accomplished," and Lydiard knew from practical experience that this would result in increased performance capacity later.

The hill climb was a substantial effort at any stage of the year, and early in the conditioning period it would be attempted steadily and cautiously. By the end of the conditioning period, this hill-

climb would consist of about 20 minutes of running with a heart rate at the edge of the anaerobic threshold zone. If an athlete ran the early miles at too fast an effort for his conditioning, he would "blow up" later in the run by using precious carbohydrate stores too early and not be able to complete the rest of the course in a fit state. Athletes thus learned to ration their efforts and fuels very carefully in this weekly run.

The uphill run provided other valuable stimuli. The fast twitch muscle fibers would be recruited to provide the extra power that uphill running requires. The prime movers for uphill running are essentially the same required for fast running; these would be strengthened by the resistance training.

Slow twitch fibers, although admirably suited to long endurance runs, do eventually fatigue as they are the only ones preferentially recruited at lower paces. One to two hours of running will often do the job, depending upon the effort and fitness levels. Although slow twitch fibers can preferentially burn fats at low intensities, with stronger aerobic efforts their readily available carbohydrate stores (blood glucose, muscle glycogen) will gradually be used up. Meanwhile, the fast twitch fibers have not been used much at all, and still have most of their glycogen stores intact, *unless* the early pace has been too fast for the level of conditioning.

Muscle tension with each stride has to be maintained, and especially on uphill climbs, this recruits the intermediary fast twitch fibers next, with their own (limited) stores of muscle glycogen. These fibers will then use up their glycogen, eventually having to resort to their third-choice fuel of fats, thereby lowering power output. This leaves only the very fast (IIB) fibers with glycogen and creatine phosphate reserves to maintain tension, and these are recruited last.

The constant pressure upon fast twitch and intermediary fast twitch fibers under the pressure of lowering fuel availability forces the muscles to adapt over time. They adapt by becoming more efficient at replenishing and storing glycogen, utilizing fats, and increasing the ratio and number of intermediary fast twitch fibers (Type IIa), which increases the potential of the body to run anaerobically when glycogen levels are restored.

Why? These fibers are primarily glycolytic, so because there are more of them across a given muscle, potential glycolytic capacity has been increased. (The downside is that the ratio of very explosive IIB fibers will decrease, but there's an answer for that in the next phase of training).

After the uphill slog, the recovery downhill and following efforts along the ridge road involved hovering at the edge of the anaerobic threshold and learning to disperse lactates at strong aerobic speeds, while starting to fatigue the carbohydrate stores in the muscles and liver.

The final miles of gradual descent and flat running were largely pure endurance/ fatty acid metabolism running, but a short sharp hill of about 700m at the 28km mark served to jolt the fatiguing athlete into short-term anaerobic metabolism again.

So there you have it: once an athlete was fit enough to get fit and had established a decent base of endurance running, the meat and potatoes of the system centered on 8 to 10 weeks devoted purely to the development of the aerobic systems and all the fuel utilization, aerobic enzyme, and cardiovascular benefits that would follow.

* Costill, D. L. "A Scientific Approach to Distance Running," *Track and Field News Publications*, 79-80, 1989.

BASE RUNNING

DO's and DON'T'S

DO

- Run every day. Then ease yourself gradually into longer runs, by running a few extra minutes every second day if possible.
- Wear correctly fitted and balanced running shoes.
- Buy several good pairs of shoes to alternate daily during the base phase.
- Run most of your mileage on firm surfaces that won't pull your legs around too much. This can be parkland, dirt, or asphalt, but concrete can be too firm. Loose sandy surfaces can be hard to gain traction on and can cause joint problems because there is no consistent footfall.
- Vary the length and intensity of your runs day by day.
- Try to eventually fit in two medium-long runs and one long run each week. At whatever level this represents for you currently.
- Increase your total mileage conservatively.
- Eat well and healthily.
- Get ample sleep and easy recovery days.
- Every few weeks have an easier week to consolidate.

If you've never done long aerobic runs before:

- Run very evenly. Start on a flat course and try to run out for a set period of time, and run exactly the same time for the return distance.

DON'T

Take carbohydrate supplements (gels, etc) during long runs *unless* it's in a long race. You'll lose the training effect on the fatty acid system and the glycogen-sparing effect.

Part 4
Recovery, Nutrition and Body Therapies

Recovery from Long Runs

When I was an active athlete in New Zealand, most Sunday mornings would be taken up by the *long run*.

If the runs are long enough to be doing their job, we start to feel "heavy" in the legs as we deplete the glycogen stores nicely, and we start to get *hungry* and *thirsty*!

In Auckland in the late 1970s, a large pack of ravenous distance runners would regularly descend upon a Chinese restaurant in downtown Queen Street for an "all you can eat" buffet meal for $5. This was accompanied by an offer of a bottomless cup of coffee or tea. Our hosts were initially very glad to see our group of about a dozen as we ate and drank everything in sight.

It was a noisy and convivial scene, and we'd stay for hours before we waddled out satiated. The word got out very quickly. When we invited a group of monstrous throws events men to join us one Sunday, after their heaviest training morning of the week, the mood shifted. We were politely informed by the proprietor that he liked us all very much, but he simply couldn't make any money at all on Sundays. With moist red eyes, he shook his head and said "How can men so skinny eat so much?"

He was given a shock course in recovery principle Number 1: endurance runners have a *huge* basal metabolic rate and need to replenish their glycogen and liquid stores rapidly after such long runs, with whatever is available.

When I lived in cold and windy Wellington, at one stage I was regularly carving up a 25 miler over big hills at under a 6 minute-mile average. Often the last five miles were a flat out run into a headwind to get a PB. This was stupid but fun. When I got back to my third floor flat in an old Victorian house, I was famished. I'd run a deep hot bath and place a wooden board across the bath. Then I'd take the kettle, teapot, toaster, electric frypan, and all ingredients and utensils into the bathroom. It was a full English breakfast, and the thought of it drove me on those last few miles. This arrangement wasn't overly popular with my lovely female flatmates, but I had a deal going where they'd cook on weeknights when I was out training, and I'd not only eat everything left, but wash up everything as well! The relationship got mildly edgy when I was caught using one of their hairdryers to dry my socks.

Some people unfortunately can't eat a thing at the end of a long run: it's the last thing they feel like doing. However, it is *extremely important* to rehydrate and get carbohydrates back into the system, even after short runs and races. Any delay in getting carbohydrates into the system beyond about 45 minutes can double or treble full glycogen recovery time in terms of days!

It's also a good idea to get some protein and a bit of fat into the system. One option for people who can't eat straight after a long run is to invest in carbohydrate gels and sports drinks, or get a high-quality juice-extractor and make a fresh fruit juice with an egg whipped in. Sounds revolting but it does the job.

You can make your own excellent sports drink by diluting dark grape juice 1:3, or by whatever factor ends up with a natural sugar or carbohydrate concentration of around 6mg/100ml. This is known as a 6%w/vol concentration, about the same as your natural blood plasma concentration should be. Dark grape juices off the shelf typically have a sugar concentration of 15-18 g/100 ml w/vol.

If it's hot weather, dilute the juice more again. Grape juice is an alkali and full of potassium. At this lower concentration, there's not the danger of making your stomach cramp with too high a concentration of sugars.

Orange juice is far too acidic and can create problems. Apple juice is an alkali and well tolerated but may have to be diluted similarly.

As mentioned earlier, carbohydrates are best absorbed with fat and protein as well: A soy thickshake with a banana and an egg might fill the bill. A toasted cheese sandwich has carbohydrates, protein, and fat: these are tolerated quite well by most athletes after long runs.

Once conditioned well, the athlete often needs just a light Monday's running to bounce back ready for more work on Tuesday. Don't plan a big work day requiring mental concentration on Monday; it may not be there.

Lydiard's athletes were so well-conditioned that they could do a strong-effort aerobic run on the Monday after a long run and come up smiling; however, they probably had more brains than me and ran their long runs at the appropriate steady effort.

Oiling the Machine

In terms of supplements, I find *simple* and *natural* is best! Endurance-based athletes need antioxidant protection more than most, because we're breathing in so much of the stuff! The best-known antioxidants are vitamins A, C, and E, but before you go spending hundreds of dollars at the pharmacist, consider getting even more powerful antioxidants from natural sources.

Fresh berries and red grape seeds have a huge ORAC rating (Oxygen Radical Absorbance Capacity). You can get freshly frozen berries at any supermarket, and grape seeds from any health food store, and juice them with grape juice, fresh beetroot and a bit of fresh ginger for a delicious drink after training.

Your joints need protection, and this is where glucosamine sulphate, chondroitin, and MSM (biological sulphur) powders come in. These natural substances are so good at protecting joints that current research shows there is nothing better. 2000mg a day is the pharmacologically effective amount for glucosamine sulphate, and it can be mixed as a powder into a yogurt-based protein shake.

Pharmaceutical companies have flocked in droves to market these natural substances under their own brand names, but they're not drugs – they're really foods, so they can't ever be patented. They're extracted from animal sources of connective tissue: cartilage, tendon, etc. You'll get them naturally by chewing all the gristly bits of any chicken you eat, and a very cheap source is beef gelatin powder, extracted from the joints of cattle. Or you can have shark fin soup (mostly cartilage!), prized by the Chinese for centuries. Your hard-working ancestors would probably have left animal joints simmering in a thick stocking pot that would provide an amazing source of glutinous connective tissue proteins for stews and soups.

Another great supplement is fish oil, rich in Omega-3 essential fatty acids, so necessary for the basis of our neurotransmitter chemicals and therefore the function of our whole nervous system. Flaxseed oil (also known as linseed oil) is also a terrific source of gamma linoleic and gamma linolenic acids, but it is very concentrated and can be hard on the liver and gall-bladder if taken too much. Cod liver oil is a great source of the fat-soluble vitamins A, K, and D. These are necessary for proper bone formation and blood clotting. Fresh wheat germ oil is a strong source of vitamin E.

If you eat plenty of canned tuna or salmon, you might think you're getting lots of fish oil, but you probably aren't. Most decent bigger fish are squeezed for their oils at the processing plant, and these are then sold off to the vitamin companies. What's left in the can is first-class protein floating in vegetable oil or brine. If there was any oil left you'd see it floating in little globules in brine, but you don't – it's gone. Sardines are a different matter; they're so flimsy they'd make a total mess if they were squeezed, so the processors usually have the sense to leave them whole with their "good oils" intact. One doctor friend of mine says that three cans of sardines a week would stop a lot of early dementia and neurological problems, and he could be right.

Fish oils rich in Omega-3 essential fatty acids will raise serum levels of HDL (high density lipids: "good fats"), and relatively lower the levels of LDL (low density lipids) associated with plaquing of the arteries by various cardiology researchers.

Apart from eating as much fresh fruit and green food as possible, we need a good source of protein and essential fatty acids. My favourite source for all these is the humble free-range egg, which for so many years has been criticized as a source of "cholesterol." (Lightly poached and runny is best!)

Food fads change every year, but what is beyond doubt is that cholesterol is a very important substance for the human. Many of our sex and growth hormones can all be derived from cholesterol. Our brains are mostly made from it, and it forms the basis of myelin, which sheaths our biggest nerves. Your own liver produces at least 80% of the cholesterol measured in transit in your blood, regardless of whether you eat buckets of deep-fried chicken or subsist on a strict vegan diet. If you're highly strung and neurotic, and follow a strict vegan diet, chances are that your cholesterol levels will be higher than those of your relaxed country cousin eating his deep fried chicken on a porch in Texas.

Consider the findings of Dr. Harlan Krumholz of the Department of Cardiovascular Medicine at Yale University, who reported in 1994 that old people with low cholesterol died twice as often from a heart attack as did old people with a high cholesterol.[1]

There is even good evidence that high blood cholesterol levels protect against bacterial infection.[2]

"To be more specific, most studies of old people have shown that high cholesterol is not a risk factor for coronary heart disease. This was the result of my search in the Medline database for studies addressing that question," says cardiology researcher and writer Uffe Ravnskov, MD, PhD.

Ischaemic heart disease was virtually unknown until earlier last century when hydrogenated vegetable oils, such as margarine, flooded the markets. Their biologically useless trans-fatty acids compete with essential fatty acids for receptor sites in our brain and nervous system, and can muck things right up hormonally. These are the nasty fats in your favourite packet of salt and vinegar potato crisps, unfortunately. Before they're processed by bleaching and coloring to make them look palatable, hydrogenated vegetable and margarine oils look like they've just been drained from the sump of your car engine.

Of course, wherever there is a "disease" or "epidemic," the pharmaceutical lobby and their researchers cloud the waters and promote their "solutions." There are even heavily-promoted butter blends out there designed to lower cholesterol, despite all the recent evidence indicating it's another storm in a teacup!

Yes, you can have fresh butter if you want, and *enjoy* it! If you're running enough, your body will suck it up and metabolize it as soon as it's in the bloodstream!

This isn't an excuse to hard-fry eggs and bacon for every meal; but the hard evidence these days is indicating that the saturated fats (i.e., animal fats like lard) our ancestors ate caused no harm and were probably an excellent source of energy. If we work hard enough, the fats are metabolized rapidly.

My brother did enormous mileages for years on end, and his meals were often too "awful" for dieticians and nutritionists to contemplate. In the middle of a crazy 300-mile week, he once proudly presented me with an unrecognizably carbonized fried egg that appeared to have half the frypan still attached to it, along with fried rice that hadn't been steamed prior to the frying. When I protested, he sat down and ate the pile of rock-hard, oily, browned pellets himself. After having to evacuate his bowels shortly thereafter, he went straight to the Chinese takeaway and ate again, with no problem. Basal metabolism at work! Somehow, from all the various foodstuffs he was shoving into his hungry frame all day, he was getting what he needed. He ate massive amounts of bananas and apples during the day too, and he never seemed to get injured either! To cut to the chase, and avoid writing a whole book on the subject of dietary myths, you can't go too far wrong if you stick with foods that are as fresh and as near to nature as possible. Fruits and vegetables provide plenty of needed carbohydrates, as do grain-based foods, such as bread, pasta, and rice. Plenty of fresh water in small amounts throughout the day is always a good idea.

The Dixon brothers, John and Rod, were huge eaters when they embarked on their ambitious training regimen in Nelson, New Zealand. Their sensible mother left a big bowl of rice with bananas in the fridge every night for them to eat when they had the "midnight munchies."

For the athlete who is rich and would like to absolutely cover all bases, consider some trace elements from natural sources: ancient lake beds at high altitude are excellent sources of "phytonutrients" and trace elements, and severable reputable companies mine these for their pristine fossil mineral sources. These colloidal mineral preparations are available for a premium but are getting more common and cheaper all the time.

Anemia is a problem for many athletes, and the best source of bio-available (easily digested) heme-iron is liver. Some people shudder at it, but chicken liver paté from the delicatessen is nice on wheat or rye crackers, and if that doesn't appeal, freeze-dried or dessicated bovine liver tablets have been around for years. Iron tablets are often made from ferric oxide (rust!), so you might as well scrape the stuff off old railway lines and eat that. They'll both constipate you equally as well, guaranteed!

Liver is a wonderful source of vitamin A and the B vitamins, including vitamin B5 (pantothenic acid), which in large amounts has cortisone-like effects on allergies, asthma, eczema, hives and hayfever. This is because the body's own cortisone can only be produced in the cortex of the adrenal gland if blood levels of vitamin C and B5 are sufficient.

Prolonged stress of any kind depletes these vitamin levels markedly. Two grams of vitamin C with an equal amount of B5 is a safe level of supplementation that I have used with clients, young and old, for a number of years to eventually get them completely off cortisone and asthma medication and return to full health. There are no reported toxic side effects. It's probably a good idea to have this supplement with a B-complex supplement or liver tablet so that all the co-factors are there.

One peer-reviewed study done in 1954 showed that the crippling auto-immune disease lupus erythmatosus, treated with massive daily amounts of pantothenic acid, and large amounts of vitamin E (tocopherol), resulted in "complete clearing of a majority of 67 subjects." To this day, lupus and similar auto-immune diseases are treated with everything *but* nutritional therapies. The amounts used in this study were over 5 times the amounts I recommend, and at those lower levels we've had terrific results with allergies, hives, hayfever, and eczema as well – all treated with cortisone previously.

Lean meat strips are terrific when quickly tossed and stir-fried with vegetables and rice, Asian style, on a wok that has been lightly wiped with just enough oil to keep things from sticking. Foods cooked this way can be delicious and satisfying.

A quick healthy meal I have always found enjoyable and nourishing is made by slicing up fresh avocado and mixing it with a selection of diced green salad leaves: cos lettuce, etc. Anything fresh and green will do. Most supermarkets these days carry several lines of chilled, freshly prepared salad leaves in sealed bags. Chuck in some sliced cherry or roma tomatoes, or sun-dried tomatoes. Dice up some feta cheese into small cubes, and pour in the contents of a small tin of tuna in olive oil or strips of smoked salmon. Squeeze fresh lemon juice over the top and sprinkle with cracked black pepper.

A little bit of this goes a long way, and it's very healthy. You're getting essential fatty acids from the avocado; calcium, protein and good fats from the feta; chlorophyll and phyto-nutrients from the green salad leaves; lycopenes from the tomatoes; different essential fatty acids from the olive oil; and first-class protein from the fish. The lemon juice, being an anti oxidant source with its vitamin C, will keep the salad leaves fresh and the citric acid will aid your digestion.

How good an an anti oxidant is the modest lemon? Try this: slice a fresh apple in two, and place the separate halves on a plate. Soak the sliced face of one half in squeezed lemon juice and leave the other half as it is. Over several hours you will see the apple half that has not had lemon juice turn an unappetizing brown color as it oxidizes and loses its freshness. The other half will stay normal for much longer. Lemon juice in fresh water is a refreshing way to hydrate.

Female Athlete Triad

The female athlete triad is a combination of three different disorders that commonly affect female athletes: osteoporosis, eating disorders, and amenorrhea.

Some female athletes in their quests for excellence become amenhorreic, meaning that they no longer have the normal menstrual cycle, and this has until recent years been associated with osteopaenia (thinning of bone) that may lead to osteoporosis (severe thinning of bone 2.5 standard deviations beyond that of a normal healthy 20-year-old). Osteoporosis is a first-world epidemic that has become the subject of a major World Health Organization incentive.[4]

It was thought that very low body fat percentage affected the normal levels and interplay of reproductive hormones, especially LH (luteinizing hormone), in the pituitary gland. The onflow from this was thought to be disruption of normal bone-protective levels of progesterone and estrogen.

However, a recent study indicates that energy availability, rather than low body fat and the stress of exercise, causes disruption in luteinizing hormone.[5] If hard-exercising female athletes have ample food intake, particularly carbohydrate, the negative hormonal spiral can reverse.

I suggest frequent, small, tasty snacks based on complex carbohydrates and proteins throughout the day to keep blood sugar and amino acid levels up. (A sardine with feta cheese on thick wholegrain bread will do the job). A hard-training female athlete who eats small meals frequently will not put on excess weight.

If you're a female athlete and have been convinced by the dairy industry that milk products are the best way to keep the calcium in your bones, here are some things to consider.

1. Full-body weight-bearing exercise (i.e., lifting heavy weights) will effectively prevent osteoporosis, due to Wolffe's Law.

   Wolffe's law states that bone in a healthy person or animal will adapt to the loads it is placed under. If loading on a particular bone increases, the bone will remodel itself over time to become stronger to resist that sort of loading. The external cortical portion of the bone becomes thicker as a result.

2. Many of us become osteoporotic because we ingest far too much meat protein, which makes our blood acidic. This forces the body to alkalise the bloodstream by liberating calcium phosphate from the bone stores, eventually to be urinated out in solution, and possibly becoming the cause of calcium stones in our urine filters: the kidneys.

3. Another cause is excess drinking of phosphate-rich soft drinks (most carbonated soft drinks) which demineralize bone due to the excess of phosphoric acid in the bloodstream. Stay away from that junk!

4. The cow that gives us all this calcium-rich milk has probably not had a drop of mother's milk since it was a few weeks old. It has grown big and strong with its own calcium-rich bones, and gallons of calcium-rich milk for you and me, on a diet of grass! Ask any dairy farmer!

Forgetting the cow for now, we see that the biggest strongest mammals on the planet are all herbivores too. There's nothing wrong with the bone strength or muscle development of the average hippo or elephant, is there? And even the biggest primate, the gorilla, is an herbivore. So there's something to be said for barley-green drinks and wheatgrass shots!

Carnivores in the wild will usually go straight for the stomach and small intestine of the herbivores they kill. Here they access the partially-digested chlorophyll (green plant pigment)and phyto-nutrients (plant nutrients) last eaten by their prey. Freshly juiced organic vegetables are a great source of these substances for the athlete, and you don't have to run down an antelope to get them. Please don't start juicing madly straight away; take your time, or the fastest running you'll be doing will be to the toilet!

Many athletes drink diet drinks and colas. Frankly, they'd be much better off with sugar in their fizz. Diet drinks are full of aspartame, a synthetic compound that binds the deadly alcohol methanol to aspartic acid and the amino acid phenylalanine. The US Food and Drug Administration and all the "vested interest" science groups have made a recent, massive push, uniformly claiming that aspartame is indeed a "safe additive" for 6000 foods, but where there's smoke there's fire. In 1995, FDA Epidemiology Branch Chief, Thomas Wilcox reported that aspartame complaints represented 75% of all reports of adverse reactions to substances in the food supply from 1981 to 1995.[6]

However, they cannot disclaim the basic chemistry. Aspartame breaks down quickly in the gut to form methanol (10%), phenylalanine (50%) and aspartic acid (40%). Methanol is the simplest of the alcohols, but is a potentially lethal poison. At 30 degrees celsius, well below body temperature (37.6 C), methanol breaks down and forms formic acid and formaldehyde. Formaldehyde is a carcinogen and neurotoxin used to embalm dead bodies. The FDA and industry body sites neglect to say exactly what happens to the methanol when it quickly breaks down in the gut and reaches the liver, but I've just told you.

High concentrations of phenylalanine and formaldehyde in the liver are strongly linked to the presence of cancers in the body. So if you must have a soft drink, be like Frank Shorter who drank flat Coke (with real sugars and caffeine) all the way to Olympic marathon gold in 1972.

Finally, we pay a tribute to the ancient practices of Chinese herbal medicine. If you want to stay free of infection and have the immune system of a rhino, have a daily swig of "Astragalus membranaceus" preparation with juice or water. Naturally, like all things that are especially good for you, it tastes like it came straight off the bottom of the compost heap, and for a month or so you'll not like it at all, but it's a taste you learn to love when you realize how much of an all-round tonic it is. The herb echinacea purpurea is also an excellent immune system booster.

References

1. Krumholz, H.M. et. al. "Lack of association between cholesterol and coronary heart disease mortality and morbidity and all-cause mortality in persons older than 70 years." *Journal of the American Medical Association 272*, 1335-1340, 1990.
2. Ravnskov, U. "High cholesterol may protect against infections and atherosclerosis." *Quarterly Journal of Medicine 96*, 927-934, 2003.
3. Welch, A.L. "Treatment by combined use of massive amounts of pantothenic acid and vitamin E in lupus erythematosus." *Arch Dermatol 70:181,* 1954.
   Amounts used: 1000-2000 mg tocopherol (synthetic & natural) + Ca pantothenate (10-15 g) or Na pantothenate (5-10 g))
4. WHO Scientific Group on the Prevention and Management of Osteoporosis (2000: Geneva, Switzerland) (2003)
5. Loucks, A.B., Verdun, M. and Heath E. M., "Low energy availability, not stress of exercise, alters LH pulsatility in exercising women." *J Appl Physiol* 84: 37-46, 1998; 8750-7587/98.
6. In a June 12, 1995 article, which appeared in *Food Chemical News*, Thomas Wilcox, the FDA epidemiology branch chief was quoted as saying, "FDA has no further plans to continue to collect adverse reaction reports or monitor research periodically done on aspartame."

Maintaining the Chassis & Electricals

The best strategy for injury prevention is to train sensibly, eat well, sleep well, and increase training volume or intensity gradually. Excellent footwear is essential when you're logging many kilometers, and I recommend alternating between two or three pairs of recently purchased running shoes all the time to constantly vary the stresses on your lower limbs and frame. Compare the heel-wear from all angles (and place the shoes on a flat surface and view from behind regularly) to see if the heel counter or sole material is becoming deformed. When one pair starts to look suspect, buy another pair and use that!

When running, our joints can really take a pounding; so protect them! You won't think so when you're young, but think of joint damage as a deferred-repayment, high-interest loan. When the body chooses to rebel in later years, it may shock you!

Research by Nike scientists in 1984 revealed that the forces of heel strike when running are 3.5 times one's bodyweight. The shock waves dissipate up the skeletal frame, so that for every 5-7grams of shock at heel-strike, 0.5 grams still exist at the runner's temporomandibular joint (jaw joint).

These forces of footstrike travel along a "kinematic chain" from the three arches of the foot. The most obvious arch of the foot is the medial longitudinal arch on the inside plantar surface of the foot, stabilised by the navicular bone. There is also the lateral longitudinal arch along the outside plantar surface, stabilized by the cuboid bone. Finally there is the anterior transverse arch in the ball of the foot, comprising the metatarsal heads. Each arch has a key function in absorbing and transmitting shock, and if it is too lax or too rigid, it can cause more problems.

Podiatry

About 90% of people tend to pronate, with their feet rolling inwards, and 10% supinate, with their feet rolling outwards. (This is simplistic, but will do for now). These patterns, according to their severity, will manifest in predictable patterns elsewhere in the body. The podiatrist is trained to subtly correct or stabilize the lower limb into a more neutral motion pattern that will positively affect the biomechanics of the rest of the body.

People with legs of nearly equal length may exhibit very little difference in pronation or supination from foot to foot. However, other people may pronate on one foot and supinate on the other! Many people will have a markedly pronated, "flat" foot on the side of their "longer" lower limb. This is very common, as we can acquire measurable lower limb length differences while we grow for a number of reasons.

Such people do not need much podiatric correction on the longer leg side, but rather need a raised shoe or heel, with suitable orthotic insert, on the short leg side. This is best discerned by a standing postural X-ray of the pelvis, where we can clearly measure relative hip height.

I have seen a person with a poorly positioned hip replacement result in a much longer leg and higher pelvis, as measured on postural X-ray. He rapidly developed a very flattened foot on the same limb as his body tried to level his pelvis and spine. His only other option was to grow his other limb longer, which wasn't probable in his late 50s. The markedly pronated foot can cause an anterior rotation of the pelvis on the same side as the body seeks to level the hip joints, or the pronation itself may simply be an adaptation to a previously undiagnosed longer limb. A sports chiropractor can assess this and refer you for appropriate correction.

See a podiatrist who will take all this into account and who'll take an accurate weight-bearing impression of your foot in a foam bed or with a scanner; this is considerably more accurate than the plaster-cast method in vogue since 1970, where the podiatrist casts the foot in a pre-determined, academically "neutral" position done while the client is sitting or lying. The plaster cast neutral position may bear no resemblance whatsoever to your true weight-bearing position and need for stabilization.

The next thing to ask for is a flexible orthotic that is long enough to stabilize all three arches: many older ones I see stabilize only the medial longitudinal arch, and the other two arches are completely ignored. There is no excuse for this in the 21st century.

The orthotic insert does not need to completely prop your arches up; rather it should allow the joints of the feet to move within their normal range and effectively limit excess motion. Some of the rigid orthotics that were used until recently would have caused numerous problems further up the kinematic chain by totally "correcting" the medial longitudinal arch and making it stiff and hypomobile, creating compensatory hypermobility elsewhere. Often this dysfunction is never felt in the rigid foot, but can manifest as imbalance, pain, or weakness elsewhere, due to the over-firing of pain-sensitive "nociceptors" into the central nervous system, and under-firing of the motion-sensing, pain-inhibitory "mechanoreceptors."

Chiropractors often work in well with podiatrists, as foot function clearly relates to whole-body mechanics and health. In chiropractic practice, dysfunction in any of the three arches of the foot is often clinically associated with three distinct patterns of muscle weakness and pelvic imbalance.

The medial longitudinal arch is associated with psoas or hip flexor muscle weakness on the same side, as well as an anteriorly tilted pelvis. The lateral longitudinal arch is associated with gluteus minimus and medius weakness (hip abductor muscles on the outside thigh and pelvis). The anterior transverse arch relates to quadriceps and hamstring weakness on the same side. These can all be readily tested for by any competent chiropractor.

Before you get fitted for a suitable pair of orthotic inserts, get your feet "adjusted" (specifically mobilized) by a chiropractor: then you won't be taking an impression of a hypomobile joint system. These little things count over thousands of footstrikes.

Massage Therapies

Everyone loves a good massage. However, for hard-training athletes, relaxation massage doesn't quite hit the spot. When we run a great deal, we can acquire very localized areas of muscle contraction that effectively stop the normal flow of blood and the proper lymph drainage in the body's secondary circulatory system.

What results is often a nasty little area of poorly irrigated, irritable muscle that has been forced to survive anaerobically. There is pooling of inflammatory agents (histamines) that make the area exquisitely tender when touched or pressed. If it stays like this, the body will adapt by laying down scar tissue as the muscle cells eventually die off.

These trouble spots are known as "trigger points" for their ability to "shoot" or trigger pain radiation into distant areas of the body through irritation of a complex network of very fine nerve endings known as "nociceptors."

Lymph fluid and venous blood require the rhythmic pumping of the major leg muscles to "squeeze" the fluid uphill, especially near joints; little semilunar valves in the vessels stop these fluids from draining downwards with gravity.

These areas of congestion can be broken down by firm, repeated pressure in the direction of the venous circulation (i.e., in the direction of the heart), or by trigger point therapy in which the practitioner holds firm thumb pressure on one spot until most sensation of acute pain has abated to a lower, tolerable level.

WARNING: If you haven't had a massage in a long time, and decide to start again, be wary. Whether it's a relaxation massage or a localized therapeutic massage, give yourself a few easy days afterwards to accommodate any possible "reactions." A massage when you're not used to it represents a massive input to the nervous system, which can make you quite tired for days. If the massage liberates pools of toxins from trigger areas back into the lymphatic and circulatory systems, then these will be floating around your system and make you feel quite ordinary too. You'll quickly get over this, and by having regular work done, it won't be a problem.

When I was 20 years old, I'd been training well for many weeks and was flying in club races. I had a major cross-country race coming up, and decided to have a massage from a (now-deceased) masseur patronized by many Auckland runners at the time. He gave me a working-over that had me off the table as his strong thumbs drove through the trigger areas. It felt wonderful when he stopped, and the next day I felt great when running.

However the morning after that I couldn't even get out of bed because my quads were so stiff and tight. I could feel his thumbs as if they were still embedded in my thighs. It took me a week or so to get back to normal, but later I trusted him again with weekly massage sessions as I accumulated a winter of big mileage, with no bad effects. I had to miss my race though.

Rod Dixon says that when he was touring Europe on the track circuit, before it became the professional circus it is now, it was difficult to access regular massage. So he'd sit in his hotel bath and methodically rub the tight areas himself, working from the foot and ankle up.

Our "HIT SQUAD" athletes often "swap rubs" after training; several have done basic massage courses. This saves a lot of travel, time, and money.

Chiropractic

Chiropractors work with the spine and central nervous system, which together have the capacity to influence the whole body. Arthur Lydiard was an early advocate of chiropractic, as it made complete sense to him. Lorraine Moller introduced me to chiropractic, as it kept her going through 4 Olympic marathon campaigns and over 25 years as a world-class competitor.

I knew nothing about chiropractic until late 1979. I badly twisted my lower back one night by diving out of the way of a car that was spinning downhill towards me on a wet road. The car slammed into a grass embankment, and I got cold and stiff as I stood in the rain until the police and ambulance came. I jogged home for another hour in the rain, and then progressively stiffened up over the next two weeks.

It got to the point where I had shooting pain from my right buttock to the tips of my toes every time I walked. The only comfortable way to sleep was on my side, curled up like a fetus. I had to walk backwards down stairs. This was probably sciatica due to a herniated lower lumbar disc that started to swell more and more over time. Any doctor could explain that. However, over the next month I completely lost my appetite and started to vomit blue-green bile regularly. Bizarrely, my gums started to discolor as if I had gingivitis. I sought help from the most well-known sports medicine doctor in New Zealand at the time, as well as a duo of highly commended sports physiotherapists.

My particular case appeared weird to all of them: especially with the loss of appetite, vomiting, and gum disease. They tried very hard to help me, but it appeared that their professional training, though very thorough, did not have the broad philosophical framework to explain how or why this was occuring. The only certain advice I can remember receiving was that my competitive running days were probably over, and that my particular type of spinal curvature was to blame. That advice went down like a lead balloon.

Lorraine told me to "see a chiropractor" as she'd been helped by one earlier that year. She recommended I see Dr. Jim Brownlie in Auckland. The first thing Jim did after examining me was to take standing postural X-rays of my spine to "see" what was going on. He showed me where my lumbar spine was twisted and unlevelled between the two lowest vertebrae, and showed me the compensatory curves in my mid-back and upper neck. Showing me a basic nerve chart of the spinal sensorimotor and autonomic nerves, he 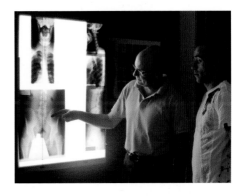 demonstrated that where I was extremely tender in the spine correlated nicely with the pathways to my abdominal organs and gums, as well as to the sciatic nerve. BINGO! I was hooked!

Fourteen weeks later, after moving cities and getting a new job, I won the Wellington 10-mile Senior road title by 21 seconds, and thereafter continued weekly or fortnightly care with Dr. Brian Kelly, Sr., in Wellington. In this time, I never had a massage, and trained or overtrained at a very high level for 18 months without even getting a cold! There has been no sign of this "spinal curvature" ever since!

As I am a chiropractor myself now, I am qualified to talk about chiropractic and how this can be a valuable part of the athlete's program. I am in no doubt whatsoever that regular massage, acupuncture, osteopathy and physiotherapy can all be valuable, and I have used them all. However, chiropractic is quite different in practice and intent. Chiropractic is a health science that was founded in 1895 in the USA by D.D. Palmer, and was developed further by his son, B.J. Palmer.

In its early years, chiropractic was lionized by its advocates and pilloried by the medical authorities, mostly because it was so simple in practice and had undeniable results that orthodox medicine was unable to achieve. Medical doctors were told by their political arm, the American Medical Association, not to refer to members of an "unscientific cult," or their licences would be revoked.

Many of the early chiropractors, like Herbert Reaver, were routinely jailed for "practising medicine without a licence", and as recently as November 1990 the American Medical Association, after a 14-year process, was found guilty on appeal in the US Supreme Court, along with 10 medical organizations as co-defendants, of "attempting to eliminate the chiropractic profession."[1]

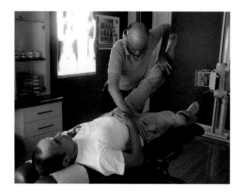

If imitation is the sincerest form of flattery, then chiropractic is flattered by the open use of its philosophy, terminology, techniques, and world-view by many other professions these days.

To quote the philosopher Arthur Schopenhaeuer: "All truth passes through three stages. First, it is ridiculed. Second, it is violently opposed. Third, it is accepted as being self-evident."

So what is this truth that chiropractic exemplifies? It's pretty basic really; the brain and nervous system coordinate the whole body. The most direct conduit of information from brain to body and back is the spinal cord, protected by the 24 spinal vertebrae and sacrum, which are all mobile. As your body is usually a self-healing, self-regulating organism, anything that compromises the normal integrity of the skeletal framework and spine has the capacity to compromise normal nerve function elsewhere in the body. Simple enough?

If these joints become stiff or hypomobile, this can create a "hyper-excitable central state" in the nervous system, known as "nociceptive noise." This is akin to background noise in a poorly tuned radio, but in the case of the nervous system, it has the effect of "scrambling" information being received or sent by the brain.

According to what is compromised in each individual case, symptoms are often very predictable, but some may be completely unpredictable, especially if they compromise the autonomic nervous system.

It is thought that gentle and subtle correction of such mechanical derangements by chiropractic adjustments can reverse the hyper-excitable central state and explain a myriad of "symptoms" that will not respond to any other therapy.

These days, a great deal of exciting chiropractic research is being carried out in universities around the world.

So, what applies to athletes? Here are some recent interesting peer-reviewed studies. One study published in May 2006 indicates improvement in cursor movement time of 9.2% for a chiropractic group following chiropractic care, compared with 1.7% for a control group.[2] This has implications for motor control.

In October 2002, a paper presented on a long-term asthma study by researchers at Sydney's MacQuarie University indicated steady reduction in blood levels of the stress hormone cortisol accompanied by an increase in salivary levels of the immune complex IgA following chiropractic care.[3]

Another very interesting study published in May 2005 indicates that there is a link between the number of dysfunctional regions (subluxations) ascertained in the spine and reaction time. The more regions of dysfunction, the slower the reaction time.[4]

References:
1. Wilk v. American Medical Association, 895 F.2d 352 (7th Cir. 1990), was a federal antitrust suit brought against the American Medical Association (AMA) and 10 co-defendants by chiropractor Chester A. Wilk, DC, and four co-plaintiffs. It resulted in a ruling against the AMA.
2. Smith, D., Dainoff, M. and Smith., J. "The Effect of Chiropractic Adjustments on Movement Time: A Pilot Study Using Fitts Law." *Journal of Manipulative and Physiological Therapeutics,* Volume 29, Issue 4, 257-266.
3. "Effect of Chiropractic Treatments on the Endocrine and Immune System in Asthmatic Patients." *Proceedings of the 2002 International Conference on Spinal Manipulation,* Toronto Ontario, Canada, Oct 2002: 57-8
4. Lersa, L., Stinear, C. and Lersa, R. "The Relationship Between Spinal Dysfunction and Reaction Time Measures." *Journal of Manipulative and Physiological Therapeutics,* Volume 28, Issue 7, 502-507.

Part 5
Hill Resistance Training Overview

The Lydiard Hill Exercises used by Olympic 400m, 800m, 1500m and 5000m champions

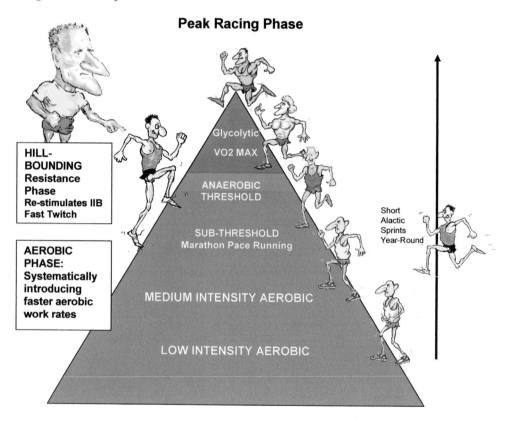

Peak Racing Phase

HILL-BOUNDING Resistance Phase Re-stimulates IIB Fast Twitch

AEROBIC PHASE: Systematically introducing faster aerobic work rates

Glycolytic

VO2 MAX

ANAEROBIC THRESHOLD

SUB-THRESHOLD
Marathon Pace Running

MEDIUM INTENSITY AEROBIC

LOW INTENSITY AEROBIC

Short Alactic Sprints Year-Round

Lydiard really saw this as a transition time where the very fine development of the aerobic system was maintained while the leg muscles were strengthened by resistance exercise. He even said that this work could satisfactorily be done in a gym if hills weren't available (and while coaching in Denmark, which has a very flat topography, he was forced to adapt gym-based work to develop the leg strength he was after).

Lydiard certainly wasn't opposed to the notion of specific strength training for athletes, but as he had to deal with athletes who often had other important demands on their time, training had to be time-efficient. He was also concerned about possible imbalances in lifting techniques causing gym-based injuries and felt that hill-running and bounding drills, done correctly, exercised the prime movers required for fast and very fast running in a far more specific manner that delivered exquisite results.

Not only middle distance runners benefited from this phase. America's 1992 Olympic 400m champion Quincy Watts, with his coach Jim Bush, acknowledged Lydiard's hill-bounding work was crucial in his speed-development program.

"I owe my success as a long sprint coach to Lydiard's hill training," says premier sprinting coach, Jim Bush, who trained, among others, Quincy Watts (Olympic 400m champion in 1992) and Mark Currier (110m H).

Olympic medalists Snell, Halberg, and Magee all did supplementary exercises in a gym under the eye of local fitness expert Keith Scott in Auckland, while also pursuing their endurance work. They'd often get a weekly rub-down too.

The important distinction here is that in hill resistance training, the focus was on strengthening the muscles most specific to running at high speeds before the faster work to come. The system employed a variety of techniques involving springing off the toes uphill, with varying sprint drills over short distances between the hill-springing exercises, and plenty of jogging recoveries.

Although the work was exacting and tiring, it never delved into sustained anaerobic energy systems because work bouts were very short and recoveries were good. Lydiard considered the hill training as an extension of the final 4 weeks of the aerobic buildup, and each Sunday the very long run would continue.

The use of slow hill bounding exercises in this way was unique and far ahead of its time. Bounding uphill off the toes at slow forward speeds will isolate the same prime movers used in sprinting, but with far less risk of injury. At toe-off, the plantar flexors will be asked to (concentrically) contract while still being (eccentrically) stretched from the landing force.

This type of contraction is known as a plyometric contraction and is exactly the sort of stimulus required to preferentially recruit the most powerful fast twitch fibers, the type IIB, before any others. This is the exact reverse of the normal recruitment and firing sequence of the "motor units" in muscle.*

Normally, whether a muscle is recruited for a slow contraction or a fast powerful movement, the nervous system will fire off muscle fibers in sequentially bigger "motor units" according to the "size principle."

Groups of muscle fibers, usually of the same type, will fire off together in a motor unit supplied by an incoming nerve. A small motor unit of slow twitch fibers requires a small electromotive charge from a small nerve axon. Intermediary fast twitch oxidative fibers (IIA) will be recruited next, with a larger incoming nerve axon and a larger electromotive charge. The massively powerful IIb fast twitch fibers fire last and require very large nerve axons and a very large electromotive charge.

This electromotive charge is electrical activity generated from the brain and delivered to the muscle in a "neural drive." It explains why some small people can be inordinately strong and powerful for their size, and to a large degree explains why this sort of training can be so useful in athletics.

As mentioned earlier, mileage wasn't the main emphasis in this demanding phase: a long run was maintained each week, and the exercise drills may have been done on three days during the week with easier recovery running on in-between days. Some articles say hill-work was done even more often. However, this wouldn't be advised by most Lydiard-based coaches today as muscles need recovery in order to repair and get stronger. It's also quite possible that today's athletes don't have the tremendous lower leg development that many New Zealand youngsters enjoyed in the 1950s and 1960s due to the national pastime of running around in bare feet kicking a football at primary school.

Barry Magee maintains that in the early days of the program, the hill exercises would be run on a daily basis, with very few athletes getting injured. Later on, as Lydiard took the program overseas, he noticed that athletes would often get very fatigued and injury prone if they didn't alternate hill bounding days with easier "recovery jogging" days. Lydiard thought that this was due to inactivity in childhood of more recent generations of youngsters. Even in third-world countries, such as Mexico, Lydiard noted that computer games and TV pulled kids away from vigorous outdoor activities.

References

Karp, J.R. "Motor unit recruitment strategy in muscle during eccentric contractions." Unpublished master's thesis. The University of Calgary, 1997.

Nardone, A., Romano, C. and Schieppati, M. "Selective recruitment of high-threshold human motor units during voluntary isotonic lengthening of active muscles." *Journal of Physiology* 409: 451-471, 1989.

Denier van der Gon, J.J., ter Haar Romeny B.M. and van Zuylen, E.J. "Behavior of motor units of human arm muscles: Differences between slow isometric contraction and relaxation." *Journal of Physiology* 359: 107-118, 1985.

Grimby, L., and Hannerz, J. "Firing rate and recruitment order of toe extensor motor units in different modes of voluntary contraction." *Journal of Applied Physiology* 264: 865-879, 1977.

HILL TRAINING:

DO'S and DON'T's

DO:

- Ease into hill training very gradually, under-doing your first sessions deliberately, and carefully monitoring your initial reactions.

- Start off with longer repetitions at steady paces with good recoveries, working your way down to shorter, more concentrated efforts, over several weeks.

- Incorporate hill sessions into your pre-track phase.

DON'T:

- Do hills when tired.

- Do too many repetitions in the first few sessions.

- Think they feel too easy to be doing any good.

- Underestimate how you may feel the day after overdoing your exercises.

Hill Training—the Lydiard Way

With Arthur Lydiard's Japanese disciple, Nobby Hashizume

"Believe me; (the effect of hill training) is unbelievable."

This is what was explained about Lydiard's hill training in the Japanese translation of *Run to the Top*.

Years later when I read the original English version, it actually read *"Believe me, it is strenuous!"* There's quite a difference in meaning, however it turns out both descriptions are true!

"If I were limited to using the type of training for every workout, I'd pick the (Lydiard style) hill workout," the late Ron Daws, the 1968 U.S. Olympian, stated in his second book, *Running Your Best*.

"It teaches technique and builds stamina and speed. It can be run at any level of difficulty and still works the different muscle groups."

Nobby hangs out with Arthur Lydiard, 1984

Marty Liquori, one of the greatest middle distance runners the US has ever produced, explains in his book *Marty Liquori's Guide for the Elite Runner* the type of hill training Lydiard advocates as follows:

"(Once you start introducing the hill training phase) the runner will notice that, almost without any effort whatsoever, his pace on long runs will drop a minute a mile or more! This will be despite the runner's own effort to keep the pace even and slow." After slogs of aerobic running during the off-season, perhaps in the snow or rain, wearing heavy layers of clothes, hill training is what prepares you to emerge as a butterfly. This is when you introduce strength and flexibility into your strides; preparing you for the next phase, which involves more race specific training such as intervals and time trials. It is physically and mentally very demanding, but the reward is immense."

Lydiard planned his Hill Training Phase between the Marathon Conditioning Phase and the Track Training Phase. It is a transition between the "slower stuff" and "faster stuff." It prepares you mechanically, as well as physiologically, for the demand of race specific training.

The original Lydiard Hill Training, or "Hill Circuit" as "Arthur's Boys" used to call it, was a loop of 1.9 miles; an 800m long uphill for springing and bounding up, 800m flat on the top for a recovery jog, 700m downhill for fast relaxed striding; with another 800m flat at the bottom where they did some wind sprints (leg speed runs), or easy repetitions (see below).

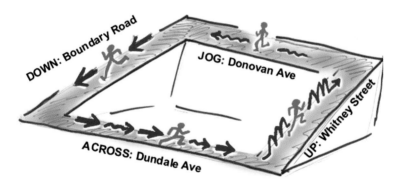

The Original Lydiard Hill Circuit:
Blockhouse Bay, Auckland

The 800m uphill section on the original circuit had a couple of slightly downhill "resting spots" in mild undulations on the way up, according to Barry Magee. It was usual to spring for two hundred meters from the bottom and then just run for 400m before springing the final 200m to the top.

The uphill work would be followed by easy recovery jogging along the top of the hill, and there would be easy relaxed striding down the hill afterwards. As we now know, downhill running is an excellent form of eccentric resistance work.

Along the base of the circuit, a few easy "wind sprints" would be included, with good recovery. Easy wind sprints are just another preparation for the Track Phase. The hill, in fact, can be as short as 50m in length if you know what you need to accomplish with it.

Barry Magee confirmed that Peter Snell would often record times of 1:50 in relaxed fast striding for 800m on the downhill section. The "official" Imperial 880 yards started just before the downhill and finished shortly after. One training day, Snell pulled out a 1:44 on the downhill with Magee flying after him but finishing well back.

The original Lydiard athletes did four laps of this circuit plus approximately 2 to 3 miles of warm up and cool down (a total of 12 to 14 miles). And they did it six days a week (though Lydiard concluded later that it could be just as effective with two to three times a week)…with a 22-mile run on Sunday!

Ideally, they would do this for four weeks.

However, many people don't grasp the specific purpose of Lydiard hill training.

There are three main queries many people have regarding Lydiard hill training:

1. **"Where can we find such a perfect circuit?"**

This can be answered with *Common Sense*. First of all, it does not have to be a circuit. The concept is to perform some resistance work in the form of hill springing or bounding followed by some recovery jogging. If you can include striding down the hill, or striding on the flat, that would make it more complete.

2. **"Isn't the risk of injury too much when you switch from Long Slow Distance to hill springing?"**

The base phase is NOT full of Long Slow Distance but includes short sharp ALACTIC sprints in fartleks and progressively faster sub-threshold runs that push up the aerobic ceiling, as well as slow aerobic recovery runs. There is no sudden switching from one phase to another in an organized program: it is introduced steadily. However, certain athletes who have scar tissue in their legs from earlier sporting injuries may find that they can't handle hill training very well. Such athletes can often handle wind sprints or short alactic strideouts with long recovery on a flat surface, and still progress, and are encouraged to do regular aerobic runs over hilly circuits.

3. **"What exactly is Lydiard hill springing or bounding anyway?"**

This is the best question! The whole point is to introduce power and flexibility into your strides, or sophisticatedly put, to introduce plyometric resistance exercise that will re-stimulate your IIB fast twitch fibers.

(Again, Lydiard understood the necessity of such resistance exercise in the early 1950s, perhaps years before scientists even named this type of exercise as plyometrics).

Lydiard just happened to use a circuit. And anybody who worries about injury should go back and double-check "Common Sense" for **Adaptation**. It is common sense to ease into any new exercise. You'd have to realize also, that most of the terrain "Arthur's Boys" trained over in New Zealand was very very hilly. So they were preparing themselves for the Hill Training Phase constantly.

Years later, Lydiard himself started to explain to people in other parts of the world where it may not be as hilly that his runners were preparing themselves for the hill training phase during the conditioning by doing easy hill exercises here and there. In fact, second and third generations of Flying Kiwis, such as Dick Quax and Lorraine Moller*, did not exactly have a distinct Hill Training Phase. Rather, they did lots of running over hilly courses to accommodate this phase.

This is basically what Rift Valley Kenyan and Ethiopian runners are still doing, running over the hills and the valleys, laying the strength foundations that enable them to become great runners.

*On reading this chapter recently, Lorraine responded with the following:

"I did in fact do formal hill training for the first 10 years of my training life, under John Davies and then Ron Daws. After that I let it slide. It's a pity, as I am sure it would have kept that flexibility in my ankles that slowly dissipated over the years."

The Three Lydiard Hill Exercises

Lydiard hill training eventually included three different types of exercise; each with a specific purpose.

1. Steep Hill Running   **2. Hill Bounding**   **3. Hill Springing**

1. Steep Hill Running

This is designed to strengthen your quadriceps, hip flexors, and knee lift. You basically run up a steep hill at a slow forward momentum, concentrating on good posture and exaggerated knee lift (see Graphic 1).

Our pictured athlete is doing this exercise very well, with one mild technical error. Her right arm is starting to go across her midline. Her left arm looks just fine. Ideally, we learn to keep our driving arms from crossing the torso.

Lydiard explained that when people start to clench their fists and struggle with their

arm swings in the last 50m of a 400m or 800m race, it's not because their upper body and arms are weak but because their quads are "gone" and they can't maintain proper knee lift or extension. (Also because the acidosis from the poorly conditioned legs affects whole-body coordination.)

"Most 400m runners are great 350m runners," Lydiard said. "In order to counter that, you need to strengthen the muscles that lift your thighs and straighten your knees. The hills are perhaps the best form of resistance work for that. You don't want to run up the hill too fast because then it becomes highly anaerobic and you start to lose form. You don't want to introduce too much of the anaerobic energy system as yet anyway (remember, "ease into the next stage"). Besides, the slower you run up, the more resistance you feel in your legs."

I saw a film of Toshihiko Seko of Japan, two-time Boston Marathon champion in the '80s, doing a hill training session in New Zealand, in 1983. The image is like spending an extra half a second longer on your foot, "grasping" the ground with your foot. A straight arm swing is a must. This is a great exercise for anybody whose knees start to go down at the end of the race.

2. Hill Bounding

I used to think Steep Hill Running comprised the majority of Lydiard's Hill Training, after some old-timers showed me the drills in New Zealand. That was until Dr. Peter Snell himself demonstrated otherwise.

Peter Snell's technique was more of a combination between Steep Hill Running and Hill Bounding. After all, it is almost impossible to "bound" all the way up an 800m long uphill as you will be sure to find out if you try, but the emphasis should still be on rear-leg extension.

(You'll notice that Peter's impromptu demonstration shows good rear leg extension and front leg lift, however, as in the previous example, his left arm has started to cross the torso. We can forgive this as it's possibly 40 years since Peter last did this regularly!).

After years of experience with so many individuals in different situations, Lydiard himself evolved Hill Training into several distinctively different exercises for more specific purposes. Bounding is designed to take a long bounding stride, much like what triple jumpers would do in their training; while Steep Hill Running is geared more toward knee lift and strengthening of thigh muscles.

The most important aspect of Bounding is to straighten your rear leg

"A lot of people run like they're sitting in a bucket," Lydiard said.

"When their knees are bent, they can't get power and stride." Lydiard always used 1972 Olympic 1500m champion, Pekka Vasala of Finland as a great example. There is a great photo of Vasala and Keino matching strides down the straight in a beautiful example of perfect sprinting form.

Vasala used to do lots of hill bounding over a 100 to 200m hill. In fact, there is a report that he did a hill bounding phase of three to five times a week for three months in his preparation for the Olympics. He continued to do some form of hill training until only two weeks before the Olympics. Lydiard's famous phrase, "like a deer going over the fence," is the best image. This is perfect for anybody who needs a good kick and particularly middle distance runners. It is best to be performed over a slightly gentler hill than the other two exercises.

This image here, from the 1990 Commonwealth Games, shows NZ 1500m bronze medalist Peter O'Donoghue exemplifying perfect form as he drives into the straight. This is a great example of the rear leg extension and upper body relaxation we're aiming to develop with these hill exercises.

3. Hill Springing

"Increase in speed comes from flicking of the ankles," Lydiard said. "If you want speed, you don't need to be like a body-builder. You need to be like a ballet dancer, with springy and bouncy ankles." He said this in the 1960s and his view had not changed since. You can see the "suppleness" and "spring" in the strides of such middle distance and distance greats as Seb Coe and Haile Gebrselassie.

Hill Springing is one of the best forms of exercise to strengthen your ankle flexibility and, hence, develop fine speed. The exercise is much like Bounding, but the emphasis is not on forward progression, it is on vertical lift.

A study published in The Journal of Biomechanics *in 1987 showed that the amount of force used horizontally during constant-speed running was one tenth the amount of force used vertically.*

Constant-speed running appears to be a series of nearly vertical thrusts against gravity, with the leg-swing phase (swing time) occupying the time till touch-down.

A long stride is therefore a function of superior vertical thrust off the rear leg. It's the vertical direction of the stride that needs our help because it is the portion most assaulted by gravity.

This use of vertical springing by Lydiard seems to be supported in recent research published by Dr. Peter Weyand in The *Journal of Applied Physiology* in the year 2000.

It appears that the determining factor in speed development is the amount of force that can be applied to the ground at foot-strike. The harder and faster the foot can "toe off" and deliver its "mass-specific-force" (MSF), the more vertical lift. This landing and toe-off time is known as "ground contact time."

According to noted US sprint coach Barry Ross, ground contact time occupies between 0.09s and 0.11s. This is much the same either for world-class sprinters or mediocre sprinters. It is the force, or *power*, that can be delivered in that contact time that is crucial.

Even slow springing, as already mentioned, invokes a plyometric stretch that recruits the very powerful IIB fast twitch fibers, and hence their massive nerve structures. Consequently, greater mass-specific-force can be generated when these fibers are recruited in a sprint.

The trick for all athletes is to generate propulsive force without increasing body mass significantly. Hill training will do this amply for middle and distance athletes. The load moved, however, is only that of the body's weight. Even more force can be developed with a very specific type of weight training that can yield big changes in power without significant increase in muscle mass. Coach Ross advocates a type of low-repetition, high load, long recovery weight training in concert with bounding or plyometric drills. We'll explore that very interesting concept later.

It appears that this sort of training, correctly performed, doesn't result in the soreness and acidosis so commonly associated with conventional weight programs. The short total lifting times involved, with big recoveries, make sure that only the alactic system gets involved heavily.

Compared to Bounding, it is probably best to use a steeper and shorter hill for springing. Here you are not taking a long bounding stride, but you are taking short steps of approximately

a foot or so. However try to lift your center of gravity as high as possible (see below). If you can do this exercise on a softer surface such as grass, and wear track spike shoes, it is most effective because your heel would go down further to emphasize greater range of motion

"I never ever had an athlete with Achilles tendonitis or a hamstring problem," Lydiard said. "Because the hill training can stretch your ankles to the extreme, both up and down, and strengthen muscles and ligaments in the front and the back in a natural way." (See below)

Downhill Striding

The original Lydiard hill training involved fast relaxed downhill striding after a brief recovery jog at the top of the hill. This was done very fast but relaxed. Peter Snell did this 800m stretch of down hill in around 1:50, so he was flying! The correct way to run downhill is to lean into the hill, not lean backward as many people tend to do on the downhill. This would create too much braking action and, therefore, landing shock.

Think about skiing down a hill. If you get scared and lean backwards, you lose control and fall. But if you lean into the hill, you can pick up smooth speed. It is best to do this on a gentler downhill if possible. You should "freewheel" and just let go of yourself down the hill. Let gravity do the work. This will help overcome muscle tension, stretch out your leg muscles, and develop faster and longer strides. You shouldn't try the forward lean if the hill is too steep (remember "Common Sense"?).

Downhill running could be even more demanding on your legs than uphill exercises. Some people, with extra caution, avoid it completely and are still successful.

Marty Liquori used to have someone drive him up the hill before he got out of the car and continued the uphill section.

John Walker was the same when he was overcoming a nasty leg circulation problem. This was myofascial entrapment, where the muscle becomes overdeveloped in its sheath, and as the muscle enlargens with the circulation of exercise, it cuts its own circulation off. This problem prevented him from training for more than half an hour, at any intensity. This was a major problem in getting ready for the 1976 Olympics, but his clever coach Arch Jelley realized the value of strong uphill running. Walker could still run a couple of repeats up the notorious Waiatarua hill and get a car trip back down for the next repeat. Walker won his gold.

Downhill exercise *can* be very valuable and should be practiced if you can (particularly if you are running the Boston marathon or other road races with lots of downhill portion) but don't strictly adhere to it if you are susceptible to knee problems.

Wind Sprints

Lydiard's runners used the circuit's bottom stretch 800m to do easy "wind sprints." This is the initial introduction to the more race specific training to follow. The speed should still not be too fast at this point, perhaps only slightly faster than all the conditioning distance work you've so far done.

Lydiard also recommended varying the distance; i.e., 4 x 100m for the first set, then 8 x 50m, then 2 x 200m or 1 x 400m, etc., with equal distance of recovery jog. Lydiard called these either "wind sprints" or "stride-outs." As the term indicates, these are not razor-sharp fast intervals or repetitions.

Remember, just as you should ease into hill training by introducing some easy hill exercises before you move into the actual Hill Training Phase you should ease into the Track Training Phase by initiating yourself with these easy wind sprints first.

A Word of Caution Here

Some people have the image of doing these wind sprints every time they come down the hill. If the circuit or the hill itself is short, this would be way too much to cope with. Originally "Arthur's Boys" were doing this hill circuit of four laps in about 1 hour (and remember: they were the "Cream of the Crop").

In other words, they were doing one 800m stretch of wind sprints in every 15 minutes. And that's about what Lydiard recommended. So if you are using, say, a 150m hill, you can repeat the hill exercise three or four times up and down with a recovery jog inbetween, then after 15 minutes of exercise, throw in some wind sprints and repeat this cycle.

More Words of Caution

Barry Magee advises that if an athlete is injury-prone, or "carrying" mild injuries, then hill circuit training should be avoided and a combination of gentle aerobic running and faster strides on the flat can be incorporated.

Hill training can "wipe out" an athlete for several days after a good session for several reasons. We found this when training two athletes of comparable ability last season.

The older athlete, 39-year-old Tony, who had been running at a high level for years, had no problem with his hill exercises, except to say that he felt "washed out" after the first week. This feeling is common and can be explained because hill circuit training directly stimulates the IIB fast twitch fibers and their massive nerve supplies. Even a small amount of slow bounding may over-excite the central nervous system initially, because it's all "new information." The points where the nerves supply the working muscle (the synapses) can rapidly get exhausted. To function efficiently, the synapses need reasonable stores of neurotransmitters (these can be derived from the fatty acids in fish and vegetable oils); these synapses also need to be "trained" to cope with this new activity.

The younger athlete, 27-year-old Stephen, felt his calf muscles get tighter and stiffer to the point that he had to cease doing exactly the same work. He was in his first year of serious running since leaving high school and had been very active in a number of sports including Australian Rules football, cricket, and karate. It was very likely that he was carrying scar tissue in his legs from contact sports. We changed his schedule to include fast, relaxed strideouts over 100-150m interspersed with jogging and fartlek, and he was fine.

Both athletes resumed training together on the track for their common goals over 800m and 1500m, with a good degree of success.

Alternatives

If you live in an absolutely flat area and can't find a hill at all, don't despair. Where there's a will, there's a way. If you understand what Lydiard was trying to accomplish with hill training, you would understand that it does not have to be a perfect hill circuit to achieve the necessary development. Lydiard liked to talk about his friend in Texas who started running when he was 63. He lived in an area where there are no hills whatsoever. But every morning he jogged down to the local high school track and ran up the stadium steps. At the age of 71, he continued to improve. "Because he's doing hill training," Lydiard said.

Stair running is perhaps the next best thing to actual hill training. In fact, Liquori used to train on a stadium steps in what he called "Pancakesville" in Florida. "If Lydiard lived in a town with no hills," Liquori says confidently, "he would have used the stadium steps." You can also be creative and use, say, the gentle incline of a local library's parking ramp, for example. If you chose to do plyometrics in the gym, you can do that too.

However, make sure you do some extra stretching for your Achilles tendon, which you would gain in running on the incline naturally. Also do some striding and leg-speed drills for stretching out and quick leg turnover to replicate the downhill running portion as far as possible. The beauty of Lydiard hill training is that you can accomplish all these things at once in a form of continuous running.

As with all other exercises, you should ease into this demanding exercise. Lydiard recommended trying 15 minutes total of hill exercise (not counting warm-up and cool-down of about 15 minutes each) in the first week and seeing how your legs felt. Then try 30 minutes, then 45 minutes, etc. He also cautioned that, because this type of exercise can be very demanding, you may feel tired and actually feel sluggish and slower in the first few weeks. "The real benefit can be felt after two weeks," he said.

Also, remember the rule of thumb in training; "start with the longer and slower and move into the shorter and faster."

If you follow the cycle of the Lydiard program, it would be advisable to do Steep Hill Running on a longer slope, capitalizing on your good endurance. After strengthening muscles and connective tissues in your legs initially, then move into Bounding and Springing. The latter two exercises can be more demanding on your legs. These also can be incorporated during the Track Phase, as 1972 Olympic 1500m champion Vasala did so successfully.

Chapter References: Weyand, P., Sternlight, D., Bellizzi, M. and Wright, S. "Faster top running speeds are achieved with greater ground forces not more rapid leg movements." *Journal of Applied Physiology* 89: 1991-2000, 2000.

Part 6
The "Anaerobic" Training Phase

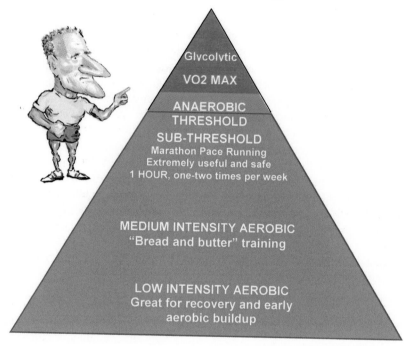

Glycolytic

VO2 MAX

ANAEROBIC
THRESHOLD
SUB-THRESHOLD
Marathon Pace Running
Extremely useful and safe
1 HOUR, one-two times per week

MEDIUM INTENSITY AEROBIC
"Bread and butter" training

LOW INTENSITY AEROBIC
Great for recovery and early
aerobic buildup

By this stage, in an ideal Lydiard preparation, the stage has been well and truly set.

The aerobic energy systems have been carefully developed to the highest level possible in the given time, without delving too far into anaerobic metabolism and the acidosis this invokes. The slow twitch fibers have greatly increased their work capacity. The circulatory system to the working muscles has become prolific. The heart has increased in size and stroke volume. Resting pulse has decreased. A higher working heart rate can be maintained aerobically. At any given aerobic speed, the body is more efficient and some speeds that were formerly in or above the anaerobic threshold zone have become aerobic.

The fast twitch fibers of both types have been prepared for faster anaerobic work via the "back door." Plenty of uphill running has put pressure on fast twitch fibers. The long runs to glycogen depletion have increased the ratio of intermediary anaerobic/ aerobic fast twitch IIA fibers, and inadvertently, potential anaerobic capacity has been increased. The very short fast sprints in fartlek sessions during the endurance base period have maintained fast twitch activity and good biomechanics, and the hill bounding phase has been a powerful stimulus to the explosive fast twitch IIB fibers.

The aerobic layers of the training pyramid have all been built, right up to the level of the anaerobic threshold, and now it's time to finish the top of the pyramid, which represents anaerobic capacity. Anaerobic capacity is notoriously limited, whether it's placed on the aerobic base of a "couch potato," or on top of the aerobic base of an Olympic rower. It's like comparing the volume of stone in the top few feet of a tiny pyramid, or the volume in the top few feet of a huge pyramid. The actual volume's much the same, but one's a lot higher than the other.

Once over the anaerobic threshold for long, increasing acidosis spoils the party for all of us. The highest "oxygen debt" anybody can tolerate is somewhere between 15 and 18 liters of oxygen; this energy equivalent has to be sourced anaerobically, and at high exercise intensity it runs out in minutes. If we're smart, we can eke out this potential capacity over the length of a marathon, or compress it into two laps of the track.

As an example, a very good runner with a VO_2 max of 75 milliliters per kilogram per minute may be capable of 5000m in 14 minutes, 3000m in 8 minutes, and 1500m in 3:45. If he weighs 60 kilograms, then he consumes (75 x 60) milliliters of oxygen per minute at his VO_2 max speed (close to his 3000m pace). This works out to be at 4,500 milliliters of oxygen (or 4.5 liters) per minute, giving him a theoretical maximum running time at that pace of between 3 minutes 20 seconds and 4 minutes to achieve the maximal oxygen debt range possible (15 to 18 liters). However, he can maintain his VO_2 max pace for 3000m, or 8 minutes. What's going on?

Having said all this, the body does have a bag of tricks it can delve into to increase this rather limited anaerobic capacity. Our ability to tolerate prolonged acidosis can be increased for sure, and this next phase does it before the first important competitions. Ironically, anaerobic training is totally necessary to develop the ability of the body to extract as much oxygen as possible at high speeds. It is both friend and foe.

The first part of Lydiard's anaerobic phase, looking back from our current understanding, actually concentrates on what we now call VO_2 max training; forcing the circulatory capacity and aerobic capacity to maximum in a sea of acidosis. This is hard going, but totally necessary to stimulate the chemical buffers required for good racing.

The next phase would be what we now call lactate tolerance training, or glycolytic training. This would involve much harder, faster, shorter work bouts with much longer recoveries, and would further increase the ability of the body to endure at very high speeds well above the VO_2 max.

Interspersed between these more specific sessions would be work bouts of lower intensity (anaerobic threshold, sub-threshold) and suitable low-intensity aerobic recovery runs that would keep the relevant muscle fibers and energy systems in a highly trained state.

Milk and Vinegar

What would you prefer to drink? Milk or vinegar? Most people would opt for milk. Milk is slightly alkali, and vinegar is mildly acidic. All of our body's systems run better in a very mildly alkali state.

Hard anaerobic running produces acidosis, so that our blood pH (the measure of alkalinity or acidity) heads towards the acidity of vinegar. Not good for our health. Prolonged acidosis can disrupt fatty acid metabolism, aerobic enzymes, and anaerobic enzymes. It can rupture muscle cell walls and harm red blood cell function. It depresses the function of the central nervous system and badly disrupts coordination.

How Gentle Aerobic Running "Restores"

Before and after any anaerobic session, Lydiard recommended lots of gentle aerobic running. The gentle flow of blood through the running muscles and circulatory system would ensure that metabolites from very hard running would get back to the liver to be recycled.

This in turn would steadily reverse the acidosis of the bloodstream. The presence of fresh nutrient-rich blood in the hard-exercised muscles would support recovery. Not only would fresh oxygen get into the region, but it would also repair enzymes and trophic (growth) hormones.

A couple of very long slow aerobic runs in a row often forgave a multitude of sins when it came to athletes overtraining or losing condition.

Developing the Ability to Tolerate Oxygen Debt

The ability of the body to tolerate oxygen debt, or acidosis, can be developed to the physiological maximum in as little as four or five weeks in trained athletes.

Lydiard conclusively proved this when working with East German sports scientists. Lydiard liked to spread this phase out a little more gradually, with hard anaerobic work sandwiched between easy aerobic sessions over a number of weeks.

It begs the question why even to this day, athletes and coaches relentlessly work on the limited glycolytic anaerobic energy systems year-round, at the cost of the aerobic systems.

There is a logical reason why many coaches choose to do this, but it's based on a profound misunderstanding of the difference between speed training and anaerobic training. They're completely different creatures, as we'll soon see.

Many coaches and athletes believe "you've got to train fast to run fast." And they're correct. This brings us to another key distinction.

What Exactly Is "Fast?"

To even contemplate running at our best potential sprint speeds, we have to develop excellent movement patterns, and explosive leg strength. This requires a relatively rested state in the first place and muscle fibers loaded with fuels.

The bad news is that as far as pure sprinting potential, we're pretty well stuck with the ratio of explosive fast twitch muscle fibers our parents handed us, although with lots of specific training these ratios can be changed somewhat.

The really good news is that running to our speed potential is also a learnable skill. It is just like taking the handbrake off when we drive. This can only be practiced with fast, very relaxed sprints over very short distances, when well rested and nicely warmed up.

For instance, a technically competent sprinter will "switch on" his big upper thigh muscles almost immediately after "switching off" his hamstrings. He literally takes the brakes off and straightaway is faster. A tired or incompetent sprinter will still be in partial hamstring contraction when he "switches on" his opposing thigh muscles. He then has to overcome the resistance of the "braking" muscle, slowing contraction, and possibly tearing the hamstring. This relationship of potentially opposing muscles is referred to as the agonist/antagonist relationship.

Top speed for anyone can only be reached and maintained for a few seconds. In the 100m sprint, top speed isn't reached until somewhere between 40m and 60m. Thereafter, good technique and leg strength may maintain a high proportion of the speed reached, but after 10 to 13 seconds the most explosive muscle fibers are running out of steam, and the body starts to cross over into acidosis as lactate is used more and more.

One of the major detrimental effects of acidosis on the system is that it affects coordination. And you need to be coordinated to practice true sprint drills and speed technique.

One only has to watch world-class runners finishing their races over 100m, 200m, and 400m to see the effects on coordination. The 100m runner struts in front of the TV cameras as if nothing has happened, and because most of the distance has been covered using intramuscular creatine phosphate stores, by the time he's finished his lap of the track most of those energy stores have replenished again.

It's a vastly different story with the 400m runner who has had to run with a bear on his back for the last few meters before yawning his breakfast over the TV cameras.

So for a middle distance runner's purposes, "fast" running can only really be trained when relatively rested, with drills lasting well under 10 seconds, to maximize the use of easily replenished creatine phosphate stores in the most explosive muscle fibers.

This sort of running can be done on an easy aerobic recovery day before a substantial low-intensity aerobic run or even when fresh and relatively rested in the warm-up before moving onto harder longer anaerobic work.

Lydiard would employ versions of this sort of work throughout the year.

Why Anaerobic Training Isn't Speed Training!

Let Arthur tell us why in his own words, (from an interview when he was 86):

"Repetitions or interval training can improve your speed to a certain degree simply because of anaerobic development and improved mechanics. This gives the false idea that you are actually improving speed.

"The actual fact is repetitions or intervals are used for anaerobic development. You are creating huge oxygen debt to develop a buffer against this type of fatigue. Problem is that when you do that, you invariably tighten up. You can not develop fine speed when you tighten up. The best way to develop speed is to use some of the American sprint drills.

"(In other words) you should be fresh and relaxed when developing speed, not fatigued from oxygen debt. But bear in mind, there's a time for repetitions to develop anaerobic development and there's a time for sprint drills to develop fine speed. You have to organize all types of training, including repetitions and sprint drills, at the right time so you can peak on the day. That is the Lydiard Way of training."

A Real Case History of "Speed Technique" Success

When I was at secondary school in New Zealand, there was a guy two years ahead of me who was good enough to make our school athletic teams in the sprint relays, but not good enough to win the school sprint titles. Several guys could regularly trounce him. He was very fast, though, in every direction except straight ahead. He ran like a spider with limbs flying fast everywhere.

Later, Auckland sprint coach Phil Temple got hold of him and straightened his technique out over a number of months with regular sprint drills and technique sessions. The same fellow (Shane Downey) eventually ran 10.53s (electronic, legal) for a NZ resident record at the time and won a number of New Zealand titles.

The Fundamental Difference Between Middle Distance and Distance Running

This book looks at the Lydiard system from the perspective of the energy systems and relevant muscle fiber types being developed in each phase. As you may have noted, Arthur Lydiard gave his middle distance specialists and his distance specialists the SAME core aerobic conditioning before they moved onto their specific race preparation. Superior cardiovascular efficiency and aerobic endurance were at the core of their respective track programs, whether it was Peter Snell chasing world 800m times, Murray Halberg chasing 5000m glory, or Barry Magee switching down from the marathon to become the world's No.1 ranked 10,000m runner.

In terms of energy systems, the middle distances (800m and 1500m) are difficult to master for athletes and coaches. This is because the high-level middle-distance runner has to master and balance the training of three main energy systems; 1) the alactic anaerobic; 2) the glycolytic (lactic) anaerobic; as well as 3) the aerobic.

The athlete at peak racing time has to have the capacity and power of each system developed to the maximal level possible in the time available without concentrating so much on any one system that it is detrimental to the others. The athlete has to have the power of a good sprinter and the endurance of a distance runner, and good lactic tolerance as well.

Australian middle-distance coach and mathematician Kevin Prendergast has a very useful definition for the problem. He defines the difference between middle distance and distance events by the relative loss of speed as we step up in distance.

In his book *A Fundamental Approach to Middle Distance Running* (available online from www.oztrack.com) he points out that a graph of speeds achieved in world record runs from 100m to marathon shows a nearly flat line (no loss of speed) between 100m and 200m, with a drop in speed to 400m of about 10%, and a further drop in speed from the 400m to the 800m of 15%.

As distances double, the most dramatic drop in average speed is that between 400m and 800m. The 800m is about 24% slower than the 200m. From 800m to 2000m, distance doubling leads to a speed loss of 8-9%. Beyond that, the effect of distance on speed loss starts to decline and doubling from 1500m to 3000m results in a speed loss of less than 6%. From 5000m to 10000m, it's only 4.3%.

Mathematically, the events from 800m to 2000m can be seen to be very different from those on either side. "Their speeds make them well separated from the sprints, even the 400m, and the fact that their speeds are so distance-dependent distinguishes them from the longer events," says Prendergast.

"Suppose we take the 1000m to be representative of middle distance. It is a reasonable representation because its speed is about the average of the two common middle distances, the 800m and the 1500. The 1000m is ten times the distance of the 100m, which can represent the sprints, and one tenth of the distance of the 10,000m, which can represent distance. The speed of the 1000m is 25.5% slower than that of the sprint, but only 13.8% faster than that of the distance run," says Prendergast.

"What does this tell us? It certainly tells us that in terms of speed, middle distance is much closer to distance running than sprinting. It might also tell us that the practice of trying to make excellent middle distance runners out of good sprinters is unlikely to be successful," says Prendergast.

"On the other hand, it would appear to be more feasible to make a middle distance runner out of a distance runner by working on speed. Seb Coe is a very good example of this. In his mid-teens, he was a competent cross country runner but did not have much speed. His coach-father Peter recognized this weakness and worked on it. His success is illustrated by Seb's second placing in the British 400m championship in 1979."

When we understand the enormously different energy requirements of a middle distance event, such as 1500m, and a distance event, such as 5000m, it makes the achievement of Morocco's Hicham El Guerrouj in winning both events at the Athens Olympics seem even more remarkable.

The Moroccan was a master of judiciously introducing faster work at specific paces as the track season progressed towards important races. He buffered his demanding race-pace work with ample volumes of low-intensity aerobic running.

Prendergast also has a great description of how the different energy systems contribute to an 800m race, and makes some very worthwhile observations on developing the *capacity* as well as the *power* of each energy system in middle distance races.

Anaerobic Capacity is increased by performing a number of intervals with recoveries just short enough to allow the athlete to incur a sizeable oxygen debt to his current limits. (This is the equivalent of the first anaerobic phase of training, where it is possible to raise systemic acidosis to a high level, gradually, by a volume of intervals with equal or shorter recoveries.)

Anaerobic Power is increased by doing only one or a few very high quality near-maximal repetitions, with very long recoveries.

Prendergast introduces 10% step-wise increases in the Lactic/Aerobic ratio of his anaerobic phase of training. The following table is a summary of how Prendergast systematically introduces this faster work. For more detail on his methods and philosophy, I suggest you purchase his book.

His work carries on from the multi-pace work popularized by British coach Frank Horwill and refined by Peter Coe. The work makes complete sense in the Lydiard context, and I include it here not because it was implemented as such by Lydiard himself but because it gives such a logical template for the coach and athlete to tailor race-specific work without "surprises" showing up.

Lactic/Aerobic	Pace	Distance	Rests
50/50	3000m	6-8 x1000m	3 min
60/40	2000m	6-8 x 600m	3 min
70/30	1500m	10 x 300m	45s
80/20	1000m	8 x 300m	90s

In the above table, you will see a progression from higher volumes of lower intensity anaerobic work (i.e., 6000m @ 3000m pace) to lower volumes (3000m and 2400m respectively) of higher intensity work. In my interpretation, all of the above sessions could be termed as quite demanding anaerobic capacity workouts, due to either the total volume of work performed in the first instance, or the number of repetitions with short recovery at 1500m and 1000m pace later. The first workout would stretch a fit athlete's anaerobic capacity quite a bit, all at maximal VO_2 pace, and during the needed recoveries of 3 minutes the heart would probably be thumping along at near-maximal rates as well. This workout could entail about 45 minutes of maximal heart rate work if a good athlete ran 8 x 1000m @ 3 minutes, with 3 minutes recovery. This is achievable but very demanding, and is the sort of work Lydiard would like to introduce early in his track preparation phase. He'd buffer this sort of workout with lots of easy jogging.

In our interpretaion of the general principles, especially with young athletes, we deal with capacity in the first general phase of anaerobic training, namely with weekly VO_2 max long intervals of 800-1000m, with equal or shorter recovery, and then we deal with power as we get into peak racing season with shorter, faster-paced glycolytic repetitions at goal 1500m or 800m pace, with much longer recoveries. We keep it very simple, and it seems to work just fine.

Our young squad has always responded very well to weekly VO_2 max paced long intervals in early track season, especially with intervals of 800m to 1000m, at 5000m to 3000m pace. Three athletes recorded PB 1500m times well under 3:50 before our current athletics season was halfway through; they all went very close to PB 800m times off this general anaerobic training as well.

This season we adopted a very gradual step-wise increment in training paces, bumping up the intensity on a fortnightly basis, and we have been very pleased with the adaptation of the group and the surprising performances. It appears to us that there's not any real advantage in pumping hard glycolytic repetition sessions into young athletes once the season's underway: this goal seems to be achieved by regular racing, which is about as race-specific as you can get! But we do reserve a bit of time mid-season to blend in a couple of quite tough faster workouts, making sure we don't risk "burning out" the athletes.

(Since Prendergast's book was written, the break-down of lactic / aerobic ratios is again in question, with recent research indicating a much higher aerobic distribution right down to 400m. This research is summarised in the *nerds* section in Part 9.)

However, the principle of gradual increments in pace still applies very well.

Finally, many athletes from the race-pace-specific school of thought see no real sense in the preponderance of aerobic work and varied pace efforts in Lydiard's successful schedules.

Lydiard would often intersperse specific middle distance pace repetition sessions with longer efforts at slower paces on other days, which we now understand kept all the energy systems highly trained. We now understand, for instance, that at the business end of an 800m, the flagging lactic acid system starts to fail at around 80-90s, and the organism slows, propped up only by a highly effective VO_2 max system, one step down the rung in intensity.

So it pays to keep the VO$_2$ max system and its supporting anaerobic threshold system trained in track season with moderate efforts at those paces, which is exactly what Peter Snell's regimen included on the way to his superlative world records in 1962.

We'll discuss Snell's approach in the next chapter, and explore the concept more in our chapter on the "H.I.T. Squad" youngsters' training program in Part 7: *How Our "H.I.T. Squad" Trains During Track Season*.

"Specific" programs need to include plenty of "not-exactly specific" variety in faster work to get an optimal outcome.

How Peter Snell Trained for 1.44.3 on Grass in 1962

Long Runs, Hill Circuits, Very Varied Track Work, Morning Runs

Interestingly, in about August 1961, Peter Snell returned from a successful European track tour exhausted from the frenetic racing and traveling, and didn't feel inspired to recommence a buildup until September 17. He established a twice-a-day routine of running to and from his work, and by October 21 won an exhibition mile race in 4.13, in the midst of accumulating the first 100-mile week of that buildup. By November, he was able to cover the 22-mile Waiatarua circuit confidently, covering 4 miles to Lydiard's home before running the full course in 2 hours 11, his best since before his Rome Olympic 800m triumph.

The following day, he started two weeks of hill circuit training, with Wednesdays given over to club races, presumably over sprint and middle distances. After the first week of circuits, he ran a picnic meeting mile in 4.14. He continued his long Sunday runs, as well as morning runs of 10 miles during the week. At the end of his second week of hill circuit training, he competed in the Owairaka marathon. He stayed with the leaders in a top field, being 4th at 20 miles. Half a mile later he was reduced to a walk and at 24 miles, he had to sit down.

He dredged himself to a very tired finish in 2 hours 41. Later that day, he played in a social cricket match, and when he batted he "lasted about three balls before being clean bowled.....my vision was obscured... there was no coordination at all." Obviously, Snell had managed to totally deplete his glycogen reserves.

He recovered all week, running another Waiatarua circuit the next weekend half an hour slower than usual, then the next Monday started track work with a 4.10 picnic meeting mile and last 440 yards of 58.6 seconds. Thereafter followed a variety of track work on several afternoons a week, with 10-mile morning runs every day and the weekly long run.

He recorded a 9.18 two mile in his first week of track training, followed soon after by a $^3/_4$ mile in 3.04.5, and for the next few weeks, in training or at picnic race meetings, a number of hard time trial efforts over distances between 440 yards and three miles.

On Christmas Day, he ran a 1.52/ 4.15 half mile/mile double. Four days later, he ran ten half-mile efforts in 2.10 average, with half mile recovery jogs. All the while, the 10 mile morning runs and long Sunday runs continued. In the next few weeks, he ran sessions including a 9.12 two mile the day before 10 x 440 yards in an average of 59.8 seconds, a half mile in 1.51, and a windy three miles in 14.23 (equivalent to about 14.50 for 5000m), a few days before a 440 yards in 50 seconds.

He then started to ease up the pressure for a few days, before winning an international race series 880 yards in 1.48.2, passing through 800m in 1.47.7. Although due to run another international half mile the next Wednesday, he felt strong enough to run his usual 22 miles on the Sunday.* The next day he ran half an hour in the morning, and 8 x 150 yards, working up to sprint speed in the closing stages of each.

(* Barry Magee says that Snell's long runs during the business end of his track season were slow and restorative, about a minute a mile slower than his best aerobic speeds achieved in his buildup.)

On the Wednesday he ran 880 yards in 1.47.1, passing through 800m in 1.46.3, tying his Olympic record time. The 10-mile morning runs continued.

A week later on January 27, 1962, he ran a world mile record of 3.54.4 with a last 440 yards in 54.8s.

The next week, on February 3, he ran a world record 1.44.3 for 800m on grass, enroute to 1.45.1 for 880 yards.

Eight months later he won the 880 yard/mile double in the Commonwealth Games. Thirty months later he won the 800m/1500m double in the Olympics.

So What?

Well, obviously regular long runs don't harm one too much. When we look at what Snell did while juggling training, working, and a racing tour around the country, we can see one certain fact.

Snell ran his world 800m record within 3 months of completing his first and last competitive marathon.

What Was the Physiology Again?

Before his marathon he'd run a number of hill circuits over a fortnight, which re-stimulated his powerful IIB fast twitch fibers with plyometric input that reversed the normal "size principle" of muscle fiber recruitment. He'd also redeveloped a substantial aerobic capacity with consecutive 22-mile runs.

In running the marathon at a constant hard pace, Snell ran to the limits of his slow twitch fiber capacity and then exhausted the glycogen stores in his fast twitch fibers to the point where he had to sit down. He recovered his glycogen reserves slowly over a week and the training effect was to force some fast twitch fibers to adapt. They were now quite possibly acting as type IIa fast twitch fibers, with aerobic endurance characteristics as well as a very large anaerobic glycolytic potential.

This potential, of course, couldn't be realized until a variety of hard fast workouts and races capitalized on their emergence. The rest is history, and we can learn from history. While most modern coaches wouldn't recommend a full marathon so close to track racing, at least one great coach of the 1970s was paying attention. John Walker ran for over 20 miles at the head of New Zealand's tough Rotorua marathon in April 1975. Then he jogged off the track, with his mission accomplished, amidst quite a few ruffled marathoners' feathers. Why?

A couple of months later he was the first man to smash the 3.50 mile barrier. His coach, Arch Jelley, was a member of Owairaka Athletic Club and applied the Lydiard principles famously.

Walker broke the world mile record with 3:49.4 in 1975 after a period of training over the Waiatarua circuit with Kevin Ryan, the top New Zealand marathoner of the time. Eight years later, in 1983, he trained on the same circuit with marathoner Chris Pilone, and subsequently he ran his PB over the mile, 3:49.08, still the New Zealand record.

First Anaerobic Phase

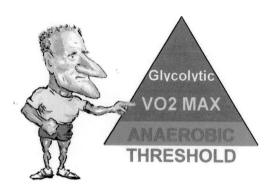

Multiple Long Intervals, Short Recovery, and VO$_2$ Max Time Trials

Intervals, for the sake of this book, are work bouts with a recovery generally equal to or shorter than the duration of the work bout.

Repetitions, which come later, are work bouts that are considerably faster and shorter, with a much-needed recovery that is far longer than the work bout.

Time Trials over longer distances are used initially to look for weaknesses in running and drops in concentration; laps are carefully timed. Time trials are never run at full effort in this first phase.

Lydiard used to refer to this first phase of anaerobic training as "tiring, exacting work." In this phase the athlete would perform numerous work bouts at paces well above the anaerobic threshold, with just enough recovery to get through the workout while still holding onto good running form, so that the body could be gradually exposed to high levels of acidosis.

The aim was to do enough prolonged harder work to get very tired, thus lowering the systemic blood pH as much as possible, without it being so fast that local acidosis in the leg muscles stopped the process too early.

The desired training effect after all this fatigue and acidic blood chemistry was an increased ability of the body to chemically "buffer" these acids so that eventually very high rates could be maintained as long as possible. A good chemical buffer is often a very weak acid or alkali: it can neutralize the effects of very high acidosis.

The work rate and paces in this first phase were very close to what we now call VO_2 max pace. We can see from the earlier example of Snell's mixed track training leading to his first world records in 1962 that there were a number of time trial efforts or low key races over 2 miles, 3 miles, and 1 mile, and several interval workouts such as 10 x 800m in 2.10, or 10 x 400m under 60 seconds, with equal distance recovery. As the major target races approached, shorter, harder races, time trials, and repetitions were run.

In Snell's case, track training started in late November. World records were delivered in late January and early February. About 9 weeks from "Go" to "Whoa." (The earlier European track tour would have left a recent anaerobic base.)

The one mile, 2 mile, and 3 mile solid time trial distances are interesting for an 800m runner. They can be interpreted as constant efforts at VO_2 max pace, or just slower.

The 10 interval work bouts over 800m in 2.10 were also at VO_2 max pace for Snell. (VO_2 max pace is extremely close to what we can hold for 8 minutes, or 3000m pace at international level). 2.10 for 800m is 8.06 3000m pace, and this would (at a guess!) be very close to what Snell was capable of over that distance at that stage of his career. The mile efforts in 4.10 to 4.15 were basically in the fast end of his VO_2 max spectrum, and the windy 3 miles in 14.23 was at the slow end.

Lydiard could give a 14-minute 5000m runner a workout like 6 x 800m at 2.15, or 20 x 400m at 67 seconds in the middle of this phase. Some days could be spent on developing leg speed with repeated fast relaxed runs over 100-150m, and long easy recoveries. Other days could involve 7/8 effort time trials over 3000m to 5000m. A long easy run would be included each week. During this phase it wasn't expected that one could race well yet, but one could if one wanted and call it "information." Lots of easy aerobic running was encouraged between anaerobic sessions to facilitate full recovery. Snell covered 10 miles every morning, or an hour's easy running, mostly on a local golf course, during his record-breaking summer of 1962. This was quite apart from his evening speed sessions and races.

The intervals were very close in principle and application to the "aerobic capacity" intervals run by Sebastian Coe, or the "multi-pace training" advocated since the 1970s by British coach Frank Horwill. Having read Peter Coe's books quite thoroughly, I would say his "aerobic capacity" intervals are really VO_2 max intervals and could be termed "anaerobic capacity" intervals for our purposes.

The basic principle was also used by 1936 Olympic 1500m champion Jack Lovelock and, later, Roger Bannister. Sebastian Coe's coach and father, Peter, even went as far as describing Coe's 5000m pace work as the "golden sessions" that got his oxygen uptake very high.

More recently, US coach and physiologist Dr. Jack Daniels has expounded the use of VO_2 max intervals, run between 5000m pace and 3000m pace, before commencing even faster anaerobic work. The beauty of his system is that he has clearly defined the paces that need to be run, based on athletes' current best performances at a number of distances. Lydiard did a similar thing by basing his classic "effort tables" on average best race times at various distances, and he maintained that any sharpening program would "fall over" if the efforts were not adhered to accurately.

All of these great coaches share a common principle when it comes to this work, despite the differing terminology and ways of arriving at similar conclusions.

I will refer to the recent work of Daniels to define the different anaerobic zones that Lydiard was using years ago. I think it is appropriate because I want to clarify exactly what it was physiologically that Arthur was doing by his intuition, in light of current thinking.

In my interpretation, Lydiard's initial phase of anaerobic work bears striking similarities to the later VO_2 max work of Dr. Jack Daniels.

Do these following tables work? Well, over two years ago we made aerobic profiles for a few of our H.I.T. SQUAD youngsters. One of them, Matthew Coloe, seemed particularly suited to 800m and 1500m but needed to work on his long endurance.

We told Matthew in 2005 that when he could run 3000m off endurance work in 8:22 or faster, that he could run 3:45 for 1500m. In December 2007, he ran 2nd in the Australian Junior 3000m champs in about 8:18, and the next month ran 3:45 for 1500m. There had been no real glycolytic work or sharpening as such; just a diet of weekly steady 5000m pace intervals, and the rest was mostly aerobic work, with the usual weekly leg speed session thrown in.

More on Time Trials

Time trials at 7/8 effort over longer distances such as 3000m-5000m during the early race preparation phase give the hard sustained exertion required for an optimal training effect physiologically and psychologically, without the acidosis and lactate of a full effort.

If an athlete can regularly run a hard sustained effort around the track at levels approaching his or her maximum oxygen uptake, this will toughen him or her psychologically for the more brutal work to come. The aim is for smooth, constant effort where lap times vary very little, concentrating on keeping effort up through the psychological "bad patch" usually felt by athletes at 66-75% of the effort distance.

Lydiard would often say things like, "Give the body something to do often enough in training, and it will adapt."

There is nothing to be gained psychologically from going into excessive oxygen debt and acidosis: exactly the same training effect can be achieved by hovering at the edge of the maximum oxygen uptake.

Physiologically, these runs would train the body to adapt very specifically to the constant high-level exertion of longer track racing without pulling hard-won aerobic condition down too much.

Later in the peaking program for middle distance events, under-distance time trials at over 600m or 1200m could be very helpful for 800m or 1500m runners respectively. Lydiard would want these run at realistic goal race-pace, *without* a "last lap sprint." For training purposes, full efforts were never wanted. Full effort was left for the first important race.

The last lap sprint could be trained in other race-speed-specific sessions in the peaking phase, and it could all be coordinated as the major races approached.

Daniels' Running Formula Tables

The following is the highlighted expected performance range of an athlete with a "V Dot" racing level of 75.0. Laboratory-tested VO_2 max is a poor predictor of race performance, but actual race performance is the best predictor of race performance at other distances, especially if they use similar energy systems. For instance, an established 10,000m time should give a realistic estimate of 5000m and 15k times to aim at. An athlete who hasn't achieved all of the times across the spectrum at his or her V Dot level may have not trained the relevant energy systems and speeds well or may have a lack of trainability (genetic) in the most dominant muscle fibers and energy systems. The 400m column is a "best-fit estimate" made by this author and is not from the original Daniels tables. It takes into account the likely required 400m time at 400 to achieve the adjacent 800m time.

How they may be applied to working out your correct training paces
The tables on these pages are excerpted and slightly modified from: Daniels, J. *Daniels' Running Formula*, **2nd Edition, Human Kinetics: 2005.**

VDOT	RACING TIMES									
Racing Level Effort	400	800	1500	Mile	3000	5000	10000	15k	21.1k	42.2k
	REP PACE				VO$_2$ INTERVAL PACE			THRESHOLD PACE		
	v.v.hard!	v. hard	v. hard	harder	"hard"			"comfortably hard"		
								World-class runners > 21k pace		
61	60	2.12	4.30.5	4.52.2	9.41	16.48	34.52	53.32	77.02	2.41.08
62	59	2.1	4.26.0	4.47.3	9.33	16.34	34.23	52.47	75.57	2.38.54
63	58	2.07.6	4.21.5	4.42.4	9.25	16.2	33.55	52.03	74.54	2.36.44
64	57	2.05.4	4.17.0	4.37.5	9.17	16.07	33.28	51.21	73.53	2.34.38
65	56.5	2.04.3	4.14.7	4.35.1	9.09	15.54	33.01	50.40	72.53	2.32.35
66	56	2.03.2	4.12.5	4.32.6	9.02	15.42	32.35	50.00	71.56	2.30.36
67	55	2.01.0	4.10.3	4.27.7	8.55	15.29	32.11	49.22	71.00	2.28.40
68	54.5	1.59.9	4.05.7	4.25.3	8.48	15.18	31.46	48.44	70.05	2.26.47
69	54	1.58.8	4.03.5	4.22.9	8.41	15.06	31.23	48.08	69.12	2.24.57
70	53	1.56.6	3.59.0	4.18.0	8.31	14.49	30.49	47.15	67.56	2.22.18
71	52	1.54.4	3.54.5	4.13.2	8.22	14.33	30.16	46.24	66.42	2.19.44
72	51.5	1.53.3	3.52.2	4.10.7	8.16	14.23	29.55	45.51	65.54	2.18.05
73	51	1.52.2	3.50.0	4.08.3	8.13	14.18	29.44	45.35	65.31	2.17.17
74	50.5	1.51.1	3.47.8	4.05.9	8.1	14.13	29.34	45.19	65.08	2.16.29
75	50	1.50.0	3.45.5	4.03.5	8.04	14.03	29.14	44.48	64.23	2.14.55
76	49.5	1.48.9	3.43.2	4.01.1	7.58	13.54	28.55	44.18	63.39	2.13.23
77	49	1.47.8	3.41.0	3.58.6	7.53	13.44	28.36	43.49	62.56	2.11.54
78	48.5	1.46.7	3.38.8	3.56.2	7.48	13.35	28.17	43.2	62.15	2.10.27
79	48	1.45.6	3.36.5	3.53.8	7.43	13.26	27.59	42.52	61.34	2.09.02
80	47.5	1.44.5	3.34.2	3.51.4	7.37	13.18	27.41	42.25	60.54	2.07.38
81	47	1.43.4	3.31.9	3.48.9	7.32	13.09	27.24	41.58	60.15	2.06.17
82	46.5	1.42.3	3.29.7	3.46.5	7.27	13.01	27.07	41.32	59.38	2.04.57
83	46	1.41.2	3.27.6	3.44.1	7.23	12.53	26.51	41.06	59.01	2.03.40
84	45.5	1.40.1	3.25.5	3.42.7	7.18	12.45	26.34	40.42	58.25	2.02.24
85	45	1.39.0	3.23.5	3.41.3	7.14	12.37	26.19	40.17	57.5	2.01.10

HOW TO ESTIMATE V DOT TRAINING PACES

This sheet shows the relevant ranges of training paces to aim at for the athlete who has achieved a V Dot of 75.0. These paces are the optimal paces to aim at to get the maximal training effect. Any faster is counter-productive. For instance, the athlete who has achieved times of 14.03 and 29.14 for 5000m and 10000m respectively, (previous page) should be able to get his time for 1500m down to 3:45.5 over a number of weeks by gradually introducing early-anaerobic phase VO_2 max intervals at 2:14 per 800m, or 2:49 per 1000m, with equal or less recovery, then gradually increasing pace and introducing glycolytic repetitions with long recoveries over 600m at 92 seconds, eventually moving to 400m repetitions in 61 seconds with full recovery. To get to the potential 800m pace, we next bring in work at the Fast Reps paces with ample recovery. This eventually will bring the 600m pace down to 82 seconds, and a few repetitions of 400m in 55 seconds, with full recovery to allow good biomechanics at speed.

VDOT	TRAINING PACES per km unless stated otherwise:				
Racing	Fast Reps	Reps	Intervals	Threshold	Easy
Level	800 pace/faster	1500 pace	5k pace:2-5 min	15k pace	40s or more slower per
Dist/Time run	200:300:400:600	200:400:600:	800: 1000: 1200	5 min-1 hour	km than thre-shold. Long
Recovery time	Full recovery	Full rec.	Equal rec./ less	1/5 rec or less	constant running.
61	33 49 66 99	37 74 111	2.40 3.20 4.00	3.36	4.17-4.36
62	32 48 65 97	36 73 109	2.38 3.18 3.57	3.34	4.15-4.33
63	31 47 64 96	36 72 108	2.36 3.15 3.54	3.32	4.12-4.31
64	31 46 62 94	35 71 106	2.34 3.13 3.51	3.29	4.10-4.28
65	31 46 62 93	35 70 105	2.32 3.10 3.48	3.26	4.07-4.26
66	30 46 61 92	34 69 103	2.30 3.07 3.45	3.24	4.05-4.24
67	30 45 60 90	34 68 102	2.28 3.05 3.42	3.21	4.02-4.21
68	30 45 60 90	33 67 100	2.28 3.05 3.42	3.2	4.00-4.18
69	29 44 59 89	33 66 99	2.26 3.02 3.39	3.17	3.57-4.16
69.5	29 44 58 88	32 65 98	2.24 3.00 3.36	3.14	3.55-4.14
70	29 43 58 87	32 65 97	2.22 2.58 3.33	3.13	3.53-4.12
70.5	29 43 57 86	32 64 97	2.20 2.56 3.31	3.12	3.51-4.10
71	28 43 57 85	32 64 96	2.20 2.55 3.30	3.1	3.50-4.08
72	28 42 56 84	31 63 95	2.18 2.53 3.27	3.08	3.47-4.06
73	28 42 56 84	31 62 94	2.17 2.51 3.25	3.07	3.46-4.05
74	28 42 55 83	31 62 93	2.16 2.50 3.24	3.06	3.45-4.04
75	27 41 55 82	30 61 92	2.14 2.49 3.22	3.04	3.44-4.03
76	27 41 54 81	30 61 91	2.14 2.48 3.21	3.02	3.42-4.01
77	27 41 54 81	30 60 90	2.12 2.45 3.18	3.00	3.40-3.59
78	26 40 53 79	29 59 88	2.10 2.43 3.15	2.58	3.38-3.57
79	26 39 52 78	29 58 88	2.08 2.41 3.13	2.56	3.36-3.55
80	26 39 52 78	29 58 87	2.08 2.40 3.12	2.54	3.35-3.54
81	25 38 51 77	28 57 85	2.06 2.38 3.10	2.53	3.33-3.52
82	25.5 38 51 77	28 56 84	2.04 2.37 3.08	2.51	3.31-3.50
83	25 37.7 50 76	27 55 82	2.02 2.36 3.06	2.49	3.29-3.48
84	25 37.5 50 75	27 55 82	2.02 2.34 3.05	2.48	3.27-3.46
85	24.7 37 49 74	27 55 81	2.01 2.31 3.03	2.46	3.25-3.48

Creating an Aerobic Profile

Creating an aerobic profile using tables such as these is very simple and easy. The charts themselves can form the "graph." Ideally, a well-trained athlete should have a "flat line" across a range of distances that are regularly raced. Below is a sample from the author's 1980/81 summer season, where his actual track or road times have been approximated to fit the chart.

V DOT			RACING TIMES						
	400	800	1500	3000	5000	10000	15k	21.1k	42.2k
69.5	53.5	1.57.7	4.01.2	8.34	14.55	31	47.32	68.21	2.23.10
70	53	1.56.6	3.59.0	8.31	14.49	30.49	47.15	67.56	2.22.18
70.5	52.5	1.55.5	3.56.8	8.28	14.44	30.38	46.58	67.31	2.21.26
71	52	1.54.4	3.54.5	8.22	14.33	30.16	46.24	66.42	2.19.44
72	51.5	1.53.3	3.52.2	8.16	14.23	29.55	45.51	65.54	2.18.05
73	51	1.52.2	3.50.0	8.13	14.18	29.44	45.35	65.31	2.17.17
74	50.5	1.51.1	3.47.8	8.1	14.13	29.34	45.19	65.08	2.16.29
75	50	1.50.0	3.45.5	8.04	14.03	29.14	44.48	64.23	2.14.55
76	49.5	1.48.9	3.43.2	7.58	13.54	28.55	44.18	63.39	2.13.23

The actual times recorded that season were 1500m: 3:54.7, 3000m 8:06.0, 5000m 14:11, 10000m 29:41. A disparity in these times is seen immediately. The highest oxygen power ranking is seen at the 75.0 V Dot level for 3000m. No specific 1500m or 800m pace training was done that season as the author was carrying a couple of minor injuries and "raced himself fit" with Saturday races once a week over varying distances between 1500m and 5000m, with the rest of his training being steady aerobic runs up to 22 miles. The 5000m and 10000m times weren't up to the level of the 3000m as

1. No pace-specific intervals were run during season

2. These races were run mid-afternoon in hot, windy conditions

3. The 10,000m was author's first attempt at distance on track.

The 3000m time was achieved because before it there had been four 5000m races, three 1500m races, and one 3000m race over a two-month period. These 5000m and 3000m races were VO_2 max workouts, and the 1500m races, though not fast, served to stimulate glycolytic energy systems above VO_2 max.

Later, the author recorded other times using differing training methods that resulted in the following profile: 1500m 3:50, 5000m 14:04, 10000m 29:19, 15k road 44:37.

V DOT	400	800	RACING TIMES 1500	3000	5000	10000	15k	21.1k	42.2k
69.5	53.5	1.57.7	4.01.2	8.34	14.55	31.00	47.32	68.21	2.23.10
70	53	1.56.6	3.59.0	8.31	14.49	30.49	47.15	67.56	2.22.18
70.5	52.5	1.55.5	3.56.8	8.28	14.44	30.38	46.58	67.31	2.21.26
71	52	1.54.4	3.54.5	8.22	14.33	30.16	46.24	66.42	2.19.44
72	51.5	1.53.3	3.52.2	8.16	14.23	29.55	45.51	65.54	2.18.05
73	51	1.52.2	3.50.0	8.13	14.18	29.44	45.35	65.31	2.17.17
74	50.5	1.51.1	3.47.8	8.1	14.13	29.34	45.19	65.08	2.16.29
75	50	1.50.0	3.45.5	8.04	14.03	29.14	44.48	64.23	2.14.55
76	49.5	1.48.9	3.43.2	7.58	13.54	28.55	44.18	63.39	2.13.23

The author hardly ever raced at 800m as he found it far easier to be competitive over longer track distances. However, he should have raced over those distances regularly in early season each year to balance his aerobic profile and achieve his potential at 1500. If the correct specific anaerobic work had been introduced, much better times could have been achieved and perhaps a different spectrum of race distances attempted.

Here's another example of an unusual profile: youngster Navin Arunasalam can run 200m any time of year in 23 seconds or under. He can run 400m in 49.6 in a time-trial. He can run 600m at the drop of a hat in under 79s, a time which could stretch many mature 800m athletes. He has a huge glycolytic anaerobic tank with muscle fibers that are probably high in IIB and IIA distribution, but with few Type I slow twitch fibers. However, his 800m time is still about 1:51.8, and his 1500m and 3000m times have lagged way behind his 800m time. He responds best to aerobic running mixed with intervals at his estimated VO_2 max pace (1000m in 2:50, repeated). He does this sort of work, or ten minutes at his sub-threshold pace, after leg speed drills in his track warm-ups. This enables him to run consistently.

We have found with Navin, and his training partner Matthew (another 1:51.9 800m runner as a junior), that a Tuesday session of VO_2 max intervals will ensure a strong last 100m in a Saturday race, even though it is "miles slower" than race pace. Why? Because when you're very tired at 700m, the energy systems change down a gear from the glycolytic system to the next-best-trained system. This is something that Lydiard always ensure, long before VO_2 max had a surname! Every system remains "trained" leading into a race. You will see from the chart below that if Nav can get his 3000m time down that his 800m time will come back down too. Imagine that the aerobic profile is like a clothesline secured against the 400m time. Lowering the "aerobic end" of the line won't change the 400m time much but will lower the line as a whole, including the region most relevant to 800m.

V DOT	400	800	1500	3000	5000
			RACING TIMES		
61	60	2.12	4.30.5	9.41	16.48
62	59	2.10	4.26.0	9.33	16.34
63	58	2.07.6	4.21.5	9.25	16.2
64	57	2.05.4	4.17.0	9.17	16.07
65	56.5	2.04.3	4.14.7	9.09	15.54
66	56	2.03.2	4.12.5	9.02	15.42
67	55	2.01.0	4.10.3	8.55	15.29
68	54.5	1.59.9	4.05.7	8.48	15.18
69	54	1.58.8	4.03.5	8.41	15.06
69.5	53.5	1.57.7	4.01.2	8.34	14.55
70	53	1.56.6	3.59.0	8.31	14.49
70.5	52.5	1.55.5	3.56.8	8.28	14.44
71	52	1.54.4	3.54.5	8.22	14.33
72	51.5	1.53.3	3.52.2	8.16	14.23
73	51	1.52.2	3.50.0	8.13	14.18
74	50.5	1.51.1	3.47.8	8.1	14.13
75	50	1.50.0	3.45.5	8.04	14.03
76	49.5	1.48.9	3.43.2	7.58	13.54
77	49	1.47.8	3.41.0	7.53	13.44

Note:

You can see that if Navin can eventually get his 3000m down to 8:13, for example, that the profile would more likely pass through an 800m time well under 1:50. Aerobic endurance can be improved much more easily over time than lactate tolerance. (A far more exact chart by Jack Daniels and Jimmy Gilbert can be ordered by sending a check for US $20 to Jack Tupper Daniels, 20 East Separation Canyon Trail, Flagstaff, AZ 86001). Another useful source of similar material is the McMillan Running Calculator on www.mcmillanrunning.com.

Why Is VO$_2$ Max Pace Anaerobic?

Isn't There Still Oxygen?

For a world-class athlete, the anaerobic threshold is extremely close to his half marathon race pace. For the rest of us, it's what we can race flat out for 50 minutes to an hour. Our heart hums along at 85% of its maximum or faster.

Running faster than this for any extended period raises acidosis in the body all along, but we're still capable of running considerably faster yet, and extracting and delivering even more oxygen from the air we breathe until acidosis gets so great that we can't possibly extract any more oxygen and are forced to slow.

That pace is very anaerobic because it's way above the anaerobic threshold and because it's the running velocity at maximal oxygen uptake (we know it as VO$_2$ max). It corresponds to 3000m pace for a world-class athlete or extremely close to what we can run flat out for 8 minutes for the rest of us.

However, once more, we can still run faster again, even though our heart is now thumping at its maximum rate and we've extracted as much oxygen as we can. This faster running is done by using the powerful short-term glycolytic and alactic anaerobic systems, but those rates of running can't be approached effectively by running faster and faster over longer intervals. Increasing acidosis prevents us from getting there effectively.

We have to go shorter, harder, and faster, with ample recovery, to develop that higher-intensity part of the anaerobic system.

Lydiard would often give his athletes specific paces to run these sessions at, and other times he was happy as long as they were "generally tired." His books and interviews don't give much detail unfortunately, as Lydiard considered the anaerobic phase as the "*least* important" phase of his schedule.

He didn't like to delve into elaborate explanations of anaerobic training, saying that it could be accomplished in "101 ways" and was "eyewash."

In one of his books, he discusses supervising such a workout in the final weeks of preparation with Dick Tayler, who was to win 10,000m gold in the Commonwealth Games in 1974 with a stunning last lap.

"The workout was at a school, and the school coach and his athletes were curious to know what times he was running his 400m repetitions in and how many he was going to run.

"Look," I told them, "he doesn't know, and I don't know. It wouldn't even matter if they weren't 400 meter repetitions. As long as he's tired, he's going to get the required physiological reactions."

That was OK for Lydiard and Tayler. One was a world-class coach and the other was a world-class runner. Of course they knew what they were doing by this stage! But over 30 years later, the rest of us need a bit of a guide. Here goes, with all due respect.

Without going into great detail, Daniels states that the safest form of VO_2 max interval is run at 95% of VO_2 max pace, which is right at 5000m pace for good competitive runners. According to all his work over the last 40 years with world-class athletes, 95% VO_2 max pace is more than sufficient to stimulate VO_2 max from "below." Recent research indicates that training an energy system such as the anaerobic threshold, for instance, can positively influence the time one can hold VO_2 max pace for. It seems that training within one general zone can have benefits for the next higher level of intensity.

(Refer back to the previous pages on Daniels' V Dot Training Paces. These findings are accurate for the vast majority of serious, well-conditioned middle distance athletes and provide an excellent frame of reference for accurately assessing and fine-tuning anaerobic sessions.)

Because it is slightly slower than 100% VO_2 max pace (3000m pace), 95% VO_2 max pace (5000m pace) is easier on the body and more time can be spent in that realm. 100% VO_2 max pace can be used, but more sparingly as it is very tough work and the objective is to train, not strain.

Any extended work faster than 100% VO_2 max pace with insufficient recovery is a total waste of time because exactly the same training effect of raising the oxidative capacity of the muscles to maximum can be achieved without the extra acidosis and recovery required. That's good news. The extra acidosis can even harm progress at this stage.

Time spent at or near VO_2 max is the biggest stimulus to maximum oxygen uptake, as one would expect. It still produces plenty of the desired acidosis and extreme pressure on the cardiovascular system but does so at a tolerable level that the nervous system and musculature can handle.

NB: A session of "20 x 400" at $1/4$ effort would often be given early season. This would have about a lap brisk jog recovery. A well-conditioned athlete would normally be able to average close to his or her VO_2 max pace on these, whether he meant to or not.

I looked at a diary from early in my 1980/81 track season where I had been given such a session and the first 10 400m intervals averaged 65.4, and the last 10 averaged a fraction more, with the last interval run in 64s. This was incredibly close to the average pace I held for a 3000m (VO_2 max pace) later in the season for a time of 8:06.

These workouts take a number of efforts to get the heart rate into the maximal zone, due to the regular recoveries. However, once "up there," the heart rate stays near the maximal level for the duration of the session.

What Should It Feel Like, Then?

The most effective work bouts or intervals for running appear to be longer than 2 minutes or shorter than 5 minutes, with equal or shorter recovery, depending on fitness. Any longer than 5 minutes at VO_2 max pace and it's too near being a race in intensity, without the adrenalin, to have training value.

Shorter work bouts of 400m (at 5000m pace) can be used, but it takes a few of these intervals in a row, with short recoveries, until the heart rate and acidosis are in the right realm. It takes some time at a hard pace (usually minutes, at first) to get the heart rate up to near maximum.

With shorter intervals, just as the heart rate starts to sneak towards maximum, the recovery interval snatches it back out of the target zone, so the first few efforts, even though they are at the correct pace, fail to achieve time in the correct heart rate zone. With longer work bouts, the heart rate keeps climbing to near maximum and stays

there for quite some time. The heart rate is still high at the very start of the recovery, near its maximum, and because of the substantial oxygen debt incurred only drops slightly before jumping back up with the next interval. More of the effort will reach VO_2 max, or very close to VO_2 max, in a session.

In fact, Dr. Gerschler, the famous German coach and physiologist of the 1940s, claimed that the heart stroke volume would increase in recovery periods between intervals.

This sort of workout can total up to 6000m at VO_2 pace, for a mature athlete who has an extensive aerobic background. More is possible, but then we are dealing with a very hard extended workload. It may be better to do a shorter session regularly that one can recover adequately from.

How Coach Bideau Approaches Interval Work

In a recent article for the Australian publication *Modern Athlete and Coach*, Nic wrote the following:

"I prefer high volumes of work when using intervals, with 6-10k of running at various speeds relevant to the athlete's current fitness level for 1500m, 3000m, 5000m or 10,000m with recovery bouts as required to maintain that pace.

"In the first stages of a training program these are initially focused on 10,000m race pace or even slower. Closer to the main target race faster speeds are introduced at the specific pace of the event the athlete is training for. I believe that too often athletes try to run too fast in track sessions relevant to their current fitness and are too anxious to focus on their cruising speeds for 1500m or 3000m races, whereas I prefer to set the bulk of these sessions at 5000m or 10,000m cruising speeds over longer distance repetitions interspersed with shorter faster work.

"For example, when training for an event such as the World Cross Country in March, Benita Johnson may begin the preparation in November with 8-10 x 1 km on a dirt path in around 3.20 with one minute rest. This develops into 3.10 and the next step is to speed up 2 of the reps, the 5th and 7th in 3.00. This may progress to 4 x 2km reps on the track with a lap jog recovery doing the 1st and 3rd rep alternating laps in 70s (current 3k race pace) and 75s (half marathon race pace), the 2nd and 4th rep all even paced at 75s per lap (10k race pace).

"There are a myriad of workouts that can be designed with this philosophy. The main aim is to always be doing enough high volume to continue building aerobic endurance while introducing some faster running that relates to shorter distance race paces and still avoid flooding the athlete's muscles with lactate during the workout.

"So varied are the possible combinations that rarely do the athletes repeat the same workout. I see a couple of distinct advantages in this – they don't go home to check their diary and compare workouts from week to week or year to year – too often athletes try to compare workouts from one period to another, which I regard as impossible to do for any real gain.

"You can never go to the track with all other elements of your life exactly duplicated from one day to the next so you will always fail to read into the effects of other situations whether they be weather, poor sleep the night before, harder training the week before, personal problems or whatever – and being different, the workouts always provide an interesting challenge to the athletes who don't know exactly how they will feel not having done that exact workout before.

"Closer to the big race, these workouts often mimic planned strategies due to be employed in the race whilst surrounding it with volume to ensure aerobic fitness is still maintained. Before the Melbourne Commonwealth Games 5000m Mottram ran a series of 3x1600m. The first one was done in 4.20 (basically what we felt was around 10,000m race pace for him or more specifically the slowest we could imagine the Commonwealth 5000m race being run at inside the last 2km).

"The 2nd rep was to practice the tactic, which we hoped could take him clear of the Kenyans in the Melbourne 5000m. His training partner, England's 5000m runner at the Games, Mo Farah, ran the 1st lap in 65 secs and Mottram went to the lead running the 2nd lap faster, the 3rd lap faster again and once more increasing the pace on the last lap. He ran those laps in 59, 58 and 57 for a final 1600m time of 3.59. He then eased back to 4.20 again for the 3rd rep and finished the workout by cruising 4 x 200m at 1500m race tempo with an easy 200m jog recovery. We felt he was ready for Ben Limo and he was. But, unfortunately for us, Augustine Choge had something else.

"These sessions are usually only carried out once per week. If a second session of repetition running is used it is usually hill repetitions. Athletes usually begin with 6-8 repetitions of running uphill for three minutes at around 10,000m race pace or effort. Then shorten the distance to something that can be reached in one minute running at around 3000m race pace effort. Sometimes they alternate three minute efforts with one minute faster efforts in a series of 8 repetitions.

"I prefer the hills to be not so steep that the athlete can't run up them smoothly for three minutes at 10,000m race pace. The recovery taken is as long as it takes to jog back down the hill easily and feel ready to go for the next repetition. I believe these workouts are fantastic for developing power and speed as well as running efficiency."

Why Lydiard Would Never Use Short, Hard, Fast Intervals at this Stage

Lydiard would never use short, hard, fast repetitions at this stage because the first phase of anaerobic training was aimed at getting the systemic circulation into acidosis. This was ably achieved by the sustainable longer work periods of the VO_2 max type work.

However, very fast running over shorter distances would not be able to achieve the initial goal of systemic acidosis because the rates of anaerobic exercise were so fast that the leg muscles would become very fatigued with local acidosis long before a systemic response was achievable. This is not unlike an athlete doing bench press until exhaustion in a gym, with local muscle exhaustion and glycolysis stopping the exercise, but the athlete is still able to go and lift heavily in another exercise using another muscle group. The fatigue and acidosis is a localized event that does not stop exercise altogether.

In terms of rates of acidosis, although VO_2 training at 5000m and 3000m pace definitely can produce significant acidosis in the general circulation over minutes, the rate is nothing compared to what happens in the legs when running at 1500m and 800m pace. At those paces there is far less likelihood that the cardiovascular system can flush all of the acids out of the muscles and back into the general circulation. So acids build up exponentially in the legs and everything stops.

The goal of reaching a high level of acidosis in the systemic circulation is much harder to achieve this way, and local muscle fatigue stops the exercise anyhow.

For instance, a runner with an estimated VO_2 Max of 75 (mls/kg/min) may be expected to have a realistic potential range of times ranging from 1.50 at 800 to 3.45 for 1500, 8.04 for 3000m, and 14.04 for 5000m, according to aerobic tables devised by Daniels. This assumes that the differing energy systems have all been well-trained, and that the runner has a degree of natural speed.

Often it can be shown that under-achievement at a particular distance is due to lack of specific training or racing at the relative paces rather than a total lack of aptitude.

If we look at the speeds involved, we are moving down from 67s 400m pace at 5000m (95% of VO_2 max pace) to just under 65s for 3000m (100% VO_2 max pace). The 1500m pace at this level is 60s per 400m, and 800m pace is 55 seconds.

100% VO_2 max pace is a full 9 seconds per 400m slower than realistic achievable 800m pace and 5 seconds slower than 1500m pace. So, obviously, those paces have to be run next, and workouts at those paces can be steadily introduced on the road to the "peak performance."

Having said this, the technical and neuromuscular aspects of fast running have never been lost. Only lactic acid tolerance ability has been allowed to drop away to some degree until this stage because the training of that part of the anaerobic system (the glycolytic) would counter the optimal development of aerobic capacity and oxidative enzymes. Very short, relaxed alactic leg-speed runs, done throughout most of the year (or within fartlek workouts during Lydiard's original base periods) would maintain and develop speed running beautifully.

The Second Anaerobic Phase

Glycolytic Exercise

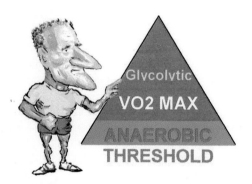

Short Fast Repetitions with Ample Recovery

When we get much beyond about 10 seconds with flat-out running (and the exact time will vary according to our training and genetics), then we enter another energy realm. This is the realm where acid wastes build up at a rate quicker than the body can get rid of or recycle them. This part of the anaerobic energy system is called the *glycolytic* energy system, where the primary fuel is glucose, which is broken down without oxygen to yield energy. The 6-carbon glucose molecule is split into two 3-carbon molecules of pyruvic acid, which in turn is rapidly metabolized into lactic acid.

Lactic acid is really a rather inert large sugar molecule that is beneficial to the function of tiring muscles. Lactic acid consists of a hydrogen ion (H+) attached to a lactate ion (La-), and this accumulation of hydrogen ions in hard-working muscle creates the acidosis that eventually stops nerves and muscles from functioning efficiently.

Lactic acid is a fuel that can be used by the heart, brain, and tissues in the absence of enough oxygen for quite a few seconds. It can be shuttled around the body rapidly. It can be re-metabolized (slowly) by the liver back into starchy fuels (glycogen) or glucose itself.

However, regardless of the biochemistry and the many benefits of lactic acid, all we really have to understand in practical terms is that *acidosis is not good* on a regular basis.

If hard acidosis-producing exercise is undertaken too regularly, without letting the body fully recover, then a cascade of nasty things will occur.

At the cellular level of the muscle, these harmful effects have been well-documented. For a start, we have the rupture of the cell membrane wall, with leakage of cell proteins and destructive hemolytic enzymes into the bloodstream and extra-cellular tissues.

According to Dutch sports medicine doctor, endurance coach, and author Peter Janssen, the aerobic enzyme system can be sabotaged, with a decrease in endurance capacity.

Fat metabolism, carbohydrate metabolism, and alactic metabolism may all be compromised. It may be days before the aerobic system recovers and the aerobic capacity is at its old level again.

It may be 24 to 96 hours before these values settle down. Recovery from the damage may take longer.

Does this mean we don't ever exercise this way? No. But we train it intelligently and specifically at our level of current development, at the appropriate time, and with *plenty* of easy aerobic exercise all around it to get the acidosis out of the systemic circulation and back to a neutral state before any further hard work is done.

Funnily enough, we need this sort of training in sparing doses to fully realize our potential in the middle distances. What we don't need is to bomb this energy system day in, day out, at a time of year when we should be "accumulating" aerobic fitness and improving sprint potential.

So many aspiring athletes and their coaches train this misguided way that I have devoted a whole chapter to it later. Every person who has contributed to this book has made major costly mistakes in training: this is why they are good coaches or athletes!

In a nutshell, what athletes and coaches need to realize is that any sustained exercise faster than threshold pace has the capacity to induce acidosis and general fatigue. The harder and more sustained the exercise, the more *rest* required. To some coaches, *rest* is just another 4-letter word. To a Lydiard coach, *rest* is relative. Very hard fast efforts can be balanced out with very low-key aerobic "recovery" of some duration. This type of "Active Rest" gets our systems back to neutral in the best possible way. Total rest does very little to flush the muscles and their aerobic systems.

Alactic exercise, i.e., very short bursts of fast exercise with plenty of recovery, is quite different to glycolytic anaerobic exercise. Alactic exercise is reasonably safe, especially if done with a good relaxed technique. Whatever speed we can repeatedly stride through over short distances like 60 meters is well and truly faster than our best possible 200m, or 300m pace, and very much faster than our 400m pace. There's no problem doing this sort of work regularly. It has to be done regularly to train fast movement patterns, which are a learnable skill.

Here we come to the tip of the anaerobic portion of the massive Lydiard training pyramid. This final work commences in the weeks leading up to the important races. At this stage, racing is the ultimate focus, not long endurance training or hard sustained training or VO$_2$ max training. That's all been done in the correct, logical sequence.

Any long running is at a very easy aerobic pace that will really tend to use fats as a primary fuel rather than stored carbohydrates. We need to save these stored carbohydrates for hard, fast efforts.

Remember that any speed potential reached over short sprint distances during the previous track season had been maintained to a degree by short fartlek bursts once a week during the endurance or buildup phase. This was then developed further with sprint drills, striding, and bounding in the hill phase. All of these developed the explosive alactic portion of the anaerobic capacity, as well as strengthening the specific muscles and movement patterns used in fast racing. So the long endurance is there, and the short speed is there.

The body's ability to tolerate systemic acidosis has now been developed to near its maximum by the extensive VO$_2$ max-pace work over a number of weeks. It does not take any longer than five weeks to develop this specific capacity of the body to maximum, although we can do it more gradually.

Easy running days between those anaerobic effort days would be used to restore more normal blood pH. Very easy running for up to an hour, depending on training maturity, would also be encouraged on the morning of anaerobic effort days.

So all we have to develop now is the specific ability of the middle distance athlete's body to tolerate the very fast rates of *local* leg muscle acidosis that will be experienced in 800m or 1500m running at the current level of aerobic development.

If the athlete has developed the aerobic capacity to a known level of longer distance performance, by utilizing the Daniels tables we can have a very accurate idea of current achievable potential at shorter distances, given specific training.

Using the earlier example of an athlete who has developed aerobic capacity to a level that corresponds with a predicted VO_2 max of 75 mls /kg /min, we see from the tables that this indicates a potential of 800m in 1.50, 1500m in 3.45.5, 3000m in 8.04, or 10000m in 29.14.

Paces down to 3000m pace have been handled in the earlier phase, as they are largely VO_2 max pace. The pace required to run 3000m to potential is about 64 to 65 seconds per 400m. This is a world away from the pace required to run 1500m to potential (60s), or 800m (55s).

Please Note: **Glycolytic anaerobic training does not have to be any faster than our current realistic achievable 1500m or 800m pace.**

These 1500m and 800m paces are what we base our realistic glycolytic repetition paces on. It's no use for a mature runner with an endurance capacity of, say, 31 minutes for 10k, or a VO_2 max equivalent ("V dot") on the Daniels tables of only 69.5, trying to do repetitions of 400m in 60s, in the vain hope he will achieve a 1500m time of 3:45, a time that requires a much higher level of equivalent oxygen uptake on the Daniels tables (V dot 75.0).

He most likely hasn't developed his endurance capacity to the level required, and his realistic goal pace is more likely 1500m in 4:00 and 800m in 1:57. By running his repetitions any faster than those race paces, he is probably running above his training level and invoking acidosis way above the level required to achieve current potential. He is actually harming his current potential.

One way to look at things in this particular example (V dot 75.0) would be to introduce 1500m pace glycolytic work (60s 400m pace) after the VO_2 max pace work (65s 400m pace), which is a reasonable increase in pace to cope with over a number of weeks. The pace can be introduced over different repetition distances from 150m up initially and working up to 600m but always with full recovery.

The next logical progression would be to introduce sessions at 800m pace, an increase in pace of another 5 seconds per 400m, and this increase in pace should be stepped up over a few weeks. If we have done our work properly and methodically, all systems will be firing, and brief glycolytic workouts at our appropriate 1500m and 800m paces are all that are required to complete the task of coming to a peak.

Remember, we have already developed our very short distance speed capacity significantly with leg speed drills, so we're just topping the anaerobic capacity or systemic acidosis training (VO_2 max pace) with an injection of brief glycolytic sessions. For the man who has run 29.14 for 10,000m, (V dot 75.0), trying to achieve his theoretical potential 1:50 800m can be achieved by running glycolytic 800m pace repetitions totaling no more than 1600m.

This could consist of 4 x 400m in 55s, for instance, with a full walk/jog recovery that may last a number of minutes after each repetition.

His total workload at 1500m pace need not total more than 3,200m.

This could consist of 8 x 400m in 60s, for instance, with a full walk/jog recovery that may last a number of minutes after each repetition.

Small total workloads of very fast glycolytic running (800m pace) will yield a terrific training response if the preceding work has been done correctly and full aerobic recovery is taken. If the preceding work has been achieved haphazardly, then the training response might be a very tired or injured athlete. It is useful to note that the average runner needs at least 5 or 6 800m races in a season before he or she hits a PB.

CAUTION!

It's here, during the race preparation phase, that we have to monitor individuals' reactions very carefully.

Once into anaerobic training, variations in athletes' genetics will dictate their responses far more loudly than in the aerobic buildup phase. Nearly all athletes will respond well to an aerobic workload and most will respond well to hill resistance work and long VO_2 max paced intervals. As already mentioned in this book, we found that it was relatively easy to get three of our squad down to PB times for 1500 between 3:45 and 3:48, but once the glycolytic work started, one went "off the boil." We know from his training diaries and from what he tells us that he responds much better to the 5k-3k paced long intervals after a warm-up with leg speed drills followed by about ten minutes of threshold paced warm-up. He "eats" sessions of 800m or 1000m intervals and can be a force down to 800m off this diet.

Many athletes and coaches think that less recovery between repetitions may be better here. Initially, the aim is to expose the body to realistic achievable 800m pace, repeatedly, not limit the workout by having to stop after only a few repetitions and slowing down. Later, as specific fitness at race speeds develops, short-recovery sessions at glycolytic speeds can be used sparingly to simulate a race effect. It's up to coach and athlete in each case, but the general rule of thumb is that developing athletes train conservatively in this energy system, and ramp up the workloads only when a very high aerobic and anaerobic training level has been reached.

We won't lose fitness by the full and long recoveries. We'll enhance it. We have designated specific aerobic recovery sessions and days in this phase to maintain the aerobic systems. Early season middle distance races and time trials will maintain and enhance VO_2 max in the best possible way too.

The same 1:50 800m pace could be practiced with 8 x 200m (1600m total) in 27s, with full recovery. 5 x 300m (1500m total) in 41s could achieve the same broad goal. It's the fast rate of acidosis in the legs we want to expose the athlete to at this stage, no more. Aerobic recovery running after the session, and the next day, will amplify the response. A time trial over 600m in 82 seconds, with full recovery, followed by 2 x 400m in 55s with full recovery, may be achievable. If the athlete starts to cramp up with acidosis at the achievable goal pace, then the session should be stopped and aerobic recovery running resumed until the next designated anaerobic effort day. It could be appropriate to then drop back to a session aimed at the current 1500m pace.

Once again, it must be pointed out that faster speeds than 800m goal pace need not be run in repetitions because those speed potentials have been amply developed with all the alactic leg-speed running, hill-bounding, and sprint drills to date.

If one has reached world-class and is searching for extra 400m potential to cope with an extremely fast first lap in an 800m with some good "speed reserve" then there may be a case for introducing a very short, sharp and sweet session of, say a 300m at 400m pace, with very long recovery, followed by a 200m at the same pace. That is certainly the sort of thing that Sebastian Coe did very well.

One may achieve almost the same ends by keeping paces of glycolytic repetitions to 800m or slower and allowing short sprints with long recoveries achieve the power goal. It is very much a matter for the coach and athlete to decide upon.

For athletes concentrating on longer distances, such top-end glycolytic capacity becomes counter-productive to develop extensively because it comes at the cost of significant aerobic capacity.

How Lydiard Would Balance Training Here

Lots of easy running on parkland or trails can be done as aerobic recovery sandwiching all hard anaerobic sessions, including long warm-ups and long-cool down runs. It's interesting to note that the great Moroccan and Kenyan athletes will do three to four aerobic work sessions at varying intensities to every anaerobic session in the midst of racing seasons. This is very much a Lydiard principle.

We have a fair idea of where we're at from training and racing "information," without being overly concerned about times and places. The big picture is what's important. In this phase, Lydiard was adamant that a good coach and athlete combination assess progress at every step, and therefore these sessions have to be "tuned" to prospective realistic race times.

Maintaining the Glycolytic Base without "Going Over the Top." "Icing on the Cake" sharpeners.

In the peak period of the season, sometimes it is necessary to maintain glycolytic activity at a high level without the full demand of a race, or the risk of upsetting the system with one session too many of glycolytic repetitions at long sprint distances.

Lydiard's way around this was a unique and demanding track workout that could only be attempted by people in peak racing shape anyhow.

He'd get his athletes to run several laps of the track, alternating 50m of flat out sprinting with 50m of recovery. This would really spike the acidosis in legs already well trained to cope with glycolytic acidosis, but it would not necessarily make the systemic circulation acidic.

Lydiard said at this stage: "If I put an athlete out on the track and say, 'I want you to go around that track five times, and every 100 meters I want you to sprint 50 meters as hard as you can,' every 100-meters, he sprints full-out 50 meters; sprint, float, sprint, float. So in 400 meters he sprints 4 times; around the track 5 times, he sprints 20 times. The athlete will probably be out there for about 8 or 9 minutes. By then his legs will be getting very very tired and start to get neuromuscular breakdown; muscles no longer contract. Now if we bring that athlete in, and took the blood from the leg muscles, and took the blood from the ear lobe for arterial blood, we are getting two different readings. We are going to get a very low pH reading in the leg muscles, but it's not going to be very low in the arterial blood."

This sort of session was intense and demanding, but for an athlete in top condition it could be recovered from well without the danger of upsetting the rest of the racing period.

Lydiard would probably say that by this stage, every athlete and coach should be able to work things out for themselves intelligently, so specific instructions for a race season are pointless. So we'll finish here with something that I've found works very well in my application of the Lydiard work. Remember the principles are what are important, not the exact days or sessions.

PEAKING

Planned peaking requires knowledge of the basic principles outlined in this book but also self-knowledge of the athlete. How does he or she respond to different types of work?

Research done some time ago by the British Milers Club revealed that an 800m specialist will not record his best time for the season until he has run 5 earlier 800m races, on average. For the 1500m, it may be 4 prior races.

The coach and athlete have to look at the season backwards from the planned "big day out," and see where they they can find suitable races. Obviously, the earlier efforts will be done when not race-sharp, but the way to get race-sharp, physically and psychologically is by racing!

Generally, in the weeks before the peak race, each week will have:

1. A long run done at a considerably slower pace than during the buildup phase. The object is to recover aerobically and take the organism back to a highly aerobic and mildly alkali state.

2. Steady time-trial efforts at or near race distances will iron out inconsistencies in concentration and reveal weaknesses.

3. Race-specific glycolytic repetitions with low total volume will be done with the aim of consistency rather than record-breaking. A potential 3:56 miler may aim to run 4 x 400m in 59s exactly, with 60s recovery. This will stimulate the response without overdoing things.

4. Alactic leg speed sessions followed by gentle aerobic restoration running.

5. Aerobic "bread and butter" filler runs at very low intensity on recovery days.

Lydiard would like to ease off from all hard training 10 days before the scheduled major competition. In this time, the athlete was encouraged to top up his or her reserves by plenty of easy jogging, and any intense anaerobic work had to be low in volume with ample recovery. Generally it should be at race-specific paces to get the body totally ready for what was to come.

Another thing Lydiard seemed to do intuitively was include some kind of solid session at each of the anaerobic intensities from threshold up in the weeks before a major competition. Why?

In competition, when we fatigue an energy system, our body will tend to kick down into the next available substrate system. If it hasn't been trained well, and rested well, then it's not available. For this reason, as mentioned elsewhere in this book, we will often give a middle distance runner a session at VO_2 max pace (well below race pace), and an effort at threshold pace, in the 2 weeks leading to a major competition.

Part 7
How Different Athletes Use Lydiard Principles

1. How Our "H.I.T. Squad" Trains During Track Season

Here's an example from our own application of Lydiard principles.

During track racing periods, we always set aside Tuesday as the toughest day of the week if racing is on Saturday. Tuesday takes the information learned from last Saturday, and earlier weeks, and applies it ready for next Saturday.

Tuesday is always very specific to next Saturday. For instance, if Johnny is aiming to run 800m in 1.50 on Saturday, Tuesday could have a variety of short, hard, fast "glycolytic" workouts tuned to exactly that *pace*. If it's a 1500, then we do work at that pace with ample recovery. Time trials at these paces can vary, but as a general rule we keep them under 600m at this stage. Longer time trials can be run earlier in the first phase of anaerobic training, if wanted. It's up to the coach and athlete to work out what sessions generate the best responses. Often the athletes will do some general easy aerobic warm up, then a few light fast strides, followed by perhaps 2-3 km at threshold speed before moving onto very fast reps with long recovery. This seems to really warm up the energy systems involved and appears to make sessions predictable and consistent.

In the height of race periods, we may do several VO_2 max runs of say a kilometer at 3000m pace, with good recovery, and this will be done instead of a glycolytic 800m pace session. The reason for this is that we like to keep all the energy systems firing and have found that this sort of workout tends to help a well-conditioned 800m runner hold his form and "kick" over the last 100m. We'll only do this if the athlete complains about "lacking speed" at the end of his latest race. More often this is a lack of specific VO_2 max endurance once the lactate tank has sputtered and the system has to change down a gear. If the next energy system down isn't trained, it can't be readily used so

sometimes an athlete who only does race-specific glycolytic repetitions and slow easy recovery jogging will get caught out over the last sprint, simply because he can't access the appropriate energy system.

A Tuesday tough session plus a Saturday race add up to two very significant stimuli for younger athletes if the balance of training is appropriate. There doesn't appear to be a need for much more than two such sessions a week in my experience: progress can certainly be attained. A balance of aerobic sessions, varied-pace fartlek runs, and easy longer runs can keep the momentum going.

We regard Tuesday at this stage of the track season as a "get in and get out" day. The total work done can be as little as 1000m to 1600m in total. Repetitions should cease as soon as the athlete finds he or she can't hold convincing form and power. The aim

is to come up "fresh" on race day, and we have to remember that a substantial amount of anaerobic buffering has already been accomplished with VO_2 max work specific to the athlete's level of development over 3000m and 5000m distances.

If preparing for 1.50 at 800m, then early in the race phase, then a typical session could comprise a 600m time trial in 82 seconds, followed by a 300m at race pace (41 s) then a 200m at race pace (27s) with ample recovery between repetitions so that the work can be achieved with good mechanics and convincing power. This work would always be done after a good aerobic warm-up, and leg speed drills over short (alactic) distances. A good long aerobic cool-down is suggested afterwards.

If in the week of a more important race, a workout of 4 x 300m at 1.50 pace or slightly faster (41 seconds or faster) could be performed. Recoveries would be just long enough to complete the work with good form and power. We're only trying to teach the body what the rate of acidosis feels like on race day, not thump the body with information overload.

If it's a very important race, and we're not "training through" lead-up races, then a fast race-specific session could be performed a good week or more away from the target race with plenty of easy jogging and light fast strides interspersed through the final days to ensure that all energy systems and fast movement patterns are "on ice" and no system is "burned."

The main thing here is to keep the glycolytic anaerobic work short, sharp and sweet the nearer you get to important races and to balance it out with ample recovery and plenty of low-level aerobic work. The human body will react to such work favourably. With anaerobic work in the glycolytic realm, at this stage of the season, a little bit of information is often enough. We try to see how little we can get away with, especially with junior athletes. The results can be surprising.

A couple of years ago, using this sort of work with 17-year-old boys following a cross-country season, one reached 3.50 for 1500m and the other reached 1.52 for 800m. More importantly, both boys are still progressing.

Wednesday for us is always a pleasant medium aerobic recovery day, perhaps over an hour of easy cross country over parkland.

In our Lydiard-based program for youths, Thursday is the day year-round when leg-speed drills, hill bounding, or light fast work can be done. Once the fast alactic work has been done, a longer aerobic run or fartlek can be done. Always a good relaxed warm-up before very short fast efforts.

Friday is a day when athletes can again run for an easy hour on parkland. If it's the day before a very important competition, the run can be shortened considerably in order to totally freshen up, but as a general principle we like to keep a strong undercurrent of aerobic activity going for as long as possible into the track season.

Saturday is race day, or a day when significant training effort is applied, depending on the stage of the year we're at.

Sunday is always a long and pleasant recovery run, depending on the development of the athlete. For young athletes of about 15 years of age, this may mean a one hour run over hills, and for athletes who have been on the program for a few years, these runs generally take 90 minutes during later track season, and are often around 2 hours during winter.

Monday is always a medium length recovery run, very easy, on parkland, and the length of this will vary according to the development of the athlete.

How Other Healthy Youth Squads Train

2. Barry Magee - Auckland, New Zealand

For the last 5 years, I have been working with teenagers 13-19 years of age with the Auckland City Athletics Club – plus some others around the country and have had great success. That success I believe has come by following the *Lydiard* schedules that Arthur has left us in his books. He has left us the blueprints to success, and those schedules are the most important dynamic of all.

Barry Magee at Auckland's famous Cornwall Park with his group.

The system is called "periodisation" training where everything comes in its right order, just like layers of the energy system pyramid. Conditioning, hill work, time trials and reps – sharpening and freshening.

The other things that have worked for me are as follows:

- Group Training. Boys and girls separated and train together as two groups to start and then splinter off according to ability and speed. Always at least two run together. It is a dynamic that they love and some even come along when injured to watch and talk to their friends.
- Give them all a schedule of their training to follow – as a guide and not an absolute. Kids have so many things going on with sports, music, ballet, school or whatever – it is essential that it is flexible and adjustable. I usually do them 6 weeks at a time. If they cannot make it to the group they then know what to do.
- Training is done on grass as much as possible and long racecourse grass when training for X/C events. The emphasis is always on aerobic conditioning with the thought that we need to be preparing athletes for the future.
- Hill training – We do all the time, as well as the Lydiard hill springing period. Even during long runs they often go over 3 Auckland hills – Mt. St John, Mt. Hobson and Mt. Eden. At other times when doing reps they do sessions uphill. Lydiard said, "Hills are the shortcut to success."
- Extra exercise —- For the older ones, I encourage an extra session most days of running or swimming in the mornings. This is not done during conditioning but

through any or all of the other phases. Particularly helpful during last weeks of sharpening / freshening.
- Being there. I show them that I am there for them and that I am available to them or their parents anytime. With my group (5-10 each of boys and girls) we have two of us coaching. I do 5 days and my assistant John does 6. When we do timed training we split them into 2 groups, male and female, and take 1 lot each. We do our best to be at every major event to see them in action.

3. Neil MacDonald - Geelong, Victoria

- Emphasize aerobic running.
- Do some speed work all year round, even if it's just 6 x "flying" 40 meters "fast / relaxed" with a good walk recovery between during winter to keep in touch with the fast twitch fibers and to continually reinforce sound biomechanics for running fast. I feel this approach means that athletes are also less likely to become injured when stepping up to the more intense training later in the year.
- Give kids regular breaks from running to recharge the batteries. i.e., two or three times a year (usually after an important Championship) the kids might have a couple of weeks off training with the group. However, this is a time for active rest as they all do other sports.
- Explain to the kids why we are doing a particular session at a particular time. Eventually, they should be able to coach themselves.
- Run on grass, gravel, dirt, bush tracks where possible to protect young growing bodies.
- Make it fun – group training helps this as the warm-ups / cool-downs / longer aerobic running is a great opportunity for talk / fun between training partners. The kids in the group are great mates.
- Plenty of variety – we are always training in different environments (in the bush / down the beach / around the river trails / Eastern Park / grass parkland / up and down hills) Geelong is fantastic for this as we have the best facilities / training venues within a few minutes. Also, there is plenty of variety in the training program – in a four-week block, apart from the weekly long run, the kids would not duplicate a session. A session might have a very similar physiological aim or stress a similar

energy system to a session from the previous week but kids don't want to be running 4 x 400 meters @ 1500 meter race pace every Tuesday during the track season. We also do a lot of circuit training that improves whole body strength, core stability and endurance (i.e., boxing, skipping, body weight exercises, very light hand dumbells, medicine ball, yoga, Swiss ball). Occasionally, we will finish off with a game (i.e., soccer) or run to the pool for a recovery swim or ride bikes around the Geelong river trails.

- If in doubt: undertrain. With kids I reckon it's important to do the least amount that achieves the desired result. Every year, the kids do a little more running (if they are coping and want to do more), but they are doing a lot less running than many other training groups

- Don't have a program that is set in stone: if the kids are looking tired or say they have been doing other demanding activities, I'm not afraid to change the session or lessen the session or tell the kids to have the night off. I like to warm up with the kids so I can see first hand if they are ready for a particular session or need an easier night.

4. How Rod Dixon Started in Athletics

Rod Dixon was a classic example of the healthy Lydiard method in action. His brother John coached him to a surprise Olympic 1500m bronze in Munich 1972, when Rod was just 22 years old. John was just a few years older! Rod was ranked world number one by *Track and Field News* over 1500m in 1973, 5000m in 1975, and US road racing in 1980. He won the New York marathon in 1983 in 2:08.59. His best 800m was 1:47.6, his best 1500m 3:33.8, and over cross-country he was third in the world crosscountry championships in 1973 and 1982. How many people could run his range of times today?

As young brothers, we kind of ran everywhere. Our grandparents had a farm and we just ran everywhere...in junior school, athletics was almost daily...and of course rugby...cricket...hockey...swimming and soccer-football...I tried them all but somehow I enjoyed the running part. Just running fast and it seemed forever, as the games we created called for lots of running....so in junior school, John Dixon was the 100 yards Champion and then 3 + years later I was. Intermediate school was much the same....I played soccer and rugby but running I enjoyed most.

John joined the running club Methodist Harriers...I wasn't able to as the minimum age was 12 years...so for two seasons John encouraged me to run for 20-30 minutes with him and his friends 3 times each week.

Our Mail delivery man, Mr Stripeman (a Dutchman) was incredibly athletic; very fit, always tanned and a great runner, more a fitness athlete, into exercise, using body weight and stretching and lifting small weights with repetitions after the run. His knowledge for good nutrition was valuable and he presented to us our very first "trail mix" of nuts and dried fruits, etc. Most non-runners scoffed at the mixture as only "fit for a horse." It was this encouragement and interest in the Dixon brothers that gave us the incentive to become runners and be fit and healthy.

Even at this young age, John Dixon was already learning many of the base skills of a coach.

Harold Nelson, 1948 Olympian and 1950 British Empire Games Gold and Silver medalist, was a member of the Nelson Running Club as was 5-time New Zealand Cross Country Champion Kerry Williams. These two world class athletes gave time and effort to assisting, coaching, and running with us all each weekend. We also had some great club runners who were ready to give advice to the younger runners. This in itself created the perfect environment to "listen and learn" for us all, and it was nothing to get hundreds of runners each Saturday at the running club.

Arthur Lydiard would travel around New Zealand in the '60s coaching and giving advice to club runners in every town, and it was during this time that Arthur shared his experience and knowledge with John Dixon. This helped to shape and mold John's own experience into an understanding that he could integrate with that of Arthur's.

I remember during one visit to Nelson by Arthur, he wasn't able to give a one-on-one discussion after his talk so he suggested to John and me that he would take time the next morning to speak with us at John's home. I took that to be maybe a hour. The session lasted over 5 hours! I believe this time, which was taped recorded by John, gave us the balance of the Lydiard method and system which complemented the system which John had developed and created through our training and running in Nelson.

I enjoyed and loved the club running, winning some races, and although this was very satisfying, it wasn't the only answer. I just loved to run and be with my mates at the club. So for 5 years that was what it was....having fun and loving what I was doing, winning some races, but mostly running my best. I did like the idea of being the Champion though!

In 1968, I decided to train hard with John and so began the pathway of the Dixon brothers, which later became the Coach and the Athlete, although John did accomplish some amazing running feats of his own in the years of the '70s and '80s.

I will say to this day, John Dixon was a great coach, equal in my mind to the very best I have ever met in my life, and in any other country in the world would have been appointed a national coach, a coach of champions.

Part 8
Exercise Physiology 101, Again!

We can't state these basics enough for most middle distance coaches and athletes. So, at the risk of overstating the obvious, let's go through the basics again.

For any exercise that lasts more than about 10 seconds, the infrastructure required for fuel delivery and waste removal becomes more and more important as the work duration increases. Under about 10 seconds, it doesn't really matter too much.

The reason for this is that our muscles have an inherent energy supply that operates independently of external fuel and air supplies, for a few seconds at most. This is intra-muscular creatine phosphate, an explosive source of short-term energy used most by our most powerful muscle fibers, the type IIB fast twitch fibers. It is the equivalent of high-octane premium unleaded fuel you pour into your high-performance fuel tank.

Alactic Exercise

Short-term explosive bursts of energy using creatine phosphate are termed alactic anaerobic exercises...meaning they are too short in duration to form lactic acid, or lactate, and they are also anaerobic, meaning capable of being performed in the absence of oxygen.

Of course, these explosive bursts can't be repeated indefinitely. It is thought that 5 minutes of rest or easy passive activity will replenish short-term phosphate energy stores to 95% of their starting levels. The high-energy phosphate molecules are recycled back into use over a few minutes if rest is sufficient.

So, as an example, it would be possible for a highly trained athlete to perform a few highly explosive bursts of exercise lasting a few seconds without producing the acidic wastes associated with lactic acid as long as ample recovery was given.

With very long recoveries lasting many minutes, explosive short bursts could be performed throughout the day without large losses of power. But shorter recoveries would eventually deplete the intramuscular stores, and other sources of fuel would have to be deployed by other less-explosive muscle fibers using lower-grade fuels, such as glucose or fats.

For a middle distance runner, short bursts of alactic sprint drills won't create acidosis but will reinforce useful fast movement patterns if enough easy jogging recovery is taken. We've used such drills right throughout a winter's aerobic base period on easy days, and the end-product has been exceptionally quick teenagers who can run endurance distances with anyone.

Running on Empty

We can induce glycogen depletion and systemic acidosis with too many long hard runs, as well as with too many fast repetitions over short distances like 300m and 400m. This became very obvious to me a number of years ago when discussing the decline of British middle distance and distance track performances with a British coach.

Stuart Hale, an expert in the use of heart rate monitoring, had written a number of extremely good articles on training by heart rate for *Athletics Today*. I corresponded with him and visited him while in England at his base near Peterborough.

Stuart told me of a number of national-level and international runners in Britain who had embraced 'OBLA' training, with erratic and underwhelming results.

OBLA training, or Onset of Blood Lactic Acid training, was very much in vogue for a few years, and possibly still is, with top athletes and coaches often considering slower aerobic efforts as "waste." They cut their mileage back and did plenty of sustained running at or around the anaerobic threshold level. Long runs were cut back to cope with the general fatigue, so more and more was expected from less and less. They simply didn't understand the benefits of easy aerobic running or where lower intensity running fit into the whole picture.

One of the most astounding observations that Stuart made when he took a few disillusioned athletes on was that they were *totally inefficient* at any slower aerobic paces. These athletes were physically uncomfortable at slower aerobic speeds, often having erratic heart rates.

Stuart had to start these athletes on weekly programs of deliberately running at very slow speeds until their bodies became efficient at each heart rate level. This took quite some time, but the outcome after many weeks of very controlled running at low heart rate zones, gradually increasing heart rate when efficiency was restored at each level, was a range of personal bests over 10km on the road.

A simple way of measuring aerobic efficiency with a heart rate monitor is by estimating meters covered per average heart beat (covered in Part 1, *Training By Heart Rate: Heart Rate Monitor Tricks*).

With a well-trained athlete, the number of meters covered during a heartbeat is about the same, whether walking, jogging, or approaching the anaerobic threshold.

Nic Bideau mentioned recently that his partner, Sonia O'Sullivan, trained intensely along these lines in the early to mid 1990s but also included quite severe VO_2 max track sessions with minimal recovery. This worked effectively for some time, resulting in world number one rankings between 1500m and 5000m in 1993 and 1994, and a world championship over 5000m in 1995. (Sonia still holds the women's world 2000m record).

However, by the 1996 Atlanta Olympics, Sonia was very ill and unable to perform at her best. She turned to more steady state aerobic work under British coach Alan Storey, winning the 1998 World Cross Country title over 4000m and 8000m, and by the Sydney Olympics in 2000 she was a very close 2nd place winner over 5000m in 14:41.

The same phenomenon was mentioned by triathlon Ironman great Mark Allen about his early days in triathlon: he came from a swimming background where the emphasis in those days was on punishing workouts, every day!

"It was all I knew. So when I entered the sport of triathlons in the early 1980's, my mentality was to go as hard as I could at some point in every single workout. And to gauge how fast that might have to be, I looked at how fast the best triathletes were running at the end of the short distance races. Guys like Dave Scott, Scott Tinley and Scott Molina were able to hold close to 5 minute miles for their 10ks after swimming and biking!

"So that's what I did. Every run, even the slow ones, for at least one mile, I would try to get close to 5 minute pace. And it worked...sort of. I had some good races the first year or two, but I also suffered from minor injuries and was always feeling one run away from being too burned out to want to continue with my training.

Then chiropractor Dr Phil Maffetone advised Allen to use a heart rate monitor and train at much lower intensities. He had to keep his maximal HR below 155 when running. At first this required 8:15 mile pace, 3 minutes slower per mile than the pace he was trying to hit in every run! Over 4 months of running below this prescribed aerobic maximal HR, his aerobic comfort zone had improved to 5:20 a mile at a HR of 155.

"That means that I was now able to burn fat for fuel efficiently enough to hold a pace that a year before was redlining my effort at a maximum heart rate of about 190. I had become an aerobic machine! On top of the speed benefit at lower heart rates, I was no longer feeling like I was ready for an injury the next run I went on, and I was feeling fresh after my workouts instead of being totally exhausted from them."
(excerpted from http://www.duathlon.com/articles/1460)

Part 9
Strength Training for Athletics

Strength training is a huge arena, and it's not the purpose of this book to expound at large on every topic. However if we're talking strength and power for running, specifically getting from A to B in as short a time as possible, then I believe this chapter will be useful for serious sprinters and middle distance runners alike.

Arthur Lydiard never saw the need for athletes to spend large amounts of time in the gymnasium lifting weights. He cited the case of Olympic champion Halberg, who had a crushed and paralyzed left shoulder following a rugby injury as a teenager, but who nevertheless could run 53 second last laps in major races. He would also cite the example of the very muscular Peter Snell, whose power was a natural phenomenon enhanced by endurance training and hill training.

As for arm swing in running, experts seem to agree with Lydiard. Dr. Ralph Mann, USATF Sprint/Hurdle Biomechanist and 1972 Munich Olympics 400 meter hurdles silver medalist has written "...the relatively small upper limb muscle moments seem to relegate the arms to the simple role of maintaining balance."

Los Angeles sprint coach Barry Ross says "since the arms are very light compared to the rest of body mass, they cannot do much more than what Mann wrote (and for which he took a lot of heat from coaches!) and therefore don't require any more than isometric work for runners."

That having been said, some degree of good upper body and torso strength is desireable, in my opinion. Years ago, I ran with Steve Austin, a very wiry and tough Australian runner who worked full-time as a bricklayer. This physically demanding work did him no harm: he'd recorded times as good as 3:57 for the mile and 13:22 for 5000m, as well as a 27:53 10,000m. I'll always remember how he described most distance runners: "They don't have enough strength to tear open a Wheaties box!" I agree fully: some of the specimens struggling at the business end of races look like they'd have trouble sneezing into a tissue.

If you've read the book so far, you'll realize that the "secret" key to power and efficiency is the short-term alactic energy system, which recruits our IIB fast twitch muscle fibers. Hill training is certainly a very effective method of activating our fast twitch muscle fibers, but I believe the very serious athlete can go one better. Heavy lifting can increase leg muscle strength far more than hill resistance exercise because we are loading the legs with far more than just bodyweight. But for best results, it should be the right type of exercise, of exactly the right duration, at the right intensity. At some stage, you'll still need to translate this newfound strength into *power*, and Arthur's hill exercises are excellent for that, especially if the active bounding or springing phase is kept to less than 10 seconds in each work bout, with plenty of recovery.

How much power can a small person develop? Think of the legendary martial artist Bruce Lee, a tiny man who weighed about 130lbs. According to one article, he could spin-kick a 300lb sandbag that would smash violently into the concrete roof of his Hong Kong apartment's verandah. That's *strength* and *power*! Haile Gebrselassie is probably less than 5'4" in height and under 54 kg, (120 lbs), but he could pass for a bantamweight boxer with his upper-body development. He has just enough useful muscle for what he needs and not an ounce more.

I once had a teammate who had run 1:48 for 800m and 3:39 for 1500m, but he couldn't even do a single "pull-up" with his bodyweight on a bar! That is extremely weak! His legs looked like tree trunks, but his upper body was woeful. He did a lot of steep uphill reps year-round, so he had terrific leg strength and anaerobic capacity from that, but he was very vulnerable in a tight finish because he didn't have the upper-body strength to match his leg strength. I put him on a program and within a few months he was able to do a dozen pull-ups in several sets. His finishing ability improved considerably, and later his range extended to a 13:38 5000m and a win in the Canberra marathon.

Every athlete wanting to reach world-class these days should do general strength training as an injury-preventive strategy if nothing else. The exercises should be compound movements that resemble real-life activities. Compound movements use many muscles in coordinated effort, across several joints, and don't just isolate one. It's possible to get extremely strong with 3 half-hour gym sessions a week or less, and most of that half hour can be recovery time!

In everyday activity, we usually push, pull, twist, lift, and jump: our strength training program should reflect these movements. (Lydiard recommended getting a ton of gravel dumped on the side of the driveway, and then shovelling it into another pile, then back again. "That'll work every muscle in your body!" he chuckled.)

When using resistance exercise, we are looking for "closed chain" movements that lift weight upwards and away from the ground as our trunk opens up and extends, just like when we run. One particular exercise, the deadlift, can accomplish what we want for 90% of the skeletal muscle used in running! And it only needs a few very heavy repetitions, in a few sets, with lots of recovery inbetween, to get maximal strength gains without unnecessary mass.

The underhand pull-up or "chin-up" is useful for runners. It is a compound exercise that uses some of the same shoulder, back, and upper arm muscles we use in hard sprinting. The most useful part is the slow descent phase. Once you've built up to about 12-15 repetitions with body weight, it is useful to get a weight belt, strap a weight disc to it, and do fewer repetitions with the increased weight. See how heavy you can go within the 10 seconds alactic zone, with ample recovery after sets, and when you get to try your strength with bodyweight-only again several days later, you'll do several more repetitions! I've seen skinny guys do repeated chin-ups with 100lb strapped to their weight belts!

Another useful exercise is the bodyweight dip. The same principle applies with use of weight belts to recruit fast twitch fibers once the exercise is established.

Barry Ross maintains that even the use of these last two exercises is not needed for runners if they do very heavy lifting in the deadlift. He maintains that a heavy deadlift works the biceps, triceps, and forearm muscles isometrically, and "the only muscles left hanging are the pectoral (chest) muscles." Push-ups or bench press can therefore complete the picture of whole-body development for the runner.

The tonic postural abdominal and core muscles tend to have far more slow twitch muscle content and will respond to higher numbers of repetitions, or even static isometric exercise, but resistance with weight plates is also useful for these exercises. It saves a lot of time. If you want to get strong, lift heavy.

Some sprinters and footballers, particularly, get hung up on the bench press. The muscles employed in the bench press are not really useful in fast sprinting, but may be very useful in hard contact sports. According to US sprint coach Barry Ross, a good strength training program must produce superior strength with minimal mass, regardless of the sport it is intended for (other than sports with a super-heavyweight class!).

With all of the energy systems optimally trained and developed, an increased sprint potential without unnecessary muscle mass becomes a potent weapon.

However, if we put the cart before the horse and get it wrong, as do conventional training program, we could be the fastest kicker at the back of the pack. I know from my own experience that mixing an endurance-based running program with conventional weight training can be counter-productive for endurance but there is a way to do it properly that we can still explore.

Heavy lifting at near-maximal is thought to recruit the fast twitch fibers very early in the lifting phase and bypass the slow twitch fibers. A similar process is probably at work when we sprint: we tend to bypass slow twitch fibers and recruit fast twitch straightaway. Whatever fibers we have in a muscle will increase in size with heavy lifting, but the ones that are most likely to increase with very heavy lifting of short duration are the fast twitch fibers.

We are all likely to have a spectrum of fiber types in our muscles that will respond to specific training in different ways. We don't quite know what we have to play with until training has been done for quite some time; this applies to resistance training as well as running. It is not something that a muscle biopsy can "predict," because muscle fiber types can vary enormously within any individual. Just like the chicken, with its white fast twitch breast meat and redder slow twitch leg meat, we can vary enormously. The chicken can flap its wings mighty fast, but the slow twitch fibers in the legs are what get it places.

In the human, postural muscles like the abdominals and trunk muscles tend to be slow twitch, and prime movers like the quadriceps (thigh muscles) tend to have more fast twitch fibers.

Very heavy lifting (above 85% of your 1 rep maximum) with few repetitions, in a few sets, with plenty of recovery between sets, will primarily recruit and train the fast twitch fibers and their huge incoming neural pathways. The key to heavy lifting for IIB development is to make sure the total "load time" or lifting time is well within the *alactic* time zone of 10 seconds.

Longer duration lifting will naturally enough cross over into the glycolytic and even aerobic systems, and the muscle fibers that will respond most to that are *not* the IIB fibers, but the less powerful fibers. This might seem OK, but it comes at a cost to a runner. Because the less powerful fibers function best in longer time frames, their cell structures have far more fluid volume and complex organelle development. This is all a cellular payload we don't want to develop as a trade-off for increased power.

Once we get past about 10 seconds, the muscle cells involved require complex oxygen and fuel delivery systems (capillaries) and an array of glycolytic and aerobic organelles (including mitochondria) and a lot of fluid in the cell body (the sarcoplasm or cytoplasm) to function. So we're doing a type of lifting that increases muscle volume and weight (which we don't want), at the same time as increasing the density of the actual contractile proteins (which we do want).

Think of the intramuscular alactic fuel, creatine phosphate, as the sole fuel for this heavy burst of lifting we're after. We want to fire the V8 engine for 10 seconds on the teaspoon of petrol already in the fuel injector, and then let it naturally replenish itself over minutes via the "phosphate battery" during a long recovery.

Less intense lifting with many more repetitions will more likely recruit and increase the size of slow twitch fibers without a specific effect on the fast twitch fibers, due to the "size principle" of muscle fiber recruitment.

The aim for the middle distance athlete or distance athlete is to have a big engine with a small frame and very high efficiency

The danger, if we can call it that, of conventional weight training is that we increase our non-specific muscle mass too much, thereby creating a larger payload to be carried around the track.

The muscle has to be very specific to running at high speeds; otherwise it is a liability that will come at a high energy cost. Even a sprinter has to be very careful that his or her muscle mass is totally functional, as even a couple of extra kilograms in weight can upset the physics of mass-specific force and ground-contact time.

Once I went from a racing weight of 57.6 kg (126 lb) to 63.7 kg (140 lb) within a couple of months of intense weight training, based mainly around half squats with as much weight as I could lift in several sets of 10 reps, two to three nights a week. Although I felt magnificent from the all-day adrenalin and testosterone surge that heavy lifting invoked, my results were "good and bad."

At the higher body weight, I could half-squat 150kg or 330 lbs (thighs parallel to floor, backside touching bench) the ten times. If that sounds very heavy, it is (ample padding over the bar is suggested), but it is nothing compared to what a trained power lifter of the same weight can lift. Don't rush out and try to lift the weight I did: I'd been training regularly with weights for 6 years when I did that and have some very good strength genetics. But it shows you that small guys can develop serious leg and back strength.

On one occasion, on the tenth half-squat rep (without a "spotter"), I found myself losing the weight and it dropped with a huge crash to the concrete floor of the gym, which was on the 1st floor above the ladies' changing rooms of a swim center. Lots of wet partially clad ladies and girls in towels emerged upstairs to see what had happened, and I made myself scarce. It pays to have a friend "spot" for you when lifting decent weights off a rack. However, several guys started dropping weights regularly after that.

I found heavy lifting very good to do at night, after any hard running session was over and usually on the night before an easy recovery day. The body was well and truly warmed up, and there was no danger of depleting the body's energy stocks before a fast running session.

This sort of conventional lifting was certainly effective for short sprint power. My average 100m (jog start) time came plummeting down by a second to about 11.3 seconds. I repeated this on several occasions, so it wasn't a fluke. My 300m time got under 37 seconds. I could do 4 x 300m runs in less than 40 seconds, with just 300m walk / jog recovery.

However, I was *training the wrong system*! Sets of ten repetitions with quite heavy weights take at least a minute to complete, without rest, so they're very lactic or glycolytic. There's the time of the lifting or concentric contraction phase, as well as the lowering or eccentric lengthening phase, ten times in a row. I was most probably training my IIA transitional fibers, with the accompanying increased muscle cell mass that invoked. I'd have been much better off halving the number of reps, and lifting a bit heavier. I might then have put on only a couple of kilos, got stronger again, and translated this strength more effectively into 800m and 1500m times.

Despite my increased strength and short-distance power, I couldn't get my 400m time under 51 seconds and my 800m time was pathetic. Not knowing what I know now, I hadn't worked on running sessions that could translate this strength into sustainable power past 45 seconds. My short-term power delivery had increased but so had my total mass by 6.1 kg (14 lbs). This was more than a 10% increase in body mass that my aerobic and glycolytic systems were expected to cart around the track.

Most conventional weight training is based on several sets of several repetitions, (usually between 8 and 12), with the weight heavy enough to cause "failure" towards the end of the exercise. This, by its very nature, forces the muscle into very localised glycolytic acidosis, and as we already know from the rest of this book, acidosis is not good for muscles, or the nervous system.

Such lifting will force a longer recovery time as the contractile proteins and cell membranes get damaged by lifting to "failure." Even worse, the inflammation caused by acidosis will invoke intracellular fluid retention, so that the weight of the muscle tissue is greatly increased. The contractile proteins have to contend with the "double whammy" of repairing serious damage at the same time as being terribly inflamed. Eventually this damage will repair, because the body is simply amazing, but if it occurs several times a week, it's no wonder it takes so long to increase strength this way. The muscle simply looks bigger because it is damaged; just like your cheek would if it was punched. So why even go there?

Conventional weight training is really glycolytic overtraining

If we lift alactically in small sets of heavy repetitions, with long recoveries, this downside of conventional weight training is avoided, and the plus side is that the first type of muscle to develop will likely be whatever fast twitch fibers we have, packed densely with useful contractile proteins and very little else, and this will happen relatively quickly. Only useful muscle will develop in the specific region trained, and because the muscles aren't bathing in a sea of heavy acidosis, they will set about the job of repairing themselves almost immediately. Alactic lifting for the IIB fibers will increase strength and speed potential without increasing useless mass.

CAUTION!

Another thing to watch out for is excessive soreness after initial heavy lifts. The shortening phase of muscle contraction is concentric, and the lengthening or lowering phase is eccentric. It is the eccentric or lengthening phase with a very heavy weight that excites the large nerve pathways most and invokes the fast twitch fiber response, but it is this same muscle action that can cause DOMS, or Delayed Onset of Muscle Soreness. So there is a case for starting gym-based work very gradually with lower weights and higher repetitions initially to prepare the muscular system for the intensity to come.

The number of repetitions we can lift at lower intensities before fatiguing has a direct mathematical relationship to our maximal potential, and this is often a very safe way to determine potential lifting goals. For instance, a 10RM weight is about 75% of one's 1RM, and a 15RM is about 60%.

The best way to warm up for heavy lifting is *not* by hopping on an exercise bike or treadmill, as most gyms have their patrons do, but by dynamically moving.

Barry Ross says, "We do a dynamic warm-up prior to lifting, then start at the heaviest weight and work down to lighter weight. New lifters I've trained *never* question the concept, and we've never had any injuries. Experienced lifters I've trained always start with the concern that they will injure themselves by lifting "heavy first." After a few sessions, they adapt and never question the concept of 'heaviest first' again.

"I recently spent time with a very experienced strength and conditioning coach who had the fear of 'heavy first' injury. He decided to try it out with 2 of his experienced trainees. Over a 4-week period, both improved bench press by more than 50 lbs and their deadlift by more than 80 lbs. Needless to say, all of his athletes lift heaviest first."

Naturally, we work our way into gym-based training gradually, with expert help where possible. Heavy lifts are safe if done with good technique; if done with lousy technique, you can rupture a disc in the spine, which is not recommended. So what is excellent technique?

The Deadlift

This is a much safer exercise than the squat, because the weight is lifted off the ground, rather than off a high rack. Therefore, it can be done without specialist equipment and you shouldn't need a "spotter." It also uses a lot of shoulder and arm muscles not recruited in the squat.

"The deadlift works the biceps extensively but isometrically. Bodyweight dips work the triceps, but so does the deadlift! Only the chest muscles are left hanging by the deadlift," says Barry Ross, whose proven strength training program is extremely uncomplicated but effective.

I recommend Frederic Delavier's excellent book *Strength Training Anatomy* (Human Kinetics, Second Edition) for any serious students of gym-based lifting. In his section on the deadlift, he recommends that the deadlifter create a "block" with his torso.

1. Expand the chest and hold a deep breath, which supports the rib cage and prevents the chest from collapsing forward.
2. Contract the abdominal group. This supports the core and increases the intra-abdominal pressure, thereby preventing the torso from collapsing forward.
3. Arch the lower back into extension by contracting the lumbar muscles.

Another advantage of the deadlift is that it uses more muscle mass across the body than any other lift, so it gives a lot of bang for its buck. The major muscles used all extend the trunk and legs as they lift; the same basic motion used in the drive phase of sprinting.

The heavier we can lift in a maximal lift (I rep maximum, or 1RM), the more we can lift in repetitions at every level below that weight; so our relative "endurance" increases with our strength. The number of repetitions we can lift at lower intensities have a direct mathematical relationship to our maximal potential, and this is often a very safe way to determine potential goals. For instance, if a 10RM weight is about 75% of one's 1RM, then this repetition range could be used early in a strength training program to test current maximums without blowing a gasket.

A stronger leg extension manifests in a longer stride without any increase in cadence, and therefore we can cover more distance efficiently. Leg strength has benefits at every race distance.

One study[1] demonstrated a statistically significant improvement in 5000m time in well-trained individuals despite no significant improvement in VO_2 max or anaerobic threshold. These individuals (experienced orienteers) trained with low repetition, heavy weight protocols and reduced total aerobic training by 35%, yet improved. The increased leg strength translates to an increased stride length at every level of running intensity.

For example, if we had a 2-meter stride length and ran 5000m in 14 minutes, it would take 2500 strides to cover the distance. But if we could increase our stride length by 2.5% (5 cm), then over 5000m at the same cadence and oxygen uptake intensity, this would translate into a time of 13:39.0 with no increase in oxygen uptake or lactate tolerance, but merely better efficiency in getting from A to B.

5000m Time Improvement						
% increase stride		0.5	1.0	1.5	2.0	2.5
Distance	5000	5000	5000	5000	5000	5000
Stride length (meters)	2	2.01	2.02	2.03	2.04	2.05
Number of strides	2500.00	2487.56	2475.25	2463.05	2450.98	2439.02
Stride reduction quotient		0.995	0.990	0.985	0.980	0.975
Theoretical time (secs)	840.0	835.8	831.7	827.6	823.5	819.0
Minutes: seconds	14:00	13:55.8	13:51.7	13:47.6	13:43.5	13:39.0
800m Time Improvement						
% increase stride		0.5	1.0	1.5	2.0	2.5
Distance	800	800	800	800	800	800
Stride length (meters)	2	2.01	2.02	2.03	2.04	2.05
Number of strides	400.00	398.01	396.04	394.09	392.16	390.24
Stride reduction quotient		0.995	0.990	0.985	0.980	0.975
Theoretical time (secs)	110.0	109.5	108.9	108.4	107.8	107.3
Minutes: seconds	1:50	01:49.5	01:48.9	01:48.4	01:47.8	01:47.3
1500m Time Improvement						
% increase stride		0.5	1.0	1.5	2.0	2.5
Distance	1500	1500	1500	1500	1500	1500
Stride length (meters)	2	2.01	2.02	2.03	2.04	2.05
Number of strides	750.00	746.27	742.57	738.92	735.29	731.71
Stride reduction quotient		0.995	0.990	0.985	0.980	0.975
Theoretical time (secs)	220.0	218.9	217.8	216.7	215.7	214.5
Minutes: seconds	03:40.0	03:38.9	03:37.8	03:36.7	03:35.7	03:34.5

There is also evidence that the increased force of delivery at footstrike means slightly quicker ground contact time is possible, and this can translate into sustainable higher cadence. This is not demonstrated in the above table.

Of course, near-maximal lifting will require a massive electromotive charge from the brain to the working muscle, and this will require activation of the massive IIB neurons and their attached IIB fast twitch muscle fibers. A massive weight near our maximal lifting capacity will have to be lifted slowly, and by definition cannot be lifted quickly, but still at the highest muscle tension possible. So this is not a speed exercise by any stretch of the imagination.

The whole intent of heavy lifting is to reverse the size principle of muscle fiber recruitment and hit the massive fast twitch fibers first.

For a weight to do the job of reversing the size principle, the weight lifted has to be very heavy, and that means at least 85-100% of one's 1RM. That means 5-7 reps or fewer of a very heavy weight. We can't lift big weights quickly, and it is ridiculous to think so. But once we have increased the cross-sectional area of IIB muscle fibers, we can certainly do power exercises with body weight only (i.e., bounding, plyometrics, etc) to attune the neuro-muscular system. This is nothing new.

"I am convinced all middle distance runners should train with weights using the accepted strength training techniques of low repetitions and heavy weights. The pyramid system of the three sets of not more than 6 repetitions should prove ideal for the middle distance runner."
Wilf Paish, former Great Britain Olympic team coach, 1978

Wilf coached 1:42.97 800m runner Peter Elliott, one of the world's greatest ever middle distance athletes, and a multiple medalist at all major championships over 800m and 1500m between 1986 and 1990.

I have even seen in specialist strength training books a recommendation that "power" exercises be done by lifting heavy weights as fast as possible. The logic of this escapes me. If a weight is very heavy, it *can't* be lifted quickly! As a chiropractor, I can tell you that this would result in joint and muscle damage eventually, if the feat were either possible or attempted. Those sorts of exercises, with more moderate weights, are useful only for specialist Olympic lifters to get past "sticking points" in competitive lifting.

If the number of repetitions can be kept very low, at a maximal level that will keep the muscle tension very high, it should be possible to keep the load time of the whole set under 10 seconds, particularly if the weight can be dropped at the height of the lifting phase. Perhaps a Smith machine can be adapted so that a deadlift can be done and weights dropped on the springs, or perhaps large rubber-edged weight plates can be used.

The reasoning behind all this becomes very clear if we realize that the short duration is extremely important here. If we dropped the weight back a bit and did more repetitions, as we've been brainwashed to do over the years, we *will not get the result*. Why?

The answer, as we already know from earlier in the book, is that the *alactic* energy system is primarily recruited, and this almost totally involves the specific IIB fast twitch fibers, and their huge intramuscular creatine phosphate energy stores. If we spend any longer than about 10 seconds lifting heavy weights, as far as the energy systems in the muscle are concerned, then we're in danger of going from the alactic system (no real acidosis) to the glycolytic system (exponential buildup of acidosis). It is this acidosis that causes the "burn" in conventional strength training, and therefore causes the "necessity" of days of recovery from the cellular damage before new muscle proteins can be properly synthesized.

So what are we saying here? Yes, to get massively strong for your size, you can simply bypass all the gym traditions associated with pyramid sets of 12, 10 and 8 repetitions, etc. and lift very heavily, in strict form, with few reps, and take as long a recovery as needed before repeating the dose, intermingled with good core exercises and upper body strengthening work.

The downside? What downside? Once training regularly with weights, there's no real muscle soreness, and you'll acquire a healthy local muscular system that can start synthesizing new proteins almost immediately after every workout. It's the way everyone will be training in the near future if they're serious.

If this is true, then surely everyone would train this way right now?

What we can tell you is that this is exactly the way the strongest weight-class power lifters and Olympic lifters in the world train, and they can't afford non-contractile muscle mass that would force them up a weight category.

For detailed information on these methods, Barry Ross's website is well worth looking at (www.bearpowered.com).

Other Useful Exercises

I have always found that boxing exercises are terrific for upper body and core work. Boxing drills after track training are a fun way to get in some much-needed upper body development.

"Floor-to-ceiling" punchball exercises develop excellent hand-eye coordination and quick reflexes, and speedball exercises can develop powerful chest, shoulders, arms, and abdominals. There is a small but effective trunk rotation that is repeated hundreds of times in a good speedball set, and this can be very good for oblique abdominal development.

The most famous proponent of speedball exercises in athletics was 1980 100m Olympic gold medalist Allan Wells, but the conditioning system of intense circuit training and speedball exercises has been used for many years by "professional" sprinters in Scotland and Australia.

Work with focus pads provides excellent conditioning, as does skipping. Skipping was an exercise used by Lydiard's athletes.

*Paavolainen, L., et al. "Explosive-strength training improves 5-km running time by improving running economy and muscle power," *Journal of Applied Physiology* Vol. 86, Issue 5, 1527-1533, May 1999.

Strength Training Terms

Muscle Actions

Concentric contraction: The muscle shortens while it contracts: i.e., biceps curl exercise. Eccentric lengthening: The muscle lengthens while it still holds tension: i.e., lowering the weight in a biceps curl.

Isometric Contraction: The muscle holds constant tension while neither contracting nor relaxing (i.e., holding the weight still halfway through the curl).

Terms for Resistance Exercises

Open-chain exercise: The extremities (hands or feet) are not fixed in place during the movement: they move away from the body. (e.g., bench press pushes weight away from fixed upper body: Leg extension lifts lower leg and weight away from fixed knee and thigh). These exercises tend to isolate one joint, and bear very little resemblance to real-life activities. They can put immense "shearing stress" onto joint surfaces designed for completely different loading forces. **Avoid these in resistence training for track athletics.**

Closed-chain exercise: The extremities are fixed in place during the exercise. e.g., deadlift, squat: where the feet are firmly fixed as the body extends and opens up. Push-up: Feet and hands firmly on the ground during exercise.

Compound movements: Movements that involve several joints and muscle groups at once: these tend to mimic real-life activities, and many are closed-chain exercises. These include pulling and pushing exercises such as the overhead chin-up, the push-up, as well as the dip, the squat, and the lunge.

Plyometric exercise: Any exercise where there is a very rapid change from a lengthened (eccentric) muscle action to a shortened (concentric) muscle contraction, i.e., skipping, bounding on toes. Also known as SSC exercise these days to confuse us further. (SSC stands for *stretch shortening cycle*). These exercises are thought to immediately activate fast twitch IIB neurons and muscle fibers.

Ballistic exercises: Ballistic means "airborne." **Concentric ballistic exercises** include jumping and medicine ball throws. **Eccentric ballistic exercises** include depth landings, like a gymnast would perform, or catching a medicine ball. The airborne object comes to a sudden stop. These exercises are thought to immediately fire IIB fast twitch neurons and muscle fibers.

Part 10
The Times – They Are A Changin'

Comparing the Principles Used by John Walker & Hicham El Guerrouj

This excellent 2004 article by Robbie Johnston is reprinted here with permission of *VO$_2$ Max* magazine, New Zealand's premier endurance sport magazine.

Robbie Johnston became a runner after being inspired by the deeds of John Walker, Rod Dixon, Dick Quax, Lorraine Moller, and Allison Roe whilst growing up in southern New Zealand in the 1980s. He went on to become a two-time Olympian under the guidance of coach Arch Jelley, won numerous New Zealand titles from 1500m to 10,000m, and remains one of New Zealand's fastest ever distance runners.

He coaches a select group of athletes from his Auckland base, as well as acting as the New Zealand Distributor for the sportswear brand 2XU.

When Hicham El Guerrouj claimed his elusive Olympic 1500m gold medal in Athens it marked seven Olympiads since New Zealand's own John Walker had won the very same crown in Montreal in 1976. NZ double-Olympian ROBBIE JOHNSTON takes a closer look at the two athletes and asks the question "what has really changed in middle-distance running over the last 28 years?"

It is fair to say that both John Walker and Hicham El Guerrouj were very much products of their own particular era and the nature of society at those times. When John Walker dominated the middle distances in the mid-1970s athletics was very much only taking its first shaky steps down the path towards professionalism. Walker's "have spikes, will travel" attitude ensured that he played a lead role in the development of the sport away from the days of strictly amateur, or "shamateur" competition.

The realities for the top echelon of the sport in the 1970s meant athletes were often forced to line up outside meet director's doors at 2am to collect relatively meager returns for their efforts. As few athletes were busier on the European circuit than Walker, it was he who essentially pioneered the athletes' collective demand to be treated in a more professional manner. His actions made it almost inevitable and acceptable that the sport had to reward the athletes whom filled the stadiums and brightened up many a living room television set.

He may well have blazed the trail towards a more professional sport, but John Walker was still very much the athletic product of 1970s New Zealand. Like Peter Snell before him, Walker was good at all sports at school, and he similarly excelled at tennis as a teenager.

Interestingly, it was the sport of cross country running, and not track, in which Walker also competed as a teenager. This path of development could be seen as the first early steps down the road to middle-distance success, as it exposed Walker to a strong New Zealand distance running culture and began to develop his aerobic base. It was also coupled with Walker's semi-rural life at home, where his large amount of manual labour and running to and from school gave him, it could almost be said, an African-type childhood.

Upon leaving his teen years, in which he had been a successful cross-country athlete, Walker sought to extend his talent to events on the track. In the early days it was the 800m, and Auckland coach Arch Jelley was the man who Walker sought out to guide him. As was usual in 1970s New Zealand, Walker worked a normal job – including a stint at a quarry – and did all of his training on top of this. As for coaching, Jelley was a full-time school principal. Only perhaps Eastern-bloc countries and US Universities were employing people to coach full-time in this era. Whilst not a professional coach in today's sense of the concept, Jelley was a very astute coach having developed his methodologies from his own personal experiences and observations of the sport and through many years of working with athletes at all levels, his approach was nothing but professional.

Walker's training environment was largely constituted by a large Auckland running community of the time, based in Auckland's Cornwall Park, Domain, and Mt.Smart Stadium. It was running's hey-day in terms of participants. While he trained with many athletes, Walker found it increasingly hard to find suitable training partners as his ability and career progressed. This was because over time his training pace increased, and also because these athletes were also in the sport for their own reasons – not singularly to aid in the development of John Walker. As we will later see, this is in stark contrast to Hicham El Guerrouj's training set up.

It was from this environment that Jelley was able to quickly shape a talented young Walker into an international athlete. By the age of 22 Walker had broken the World 1500m record, although in the process he was beaten by Tanzanian Filbert Bayi in one of the all-time great 1500m races in the 1974 Commonwealth Games final. Over the next few years Walker became the dominant middle distance runner on the planet, smashing both the 2000m and Mile world records and winning Olympic gold in Montreal. Despite a frustrating few years grappling with debilitating injuries following his Olympic triumph, Walker remained one of the worlds premier milers right up until the late-80s and in the process became the first man to run a remarkable 100 sub 4min miles. Walker only retired from European competition in 1991 at the age of 39 when he was still ranked amongst the world's top 20.

Two key components are evident when analyzing John Walker's development into the dominant miler of his era and his longevity in the red-hot cauldron of world-class middle-distance racing, a longevity that was largely unprecedented until more recent times.
- Firstly, his career-long emphasis upon quality aerobic training.
- Secondly, his preparation for and competion in two seasons per year (double periodisation) as opposed to the more traditional approach of one season per year.

Walker's development as an athlete was seemingly accelerated through the use of double periodisation – completing two seasons a year with a large amount of racing at the ascribed time in firstly the New Zealand/Australian summer season and sometimes in combination with the US indoor season, then later, a European summer campaign.

Walker's seasonal preparations would be split into three distinct periods, generally involving,

1. 8-10 week general conditioning period;
2. 4-6 week specific conditioning period;
3. 8-10 week competition period.

A typical Walker training week in his general conditioning period:

Sunday	Aerobic Run 80-90 min steady
Monday	Aerobic Run 30-45 min easy
	Aerobic Run 30-45 min solid
Tuesday	Aerobic Run 30-40 min easy
	1000m x 5 (2min rec) @ 3k-5k race pace
Wednesday	Aerobic Run 50-60 min
Thursday	Aerobic Run 30-45 min
	Aerobic Run 30-45 min
Friday	Aerobic Run 30-45min easy
Saturday	5k – 7k Tempo run approx 2m45-2m55/km pace
	Aerobic Run 30-40 min easy

Along with double periodisation, the other key aspect in Walker's rise to, and longevity at the top was Jelley's emphasis upon quality training, or more specifically quality mileage – finding the right level for the individual athlete, John G. Walker. A volume and quality that was not too much and not too little, not too fast and not too slow, but just right! Generally for Walker this was in the 110-145kms per week region through both his general conditioning and in the specific preparation period as well. All Walker's aerobic runs were done at a steady tempo (3min45-3min20/km pace generally) – which for most of his local contemporaries meant fast runs!

This last point regarding Walker's continuation of his optimum mileage, after transitioning to a specific phase, is of great importance to his success. This is because his maintenance of good aerobic condition – both in terms of volume and quality – through his specific phase allowed him to continue to improve aerobically while "putting the icing on the cake" with his specific race oriented track work. While other athletes in the USA and Europe blunted their swords by eating into their aerobic capacity with too much over exuberant track work.

Walker by contrast was able to race for periods of months on end, while others fell by the wayside. Walker explained to Tim Chamberlain in a 1984 article that "when we are on the track, we do a lot of 6 laps, 8 laps – steady type running. We call this track work, but it is not really anaerobic work, rather it is aerobic in nature." Track work was always limited to the specific preparation period and carried out no more than 2-3 times a week. In practice, this meant a similar year round framework for training where the emphasis throughout was on good quality mileage, and an avoidance of too much work on the track – an important explanatory factor in his long career.

A typical Walker training week in the specific conditioning period:

Sunday	Aerobic Run 80-90 min steady
Monday	Aerobic Run 30-45 min easy Aerobic Run 30-45 min solid
Tuesday	Aerobic Run 30-40 min easy Mile x 3 (3-4 min rec) @ 3k-5k race pace
Wednesday	Aerobic Run-60 min
Thursday	Aerobic Run 30-45 min 400m x 10 (60sec rec) @ 1500m race pace
Friday	Aerobic Run 30-45 min easy
Saturday	3k – 5k Tempo run @ approx 80-90% race pace effort Aerobic Run 30-40 min easy

The competition period would then focus upon racing and recovery, with training very much being geared around maintaining peak form. This would mean easy aerobic running and fast-paced short distance speedwork / strideouts.

Of course, given the tenure of Walker's career his training did develop over time. This however was really only a fine-tuning, as these key fundamental concepts of his preparations remained constant. Essentially what Walker was able to achieve as his career progressed was to improve his "cruising pace," whether this be from 62sec per 400m as a young athlete down to 57.5sec pace over the mile as his best, or from 6m30 per mile long training run pace down to 5m30 pace, Walker's training enabled him to maintain an improved velocity for the same effort.

This was achieved quite simply because the bulk of his training was aerobic and of high quality – that is a high percentage of Walker's running was close to, what we know today as, his anaerobic threshold. Walker essentially ran the bulk of his training close to his anaerobic threshold – the primary factor around which his training was based. This meant that before even stepping onto the track in his specific conditioning phase Walker was not only very strong from his general conditioning mileage, but he was also already relatively fast from having done a large percentage of his training around his anaerobic threshold. His specific preparations really provided the icing on the cake through assisting him to better withstand the rigors of lactate and race pace. So that was the basic recipe for success for the leading middle-distance runner of the 1970s, but what of today? The sport of track and field, like the rest of the world, has changed quite dramatically in the past 28 years, but just how much do things differ in the early 21st Century when it comes to middle-distance running?

Today track and field at the top level is big business. In Europe, the hotbed of the track and field world, the sport has largely become a sporting version of Cirque du Soleil, with the same athletes performing the same events in the same staged manner, as part of a traveling road show going from city to city, country to country, in a in a never ending quest for performances that will quench the public's thirst for record breaking entertainment.

That Hicham El Guerrouj can nowadays command upwards of US $60,000 for simply lacing up his spikes should be seen as a continuation of a legacy begun by athletes such as Walker in the '70s. More money for the athletes has come at a cost, however. In short, because athletes demand more money, meet directors, sponsors, and the general public now demand nothing short of miraculous performances every time superstar athletes hit the track. In 1998, for example, Ethiopian Haile Gebrselassie beat off three Kenyans in a thrilling 3000m, recording 7min 27.42secs. The time was one of the fastest ever run for the distance, but Gebrselassie later felt obliged to apologise to the crowd, because he fell short of a world record. Why apologise when you win a thrilling race? Because the system is now set up to churn out records, not encourage close racing; the essence of human competition has essentially been replaced by a test of physiology – or who has prepared the most systematically and scientifically (and perhaps, some would say, who has had the best "artificial assistance").

On the face of it Hicham El Guerrouj – the "Prince of the Desert" – and John Walker appear to be two very different athletes; El Guerrouj a lithe (1m76/58kg) North African, Walker an imposing 1m 82, 76kg Kiwi powerhouse. Yet both were able to be the supreme miler of their own particular era.

Just as Walker can be seen as a product of the 1970s 'slowly-coming-to-an-end-amateur-era', El Guerrouj is also very much a product of sport as it stands today. A product of professionalism and the athletic "circus" that track and field has become at the top level.

Despite largely being a third world nation, El Guerrouj's native Morocco operates one of the most systematic and professional sports programmes anywhere in the world. With El Guerrouj very much being the jewel in its lavishly supported crown.

El Guerrouj was talent spotted at the relatively young age of 16 and thereafter groomed for middle distance success by this richly resourced state sponsored national programme. Like Walker, El Guerrouj was initially inspired into the sport by the Olympian efforts of a fellow countryman – Said Aouita 1984 Olympic 5000m champion and multiple world record breaker. It was only natural then that El Guerrouj's early interest centerd upon the 5000m distance. By the age of 18 El Guerrouj had already run a very smart 13min46sec and claimed a bronze medal in the 1992 World Junior Championships (behind winner Haile Gebrselassie) over the distance.

Similar to Walker, El Guerrouj has had a career long coach, Abdelkader Kada. But coaching wise that is where the similarities end. Kada is a professional coach and heads the national programme – a programme that also contains a number of other professional middle-distance coaches, and a fulltime support team of doctors, physios, and masseurs. The Moroccan national programme is based around training centers at 1600m altitude in Ifrane and at sea level in Rabat. The athletes constantly move between these two centers depending on their training requirements at the time. Athletes are generally based with the national squad 10-11 months of the year as full time professionals, effectively only leaving mere weeks each year to spend "normal" time with their families and friends. As part of El Guerrouj's very systematic disciplined programme much emphasis is placed upon the use of altitude as a training stimulus at very regular intervals, and the use of scientific tools to monitor and aid in the fine-tuning of the programme.

Once we delve beyond the peripherals of El Guerrouj's training programme and the environment from which he comes, which are markedly different from that of Walker's, and look at what actually makes the most significant difference to his athletic abilities – that of the actual running training – we see some remarkable similarities. So much so, that it begs the question:

"Has the training required to be the worlds top miler in each era really changed as much as one would logically think it would or should have?"

Kada has pointed out that in the training of his charges they are not creating anything new. Rather, they are making improvements to something that already exists, with the use of altitude and the scientific tools at their disposal to aid in this process. The physiological parameters of the human body have not undergone any change in at least the past few hundred years or so, thus necessitating what can only be described as a fine-tuning of the quality aerobic oriented training that John Walker operated upon in the 1970s and through the '80s.

Like Walker, El Guerrouj's programme is structured by double periodisation – one season geared towards the European indoor season (as opposed to Walker's New Zealand season), the other the European outdoor season. This too has been a hallmark of El Guerrouj's preparations since a young age.

Each season is split into three periods that essentially correspond with the structure of Walker's:

1. General preparation;
2. Specific preparation;
3. Competition period.

A typical El Guerrouj training week in his general preparation period:

Sunday	Aerobic endurance 1hour + easy Rest if overly fatigued
Monday	Aerobic endurance 1hour Power in weights room with plyometrics or hill repetitions
Tuesday	Aerobic endurance 1hour 2000m x 4 (recovery 2-3min) @ 5km race pace
Wednesday	Rest Aerobic endurance 45 min
Thursday	Aerobic endurance 45 min Aerobic endurance 45 min
Friday	Aerobic endurance 50 min easy Strength in weights room
Saturday	Aerobic endurance 45min 1000m x 6 (recovery 2min) @ 3km race pace

A typical El Guerrouj training week in his specific preparation period:

Sunday	Aerobic endurance 1hour + easy Rest if overly fatigued
Monday	Aerobic endurance 1hour Power in weights room with plyometrics
Tuesday	Aerobic endurance 1hour 2000m x 4 (recovery 2-3min) @ under 5km race pace
Wednesday	Aerobic endurance 45 min Aerobic endurance 45 min
Thursday	Aerobic endurance 45 min – hilly and fast Aerobic endurance 45 min
Friday	Aerobic endurance 50 min easy Power in weights room
Saturday	Aerobic endurance 45 min Mile x 5 (recovery 2-3 min) @ 3km race pace

All aerobic runs, unless going very easy, are run at paces from 3min30/km – 2min50/km.

The key difference as El Guerrouj progresses from General to Specific preparation are that his interval runs become either faster, or longer in distance whilst maintaining a similar pace. His steady aerobic runs remain constant. El Guerrouj's workouts during the specific phase are very much aerobic strength oriented – focusing upon good strongly paced over-distance work as opposed to gut wrenching anaerobic intervals.

When we compare this with the John Walker training examples it can be seen that their structure and emphasis are essentially the same. The only real difference being El Guerrouj's gym work. It could be argued that Walker's outdoor oriented and manual labour as he grew up naturally developed his power and strength, something that El Guerrouj, being far slighter in build, has developed through his gymnasium work.

Likewise their emphasis upon quality aerobic running – a high percentage at or close to anaerobic threshold is a hallmark of both periods of training for both athletes. El Guerrouj maintains his own personal level of optimal quality aerobic running throughout both his general and specific preparation phases just as Walker did. Again, similar to Walker, El Guerrouj does not work too much on the track during the year. In fact, at his altitude base in Ifrane all his faster work is done on a one-mile dirt track as opposed to a synthetic track. It is worth noting that the longest run El Guerrouj ever does is limited to 75 mins. This has been forced upon him due to an on-going back complaint which hampers any longer duration running.

One key point of difference, and one that can be wholly attributable to the professional environment from which El Guerrouj operates, is that he is able to achieve what appears to be superior training performances in his interval work during his specific preparation phase. This is largely due to the employment of what can only be described as his training hacks – world-class athletes themselves whose sole purpose is to pace El Guerrouj in all of his key workouts. This is their well-paid role as part of "Team El Guerrouj."

Compare this to Walker where most of his hard training was performed alone due to the environment in which he found himself. One could argue that this was advantageous to Walker in strengthening his mental resolve and toughness – characteristics he displayed so capably in the tense cockpit of big time racing.

Equally, one could argue that the very systematic and controlled training programme that defines the "Moroccan system," coupled with the use of the ever present, programmed "pacing hacks," created an environment that for El Guerrouj, while perfect for gearing him to run the type of races required of today's "athletic circus," was nevertheless to his detriment in out-an-out, "mano-a-mano" championship racing.

Witness El Guerrouj's spectacular "failure" at Sydney 2000 where he was out raced by Kenyan Noah Ngeny when an overwhelmingly red-hot favourite.

Interestingly, it was not until El Guerrouj was beaten a number of times in races in championship races that he dispensed with his pacing services. It was only when he learnt to actually race that the Olympic gold flowed. His Athens triumphs signalled that he had finally overcome the weaknesses that the sports 'Cirque du Soliel' model had ingrained into him.

Has middle-distance running really improved all that much in the past 28 years then? Has the training required to be the worlds top miler in each era really changed that much? Of course El Guerrouj today is running times faster than Walker did in his day. Times that are approximately 2.5-3% quicker. But can this level of improvement really be attributed to training improvements? I suggest not.

From the observations made here we can confidently say that improvements in performance are much more attributable to environmental and societal factors, or what may be described as "variable factors" – the total professionalism of "Team El Guerrouj," his full-time coach, his training hacks, his coterie of medical advisers, his investment planners, and the track and field "circus" he competes in being prime examples of such. Secondly, we can just as confidently assert that training for middle distance success at the highest level has changed minimally, if at all. This conclusion is simply based upon observing the physiology and training of the two athletes – factors which can be thought of more as "fixed" variables.

As far as physiology goes, both athletes were exceptionally gifted in that they were able to sustain large volumes of aerobic conditioning at a steady pace. As the human body has not changed since the 1970s, and as both athletes were similarly blessed talent-wise, it cannot be said there is much difference when it comes to the actual physiology. The development of their talent – by finding the optimal amount of steady-state aerobic conditioning, in combination with dedicated, systematic training and a willingness to subject themselves to physical hardship – is where the coaching element comes in. Again, while Abdelkader Kada has at his disposal more scientific tools and a more conducive environment than Arch Jelley, both were similar in that they employed whatever means available to discover their respective athlete's "optimal aerobic mix" of quantity and quality; Kada relies on a mix of intuition and science whereas Jelley was more a student of human behaviour – a knowledgeable and astute teacher.

In the end, it all really gets back to one Arthur Lydiard and his journey of "self-discovery" in the 1950s and 1960s that lead him to conclude that aerobic conditioning forms the basis of middle-distance success. That the premier miler in the 21st century uses a schedule based on Lydiard's founding principles, notwithstanding all of the improvements in science, technology, economy and training environments, says it all and how simple the sport of running can really be when we strip it back to its fundamentals. And, to paraphrase Winston Churchill, those aspiring middle distance greats "who do not learn from history are doomed to fail," may be something worth remembering.

The Stats:

Hicham El Guerrouj	**John Walker**
1m76/ 58kg) 14/9/74	(1m82 / 76kg) 12/1/52
800m 1m47.18	800m 1m44.9
1500m 3m26.00	1500m 3m32.4
Mile 3m43.13	Mile 3m49.08
2000m 4m44.79	2000m 4m51.4
3000m 7m23.09	3000m 7m37.49
5000m 12m50.24	5000m 13m19.28
Olympic 1500m & 5000m Champion 2004	Olympic 1500m Champion 1976
Athlete of the Year 1999, 2001, 2002	Athlete of the Year 1975
World Records 1500m, Mile, 2000m	World Records Mile, 2000m

Part 11
For the Nerds

A Review of Recent Research

Physiology researchers all seem to use differing expressions and conventions for various running intensities. From what I can see there is no "one convention," and intensity levels are all expressed differently in the various endurance sports and in different research papers.

So, in this review of current literature, I've standardized the terminolgies so that I don't confuse myself or you. (My apologies to the researchers.)

For instance, vLTP (velocity at the Lactate Turnpoint) mentioned in one study is exactly the same as vLT (velocity at Lactate Threshold) mentioned in another. I'll just call it vLT in this chapter. Similarly, there are various ways of expressing maximal oxygen uptake and the pace at which it is reached: I just call it VO_2max or vVO_2max in this chapter.

Is There an Optimal Training Intensity for Enhancing the Maximal Oxygen Uptake of Distance Runners?

This was the question posed by a recent study published in the journal "Sports Medicine."

The bottom line appears to be that at lower levels of initial cardiovascular fitness, high volumes at lower percentages of VO_2 max are all that are required to be run at to elicit a significant training response, and this may be true up to moderate levels of performance. In other words, the less fit one is, the easier it is to raise one's maximum oxygen uptake through volume training at lower intensities. However, it gets harder to elicit a noticeable change in VO_2 max once very high levels of fitness have been established.

This may be because "all cardiorespiratory adaptations elicited by submaximal training have probably already been elicited in distance runners competing at a relatively high level."

To quote further from the study's abstract:

"Well trained distance runners have been reported to reach a plateau in VO_2max enhancement; however, many studies have demonstrated that the VO_2max of well trained runners can be enhanced when training protocols known to elicit 95–100% VO_2max are included in their training programmes. This supports the premise that high-intensity training may be effective or even necessary for well trained distance runners to enhance VO_2max. "

So the bottom line for Lydiard-system athletes is that sub-maximal oxygen uptake and efficiency can increase for years (explaining why performances can get better each year despite no change in measured oxygen uptake), and once the highest possible level of aerobic efficiency has been reached, intense running at 95-100% VO_2 max is necessary; i.e., longer intervals with equal or shorter recovery at 5000m to 3000m pace but no faster.

Midgley, A. W., McNaughton, L. R. and Wilkinson, M. "Is there an Optimal Training Intensity for Enhancing the Maximal Oxygen Uptake of Distance Runners?" Source: *Sports Medicine,* Volume 36, Number 2, 2006, 117-132(16).

The Relationship Between the Lactate Turnpoint and the Time at VO_2 Max During a Constant Velocity Run to Exhaustion.

This investigation examined the relationship between the running velocity at threshold pace (vLT, velocity at Lactate Turnpoint) and the time that VO_2max can be sustained for (TVO_2 max) during a continuous run to exhaustion at the minimal running velocity that elicits VO_2 max (vVO_2 max).

The main finding of this study is that the relative time an athlete can hold at threshold (vLT) demonstrated a significant positive correlation with the relative time he or she could hold at vVO_2 max.

The physiological mechanism by which the lactate turnpoint may influence the relative time held at VO_2max has not been elucidated, and further research is required to substantiate these findings.

In other words, the faster you can run at threshold pace, the longer you can hold your VO_2 max pace.

The author's interpretation of this study for athletes and coaches is that each anaerobic intensity on the training pyramid depends on the level of development of the intensity levels below and, by definition, this continues all the way down to the lowest levels of aerobic threshold.

Midgley, A. W., McNaughton, L. R., Wilkinson, M. "The Relationship between the Lactate Turnpoint and the Time at VO_2 Max during a Constant Velocity Run to Exhaustion." *Int Journal of Sports Medicine.* 2006. Apr; 27:278-82.

Kenyans Need to Train at the Right Intensities Too!

French running physiologist Veronique Billat's team analysed the training diaries and physiological profiles of 13 male and six female Kenyan 10k runners. The major significance of this study is that the subjects were élite athletes competing on the international circuit.

The study focused on training time spent at three discrete physiological paces:

- vLT (velocity at lactate threshold). Billat defines vLT as the pace at which the blood lactate concentration rises by 1 mmol/L to between 3.5 and 5mmol/L.
- vVO_2max (velocity at maximal oxygen uptake). This is a very intense pace that can be maintained for only about six minutes, with blood lactate levels around 8-10 mmol/L.
- vΔ50, the intermediate pace between vLT and vVO_2max, which is, as this study confirms, very close to 10k race pace.

Training at vVO_2max for the Kenyans took the form of interval workouts – e.g., 20 x 400m or 6 x 800m;

Training at vΔ50 involved long repetition interval sessions – e.g., 4 x 2,000m – with short recoveries.

All other weekly distance not specified in the study was run at less than vLT, e.g., 90-minute runs at an easy pace.

There were three groups studied:

M1 was one of two male groups, whose members performed faster-paced interval sessions with a significant proportion of weekly kilometers run at vLT (10.9 km), vΔ50 (6.8 km) and vVO_2max pace (7.8 km). They averaged 158 km/wk, with an average best 10k time of 28:15.

M2 men focused on training at vLT (25.4 km/wk) with minimal vΔ50 work (2.4 km/wk) and no work at vVO_2max. This group averaged 174 km/wk. The average best 10k for this group was 28:54.

The **F** (female) group completed significantly shorter weekly distances than the men, but included fast-paced intervals sessions at vΔ50 and vVO_2max pace, but no work at vLT pace. Their average best 10k was 32:22.

M1 athletes were significantly faster than M2 athletes over 10k, a feature that is associated with superior VO_2max, vVO_2max and vΔ50. vΔ50 and vVO_2max were the two biggest predictors of 10k performance. vLT does not relate as strongly to 10k performance, probably because 10k pace is at greater than vLTP pace – ie at v¢50.

A number of athletes in the M2 group were unable to reach a true VO_2max during the step test as they fatigued too quickly at the fastest running pace. Their performance was not limited by oxygen consumption, as this had not yet reached plateau. Thus it was not their cardiovascular systems that failed them. Their lack of training time at vVO_2max pace meant they were very inefficient when approaching this pace on a treadmill.

It does seem to make physiological sense to train at all three of these paces.

The Kenyan women in the study trained in a similar fashion to the M1 group but did no training at all with vLT. It is possible that their vΔ50, and therefore their 10k pace, could be boosted by adding in sessions at vLT.

References
Medicine and Science in Sport and Exercise, 2003, 35(2), 297-304 and 305.

Aerobic Processes Far More Involved in 400m-1500m Racing Than Previously Thought

It appears that there are large inaccuracies in the old methodology used for calculating Oxygen Debt (The Oxygen Debt Method or OD method), and recent research has corrected this as follows. The new and more accurate method is called the Accumulated Oxygen Debt Method, or AOD.

The consequence of this is that the aerobic work content of these distances has been significantly underrated by theorists up until now.

Distance	AOD new method	OD old wrong method	Difference %
400m	46 +/-4% aerobic	25% aerobic	21-25%
800m	69 +/-4% aerobic	50% aerobic	19-23%
1,500m	83 +/-3% aerobic	65% aerobic	18-21%

References:
AOD data: Spencer, M. R., Gastin, P. B. and Payne, W. R. "Energy system contribution during 400m to 1,500m running, *New Studies in Athletics*, no. 4/1996.
Oxygen debt data: Newsholme, E., Leech, T., Duester, G. *"Keep on Running. The Science of Training and Performance."* -1994 -John Wiley & Sons Ltd.

More Discussion on VO_2 Max

Anyone can achieve significant increases in VO_2 max readings by training at VO_2 max intensities, but without working on the lower intensities to raise the aerobic ceiling as well, this spectacular increase in efficiency and capacity isn't sustainable and definitely not repeatable from year to year.

Other questions are raised about the true meaning of a very high VO_2 max reading; it is a measure of oxygen consumed, but how effectively that oxygen is used in the system or how long this maximal consumption can be maintained are more important.

We now know from good research that there is much more to world-class middle distance or distance performance than a huge VO_2 max. How fast one can get from A to B is what's important, and this can be dictated by factors completely out of the oxygen uptake arena.

Many years ago, athletes of the caliber of Olympic marathon champion Frank Shorter, world marathon record holder Derek Clayton, and legendary US Olympian Steve Prefontaine all had their VO_2 max readings accurately ascertained. Prefontaine's was well and truly above that of Shorter or Clayton, however he was certainly not dominant over Shorter on a regular basis over track distances such as 3000m through to 10000m. Shorter was able to perform at world-class levels right down to 3000m.

Here are their respective best performances, along with their laboratory-measured VO_2 max readings: note that the three mile times, representative of 95% VO_2 max pace, were done in the same race, where Shorter lead with 200m to go and Prefontaine just got by. It's also apt to point out here that Shorter was able to outkick 1972 Olympic 1500m bronze medalist Rod Dixon over 3000m in the lead up to winning his 1972 Olympic marathon crown.

Shorter (VO_2 max 71.3): 3000m: 7:51.3 miles- 12:51.8, 5000m- 13:26.6, 10,000m- 27:45.9, Prefontaine: (VO_2 max 84.4): 3000m: 7:45 3 miles-12:51.4, 5000m- 13:21.87, 10,000m- 27:43.6

When we realize too that the great female marathoner Ingrid Kristiansen had a VO_2 max measured at 71.2 while running the marathon at 2hr 21:06, and Shorter ran the marathon in 2hr 10 at virtually the same measured VO_2 max (71.3) we see that there's more to this than meets the eye.

To confuse things further, the great Derek Clayton twice smashed the world's best marathon time in the 1960s, ending up with a 2:08.33: however, his VO_2 max was measured at "only" 69.7.

Despite a huge ability to consume oxygen, Prefontaine was nowhere as efficient a runner as Shorter, and Clayton was incredibly efficient. The actual amount of oxygen required to power an athlete through a 5000m at the elite level isn't as important as the efficiency of the athlete. The important factor is at what level the body starts to run into acidosis; this is defined by the anaerobic threshold, which is most safely developed by running at high sub-threshold aerobic efforts, and by TVO_2max: how long VO_2 max pace can be maintained.

Part 12
Winter Running &
Cross-Country Training

Winter, for any athlete not on the international circuits, is a time for getting strong and developing the aerobic systems to maximum. Winter races are all at "aerobic" distances, and therefore a highly aerobic winterlong preparation is not only a very good idea but highly desirable for any serious middle distance athlete wanting to improve on the track.

Steve Ovett, 1980 Olympic 800m champion and 1:44.0 runner, won UK titles over 400m *and* cross country as a junior. Sebastian Coe also won youth titles over cross-country before developing his speed and anaerobic capacity. Peter Snell won a New Zealand cross country title as a senior. Rod Dixon was third in the world cross country championships twice. John Walker was 4th in 1975, his world record year for the mile. Middle distance runners with an endurance base can run cross-country extremely well because they have usually developed a large aerobic and anaerobic capacity, and cross country is often a series of surges and fast running interspersed with relative recoveries. Who better trained than a 1500m runner to cope with that sort of running? It is different from the unrelenting pressure of a road race, where anaerobic threshold dictates the outcome far more.

It is not necessary to delve too far into anaerobic sharpening work in preparation for major winter races, such as National cross-country titles over 12km. VO$_2$ max intervals on cross-country courses can be a very fun way of getting ready for an aerobic peak, and these can be done once a week, or alternated between races.

Winter can also be a great time to develop and sharpen leg speed, as the preponderance of aerobic running can leave the legs quite nicely recovered. A winter spent developing the aerobic systems, and sharpening leg speed on short easy days, can pay big dividends in summer.

Writer, historian, and cross-country master Roger Robinson joins us here to expound on the virtues of sausages in winter. I include his very good writing here because I believe Roger's famous "sausage sessions" can be adapted to any team's winter cross-country preparations on hard training days, and sausage sessions can be progressively raised in intensity as peak racing periods approach. Lydiard would call it a structured fartlek, but "sausage session" sounds like more fun.

(**Roger is an award-winning writer who made New Zealand and English cross-country teams to the world champion-ships, and was Professor of English at Victoria University, Wellington. He learned his craft at Cambridge University in England, and throughout the 1980's was one of the best masters runners in the world.**)

Training for Cross Country

A Study in Sausages

Roger Robinson

Winter is here. I can tell. In Wellington, the wind has dropped. The cat takes her fresh air by sleeping on the chimney pot. My nylon fashion shorts feel chilly round the cheeks. Halfway through a run, I get cravings for beef tea. The moist earth, fermenting underfoot, smells richly as you run along. It is the season for cross-country running, the second-oldest sport in the world.

First Principles

People have run cross country since the first sabertooth chased the first caveperson, and the first nymph ran away with the first shepherd. When Pheidippides ran his 240 kilometers from Athens to summon help from Sparta, he did so along mountain paths described to me by a historian of ancient Greece as "little more than glorified goat tracks." Not on roads, not even cart tracks in 490 B.C. Nor did he go near Marathon, but that's another story.

For messengers and soldiers, shepherds and goatherds, gamekeepers and poachers, cross-country running through history has been a profession, and for every able-bodied person, a necessary part of everyday life. Modern African runners like Keino or Bayi who are reputed to have run awesome distances to and from school look utterly normal against the full scope of human history. Those of us confined to cars and concrete are the freaks.

Cross country is thus not only ancient, it is absolutely natural. The runner who does no running on the country is, in my view, missing one of the most essentially human and innately pleasurable of all forms of exercise. Yet, too many new runners of the modern running boom are coy about cross country, reluctant to get their colourful shoes wet. You can see them running wholly on the tarsealed roads in Cornwall Park and Central Park. To be only a road runner is like being a swimmer yet never leaving the municipal baths for the beach or the river. We are mechanically designed to run cross country rather than on roads.

That is the second major point. Cross country, as well as being natural, is infinitely varied, and therefore physically beneficial and mentally stimulating.

The country changes from area to area, from season to season, from day to day. I remember with delight how the 1976 NZ Nationals course at Invercargill was a hard-baked racetrack on Friday and a slushy swamp by Saturday afternoon. Things can even change during the race, as the ground cuts up or packs down under the eager feet. I remember with less delight getting caught in spikes too short for the increasingly slimy topsoil when it came on to rain at Whangarei in 1974. There is never a dull moment, and training must somehow take account of all these eventualities and variables.

So the underlying principles of any program of cross-country training should embody these two essentials:

- make it natural
- make it varied

And the third, if you plan to race, or just to get maximum benefit from your training, is

- make some of it fast

Why Run Fast?

One of the beauties of cross-country training is that often the terrain does a lot of the work and makes many of the decisions for you. Runners in cities from Dunedin to Aberdeen willing to venture off the easy harbor roads gain enormous cardiorespiratory and muscle-building benefits from simply running those formidable hills. At the top level,

Bryan Rose and Jack Foster have shown that constant-effort running on rugged terrain can bring results that might take years of mentally destructive track repetitions.

But one of the hidden enemies of continued progress for any runner is habit. You can get too good at one kind of training, and then you simply retain efficiency at that session. More common among cross-country runners are the many I have known who operate all the time at what I call three-quarter effort, and who fail to rise above that in races. To improve, you have to keep pushing the body a little into the unknown. That is why I would qualify Jack Foster's advice that you should find a form of training that works for you and stick to it.

Yes, fine, provided that you have something of Jack's adventurousness and irrepressible capacity for work. I believe there should always be some modification of the successful system, a new element, a new stress for the body to learn and adapt to. The country does much of this for you – a day of rain, a stronger wind, a fall of leaves, and you have got your new factor. You should also build it in more systematically to a well-constructed program of speed running.

What I want to propose is a training pattern which makes possible that push into the unknown for runners of absolutely any level of ability. It is a way of working for speed over the ground – all kinds of.ground – that remains faithful to the true character of cross-country by being natural and varied. It is suitable for a solo runner and even better for groups. It works on any kind of terrain. It is economical of time, fun to do, and it gets results. It is called the sausage session.

The Structure of the Sausage

The principle is easy. Instead of running round a measured lap against the clock, you simply run repetitions of a period of time, making up the route as you go along. The permutations then are countless. The "sausages" or efforts, can be of any period of time from 1 minute to 15 minutes (4 x 15 is marvelous marathon training); or they can be mixed (alternating 2 and a half and 5 minutes makes a good, psychologically manageable early-season session); or they can taper up or down; as what we call, not very accurately, a pyramid (e.g. 2m30s, 5 min, 7m30s, 10min, 7m30s, 5min, 2m30s: that's quite a tough one).

Studying the Menu

I rarely know beforehand exactly what form a sausage session is going to take. If it's sausage-day, we gather and gossip as we jog out to the chosen area – about 15 minutes warm-up. The last moment is soon enough to decide the format of the session. Spontaneity is the essence.

Where we go and what we run depends on a number of factors:
- The time of season (see The Sausage Season: p. 208)
- The current racing program (do nothing too hard close to a major race)
- The company and their preferences
- The weather (it's good to get accustomed to wind and rain, but there are limits)

But the main point is not to plan in too much detail. The route, especially, should be improvised as the session proceeds. Many places possess a spacious area of varied country like Auckland's Cornwall Park or London's Wimbledon Common or the numerous Lincoln and Washington Parks around America. Wellington, where I now live, is rather limited in this respect, but the following typical mid-season 6 x 5 minute session should give the idea:

- Round the two sportsfields at Prince of Wales Park, behind the Showgrounds – muddy grass with one small hill
- More on the grass, then up the steep hill of the town belt – a real gutbuster
- Some downhill (not too fast), then fast on the good grass of Macalister Park, behind Athletic Park
- More on Macalister, including the sloppy little lowest field, then up the road and on to the Berhampore Golf Course – greasy hills
- Hilly golf course with muddy forest tracks adjoining
- Wakefield Park – grass, with some quite firm puddly paths around it

And so on. In a single session, we have run on at least six different surfaces and incorporated uphill, downhill, and fast, flat running, in the open, under trees, with the wind and into it. At Christchurch, we used to mix the sharp hillocks of Burwood Forest with the fast, open beach or springy sawdust tracks. Often the going changes radically in the middle of an effort, just as it will do in a race. And there is still ample room for variation and initiative.

Leading up to the annual Vosseler Shield we may chase up and down the steep bank at the north end of Macalister Park or even go on to Mount Victoria itself where that precipitous race is run. Close to championships time, I like to steer for all the muddiest patches. If you don't train on it, you can't expect to race on it, I have been quoted as saying.

Nutritional Benefits of Sausages

It is not easy to tabulate all the benefits of this kind of training, but here are some:

Mental
- Maintaining and generating interest: there is no repetition, the scenery is always changing, and therefore so is the challenge
- Developing what I like to call a "philosophical attitude"; i.e., you learn to accept hills or mud as facts of life, not afflictions to shy away from; and equally to make use of the good going while it lasts
- Teaching pace-control over all kinds of terrain
- Teaching transitions from one surface to another at race effort
- Familiarization with group running (see "Sausage Groups" below)

Physical
- General strength, especially leg muscles
- The posture and balance muscles, hence the speed for long sessions. Leg speed.
- Heart and cardio-respiratory system
- Ability to run well when tired
- Mental/Physical

"Proprioception:" that is, that instinctive self-awareness that enables us to move over rough ground without necessarily looking at it. This may indeed be the greatest benefit of all. I suspect it is a skill that can be severely damaged by too much road running.

The Story of Sausages

In Australia recently, I heard runners use the term "sausage session" without the slightest comprehension that I had any special connection with the phrase or the training method. So perhaps it is time to tell the story briefly.

When I was a lad in the 1950s, the formula for success was track repetition running. Bannister, Zatopek, Pirie – all the greats were the product of intensive repetitions, usually over 400 meters. Advocated by Germany's Woldemar Gerschler and espoused then by most European and American coaches, it is a very Germanic system – methodical, disciplined and measurable.

By the time I was at university, another wind was blowing, which had originated in the freer atmosphere of Sweden's pine forests as Gosta Holmer's idea of fartlek (speed play) and then traveled round the world via the sandhills of Portsea, Victoria. This was the ideal that running expresses the runner's personality, and so, in Holmer's words, "the training is fixed according to the runner's own individuality." Fartlek, like repetitions, is fast-slow training, but the efforts and recovery are dictated by temperament and terrain, not by a concrete kerb and the stopwatch.

"Sausages" blend these two opposing principles. As students, we tried everything, from old-style English hare-and-hounds, with a fast "run-in" to finish, to high-volume Zatopekian track repetitions. We began to move towards an emphasis on long intervals, x 1 mile or x 2 miles, which may be an English peculiarity, with Gordon Pirie in those days the leading exponent. I still remember the day in 1961 when Mike Turner, then on the threshold of his long international career, ran 9 x 1 miles on the Cambridge University track, wearing out a sequence of partners just as the insatiable Roman Empress Messalina was reputed to have exhausted her lovers. I submitted after seven. A remarkable decade of international runners was to emerge from Cambridge under Turner's discerning but uncompromising inspiration.

From these long intervals on the track, we moved to long intervals off the track. Five minute repetitions on the road (usually 6 x 5 minutes with 2 minutes recovery) became a Turner institution – three out, three back, no way to chicken out. Then, away from Cambridge for three years, I adapted the idea of timed intervals to a variety of 5 minute or approximate one-mile sessions up and down the sandy hills and heather-covered commons of south-west Surrey, where I was now living. Once or twice I worked up to 10 x 5 minutes, each on different ground. Meanwhile, back on the splashy paddocks and glutinous ploughed fields of Cambridgeshire, Mike was piloting a file of runners round a regular 10-mile circuit, divided into efforts of 2 minutes, with one-minute's walk as recovery. Because this somehow resembled a long succession of bulges separated by a short string, it became known as the sausage session.

I returned to Cambridge for research in 1964. Mike, also working on a PhD, was now an established international, and I was the Surrey (i.e., provincial) champion. We wanted a lot of hard running over the country, but we took sessions at least once a week with groups of younger student harriers. So my series of cross-country miles and his string of 2 ~ 5 minute efforts became combined into the general practice of running intervals without any set route, but measured by time rather than a known circuit. How far we ran in each 5-minutes depended on the going. In that fenny mud, it was often not very far.

We still called them sausage sessions, but the string now tended to become tangled as the leaders veered around to pick up tiring runners who had dropped off. We could have called them "Follow my leader" or "Country Reps." If the computer age had been born, we might have called them LIOCROW (Long Intervals On Country Run On The Watch), or FRIGS (Free Ranging Interval Group Sessions). But sausages pre-date computer language.

Sausage Groups: Legalized Cornercutting

Sausage sessions are probably the best form of group training ever invented. The basic principles are again very simple. Take it in turns to lead. Give the leader complete freedom to choose the route. Give those following complete freedom to stray off that route if they like. Like many social breakthroughs, it thus depends on the legitimizing of crime, in this case cornercutting.

What happens is that the leader should run in a series of curves or bends, looping around completely if the ability-range of the group is wide. The slower runners behind simply cut the corners. Or, if a slower runner is taking a turn in front, the faster runners behind run wide at the corners to increase their distance. The only rule is never to go in front of the nominated leader.

This means that the better runners travel further than the slower ones, but everyone, fast or slow, runs the same session, n x n (4 x 5 minutes, or whatever). They all get the same effort, the same recovery, the same terrain, the same benefits. Nobody gets left behind or deprived of recovery time, nobody gets "beaten." And even a top runner can provide for an off day by a few sneaky savings on the corners. The more unscrupulous cut the corners to save strength so they can run everyone else's legs off when it's their turn to lead.

Everyone in the group also gets the same basic experience in the pressures of racing: experience at leading a panting, spluttering, heel-tapping mob over difficult ground, and experience at hanging in with that mob, running relaxedly among feet and elbows with bits of mud in your eyes and mouth, and experience at positional running, tailing or flanking the group, lining up your approach to the corners, hills and jumps. The jostling pressures of the cross-country race will then hold no surprises.

One "caveat." Big, mixed groups are fine in the early season and do a lot for club morale. We used to have packs of more than 20 runners scampering round Hagley Park in the early Seventies at the beck and call of Brian Taylor, the other great name in the history of sausages. But by mid-June, when the pressure comes on, it's best to subdivide into small units of relatively even ability.

Sausage Country

Solo, you can run sausages anywhere. I've done them along the San Francisco waterfront and across the prairies of Illinois, in Buckingham Palace Gardens, and on the palmy beach of Castaway Island, Fiji. For a group, you need fairly open country. Sports fields, farm paddocks, golf courses, beach-and-dune country are all good.

An area like Cornwall Park, Auckland, is ideal. Narrow paths are no good, as they prevent cornercutting and string out the group too much. After dark, it's possible to run a session on a floodlit sportsground or alongside good street lighting.

My own sausage intake is twice a week in the racing season. One session is the longer intervals I have just described, aiming at about race pace. The other is shorter and faster. Typically, this will be the infamous 75/45's, i.e., up to 16 repetitions of 75 seconds fast, with 45 seconds recovery. It's really just a session of 400s, with emphasis on recovery rather than sheer speed, and run on the free-range principle instead of constipating yourself round and round the same circuit.

(Editor's note: the above constitutes an excellent VO$_2$ max interval session)

Find good, grassy footing on pleasant sports fields or parkland. Not everyone will want this session, but personally, having muscle fibers that range between slow twitch and dead-stop, I find it indispensable if I'm to be at all competitive. This is the opportunity to practice wearing spikes, too, which too many runners neglect in winter.

A Monday-Wednesday or Tuesday-Thursday pattern is easy enough to manage, though the exigencies of work sometimes intrude. With quieter days between and a long run on the weekend, this makes for an interesting, honest and profitable week's running.

The Sausage Season

One major point remains to be made. Sausages provide a wonderfully flexible and controllable training structure. The runner or the coach can control development of fitness over the season to a nicety. Quantity and intensity of hard running can be planned long term and finely tuned short term.

Again, the principle is simple. Just increase the total quantity of fast running as the season progresses. Total "quality time" is the guide. I tend to use the colloquialism "20 minutes' worth" or "30 minutes' worth." At the beginning of the season, April in New Zealand or October in the Northern Hemisphere, 20 minutes quality is enough.

So sessions this month might be:
- 2m30s- 5m- 2m30s- 5m- 2m30s (17m30s of quality)
- 4 x 5 (20 minutes quality)
- 3-4-5-5-4-3 (24 minutes quality)
- 7 x 3m (21 minutes quality)

Edge it up. Senior men should get to 30 minutes' worth by the end of May, when the first races are coming, 35 in June and 40-45 in July. Women and juniors adjust, of course, according to race distance.

So this is another secret ingredient of sausages, the quality-time factor. If you are used to running at race speed for the full race time, over varied country and in all weathers, you are equipped to do the same in the race. You will thus be in a small and privileged minority when the gun fires. Plenty of your rivals will have run more miles, or have better speed or skills, but not many runners have trained to race all the way in cross country. Yes, it's hard to convince yourself on a cold July or January day to do yet two more efforts of 5 minutes. But those are the two that will matter on the last lap of the championship three weeks ahead.

Sausages for Beginners

Whether you are a sub-30 minute 10k gun or a novice coping with his or her first cross-country season, you can benefit, I believe, from much of the above. You have to be dedicated to handle repetition 800 meters on the track, but anyone can enjoy a few 2 minute stride-outs at their own speed on pleasant country.

You should probably not try anything like the full sausage program until you are running close to an hour every day, more or less. But even before that, try popping in a couple of one-minute "efforts" into your next daily run, then do three or four next week, six a week later. Forget about taking your overall time. Never mind the length, try for quality. Train your body to recover as well as to suffer.

Scientific Sausages

I have written about this training in personal and layman's terms, but you will find nothing inconsistent with the latest studies on oxygen uptake, proprioception, the capillary system, or peaking. There are other effects, such as developing conditioned recovery-reflexes in the heart, which I suspect have not yet been studied. But my heart has its secrets, as they say in the Mills & Boon romances.

One possibly controversial point is the mixing of anaerobic work with racing. I can only say that provided you don't race too often, or train too hard close to the race, it works. What the sausage system provides is a perfectly balanced program of aerobic and anaerobic work, with the flexibility to fine-tune the balance between them from week to week and day to day. I always had reservations about the rigid divisions of the phases of training that Arthur Lydiard used to advocate (buildup, hill-springs, etc.), and I'm glad about his move over the years towards the kind of "adjustable balance" that a sausage program provides. Jack Foster, Rob de Castella and Steve Jones use much the same mix.

Winter Sausages in Summary

Sausages:

- train the skills of running fast over various kinds of terrain

- provide a training program that can be precisely modulated to control fitness and to serve the racing program

- train the ability to run hard for the whole time of the race

- are ideal for group training and developing group-racing skills

- are suitable for almost all levels of ability and states of fitness

- are interesting and (believe it or not) enjoyable

- are natural and varied (see 'First Principles', above)

- they work

I have seen D team runners become A team runners, and club runners become internationals, on a diet of sausages. Juniors and veterans are lifted to higher levels by them. Clubs can be transformed, as Canterbury University was in the 1970s (provided, of course, they are lucky enough to have a great organizer-motivator like Brian Taylor).

In essence, what I have been describing is neither a magic formula nor a pseudo-scientific 'method,' but just a practical and interesting way of carrying out certain simple and traditional training principles. It has been called "fierce" but I prefer to see it as purposeful fun. It gets you into the country of your choice. It makes you fit. It is natural and varied. It sharpens the appetite. As a way of getting through the winter, it's a lot better than watching television.

Ten Rules for Racing

1. Ease off training before the race, for about three days; more for a marathon. Recharge the batteries; take some quiet, enjoyable runs. But don't rest too much. If the body is used to a hard training regimen, you may have trouble sleeping or mentally relaxing if you cut back too severely or too suddenly. Taper off; but keep a sense of readiness.

2. Food: On the day before, eat amply but avoid anything unusual or explosive (soft or dried fruit, muesli, etc.) On race day, find what suits you. The best rule is "little and early."

3. Gear: Make sure you're comfortable. Take clothes and shoes for whatever weather conditions are remotely possible. And check that your shoelaces are not worn thin. Why waste all that training for a broken shoelace?

4. Expect the unexpected. Allow travel time for traffic jams or punctures. Carry spikes of different lengths for cross-country, in case it rains suddenly. Carry toilet paper. Check your watch. Make 101% sure you know where the start is, and 102% sure you know what time it is.

5. Check the course. Especially for cross country, work out your track over any difficult sections. Always be sure how many laps there are – top-class runners have blown their chances more than once in the World CrossCountry by getting that wrong. Know what to do at the finish.

6. Countdown to the start. Have a regular timetable of preparations, a pattern of habit. My own goes roughly: 1 hour, visit toilet; 45 minutes, start jogging; 20 mins, light strides and stretches; 15 mins, take off track pants, put on race shoes; 10 mins, final toilet (bushes, less queuing); 8 mins, drop sweats, two or three stride-outs.

7. Get warm, physiologically. That means doing at least a little fast-tempo striding before any race except possibly a marathon.

8. Keep cool. The opposition are human, even if sometimes before the start they don't look it. Ignore them, hate them, or be friendly to them, whichever suits your personality; I prefer the latter. But don't get scared.

9. Be ready for the start. Most important, have your track pants off at least five minutes before. Anything else can be thrown off.

10. Sex before the race? Fine, it will do you no harm. But try not to distract the starter.

PART 13
Chris' Corner

With Olympic Coach Chris Pilone

Drive for Gold

Like most of the rest of New Zealand, I watched Hamish Carter's disappointing performance in the triathlon at the 2000 Sydney Olympics. Carter was ranked No. 1 in the world at the time and had been expected to do well but finished well down the field. He was 29 years old at the time, and I assumed he may compete for another year or so and then drift out of the sport. I was somewhat surprised when Hamish rang me in mid 2001 proposing a formal coaching association. Hamish was a member of the Bays Cougars club where I was a distance running coach. After some discussion, I became his overall coach, and Mark Bone, a former national swim coach, remained as his swim coach.

Prior to having a formal coaching association with Hamish, I had known him for a number of years. He occasionally turned up to some sessions for middle and long distance runners I coached in the late '90s. Most of my background as a coach came via my own running career and also Athletics New Zealand's IAAF coach education programme which I found very beneficial. At this time I had become a keen road cyclist, having given up running in 1999, and had good knowledge of road cycling training. Occasionally I called upon the knowledge of well known Auckland cycling coach Paul Leitch.

At first Hamish used a system of alternating weeks where he emphasised cycling one week and running the next, with 4 days of swimming every week. Using this system he achieved a bronze medal in the 2002 Commonwealth Games. Early in 2003, Hamish proposed a dramatic change in his training whereby he did all three triathlon disciplines in training every day for between two and five days in a row. He basically waited until, in his terms, he "punctured" and then would have between one and three days easy training to recover and then repeat the cycle again. This type of training was high volume but very aerobic based. This resulted in quite a big increase in the volume he was doing, and he quite often used training camps in towns like Pauanui and Rotorua south of his home in Auckland.

This change in training produced some good results immediately and, despite doing no specific speed work for running or cycling, he won the Aussie Sprint champs, a distance that doesn't really suit him. In the mid part of 2003 he suffered from the flu, and while he performed relatively well at the 2003 Worlds (5th place) and was able to secure an Olympic berth, I wasn't totally confident with his 2month sharpening period before the 2003 Worlds. It became apparent to me that he was suited for good high quality aerobic work for both running and cycling but had to be very careful with anything even slightly harder. Although he had finished 5th in the World Champs and qualified for the '04 Olympics, I still had a gut feeling that his training wasn't quite 100% right for him.

Interestingly, Mark Elliott, the Tri NZ High Performance Manager and Bevan Docherty's coach came to exactly the same conclusion shortly after the 2003 Worlds in Queenstown. Carter was now 33 years old and, as a runner, was relatively slow. His only chance of out finishing anyone at the end of a 10km running leg of an Olympic distance triathlon was if he arrived at the 1km to go with more left in the tank than his competitors. For 2004, I planned an even more strengthbased program for Carter with his running or cycling tempo work mainly being lactate threshold type of work and any VO$_2$ max work carefully placed and carefully controlled. Although they were involved in events that are poles apart it was probably a similar situation all those years ago when Peter Snell used to be able to outkick his great rival George Kerr over 800m even though Peter didn't have as much basic speed as George.

This slightly different type of program proved instantly successful when another triathlete I coached, Nathan Richmond gained the remaining NZ Olympic place for men. For Olympic year Hamish used a single periodisation, i.e., he didn't try to peak for the 2004 Worlds which were held in May with the Olympics following in August. This race was won by Kiwi Bevan Docherty with Hamish 35 to 40 sec back in 6th. Hamish's main aim in doing the 04 Worlds was to maintain a relatively high ITU ranking just in case he decided to race in the year after the Olympics. World Champs carries double points for ITU rankings.

I was appointed as assistant manager/coach to Mark Elliot for Triathlon NZ's Olympic team. This enabled me to have direct input into all our Olympic arrangements and our pre-Olympic training camp in Pau, Southern France. I have always had a good relationship with Mark, but prior to the Olympics became aware that that he was outstanding in his job as HP Manager for Triathlon NZ. Although we were both coaching athletes who were potentially archrivals this never affected our relationship. Sadly, shortly after the 2004 Olympics, Mark resigned as Triathlon New Zealand High Performance Manager, although he still coaches Bevan Docherty and we do keep in regular contact.

Hamish had a trouble-free buildup in NZ before leaving for the France training camp. During his 5 weeks training in France he trained better than ever before, and I realized he had a good chance of perhaps winning a medal in Athens. At the training camp, we had a great environment with development athletes there as well as the Olympic athletes and, for part of the time, marathon runner Dale Warrander. At the camp the athletes trained very hard but also had a lot of fun. The hard training but low-key environment was a significant factor in Hamish's and Bevan's first and second place finishes at the Olympics.

The only slight negative in France was Hamish was so fit he started dishing out severe beatings in training to various training partners and, on occasions, Nathan Richmond. I believe this may have affected Richmond's performance in Athens. During this time, Liam Scopes was a regular training hack for Hamish. He was very good at making Hamish moderate his training. Hamish was so fit he just wanted to go harder and longer. Between us, Liam and I managed to keep him under relative control although I did have the occasional blunt conversation with Carter to do with moderating his training and also keeping Richmond and him apart. Also, despite reports in the New Zealand media to the contrary, Docherty and Carter only occasionally trained together before the Olympics. As time went by at the training camp, Mark Elliott and I realized this was a good thing and started making sure they didn't train together at all! If they had done some harder sessions together, we could well have ended up with a couple of overtrained athletes rather than medals!

Exactly two weeks out from the Olympics, Hamish did a hard bike to run session. A 2hr hard ride followed by 8 x 1000m on the track with 45 sec jog rec. The other Olympic athletes were at the Olympic opening ceremony but the other triathletes at the camp, Liam Scopes, Clark Ellice and Kris Gemmell were in attendance and took turns in pacing Hamish on the track. The session went very well despite it being in the middle of the afternoon and very hot. After this session I thought Hamish was a likely winner in Athens but refrained from telling him. He however, must have realized he was doing well because all training partners were treated to a big feed at McDonalds!

Interestingly, the above session is really the only really hard session that Hamish did prior to the Olympics. The running part of the above session I would describe as a pretty solid VO_2 session but because of the short recovery and the number of reps, athletes can't really blow themselves apart. Carter did all his VO_2 sessions conservatively before the Olympics at a controlled effort. He didn't absolutely kill himself during the sessions. I also made all his VO_2 sessions different. He never repeated the same session so didn't get caught up in the time distance/thing but carried out the sessions at an intensity that was optimum for him. Liam Scopes who had run 1500m in the low 3:50s before turning to triathlon was an invaluable training partner for Hamish during this time and was able to moderate Carter, who invariably wanted to go harder and longer!

The last two weeks before the race was easier training with one run session of 200m in 33 to 34 sec followed by 200m float in 40 sec. He did this for 5 laps, jogged for 5 min then repeated the session. Liam Scopes did part of the session making sure Hamish didn't go mad and blow himself apart. During the whole last two weeks I never discussed with Hamish a possible outcome to the race. It was mainly a case of keeping him relaxed after a superb level of fitness had been achieved. The very nice running rhythm that Hamish showed at the end of the run in the 2004 Olympic Triathlon was a direct result of a very good aerobic background and VO_2 max running sessions carried out at correct intensity and with good form.

Despite the above specific sessions, I believe the cornerstone of Carter's Olympic result was the very good aerobic buildup he did from January '04 until mid June '04. During this time, he did long aerobic running, long aerobic riding and some hillwork for both cycling and running. The hillwork for both running and riding was still aerobic. The hardest thing he did during this period for riding and running was definitely below lactate threshold intensity.

Race day for the 2004 Mens Olympic Triathlon was quite simply unforgettable, particularly if you happened to be a New Zealander. Peter Snell and Murray Halberg winning gold medals over 800m and 5000m in 1960 will, for me, always be New Zealand's greatest ever sporting moment, but it was nice to play a small part in the Carter/Docherty one-two finish that perhaps can be mentioned in the same breath as Peter's and Murray's achievements all those years ago.

Footnote:
I sometimes wonder if Arthur Lydiard had turned his great mind to triathlon coaching what he would have come up with. Quite possibly in physiological terms something very similar to the training that Hamish Carter did for the 2004 Olympics!

Part 14
War Stories & Real Case Histories

This whole chapter is a smorgasbord of true running tales that the athlete and coach may relate to. No matter what level you've reached, if you've messed up a major race, take solace in the fact that *you're not alone*!

The author and his former training partners made a number of classic training mistakes, which they are happy to share with anyone else who fancies taking the step to the next level.

At the end of the day, careful planning, execution of the plan, and a cool head win out over wild adventure every time. Take it from some "could've beens" who know!

How Craig Mottram Came Back from the Dead

In 2006, Craig Mottram made a stunning comeback from a patch of very poor form in Europe. After a great Commonwealth Games campaign where he dominated the 5000m final and broke up the African pack a kilometer out, he was outclassed by the brilliant Kenyan youngster Augustine Choge over the last 200m.

After a short phase of recovery and more endurance base running, he returned for a European campaign in good form, recording a stunning 7:32 winning time over 3000m early on his tour, but the emotional and physical toll of his previous summer caught up with him, and he lapsed into a series of poor results. His results became unpredictable, with finishes at the back of fields that he would have been consistently dominating a few weeks earlier.

Craig's 3000m time dropped from a winning 7:32 in a world-class field to an "out the back" 7:47. His flat-out 1500m dropped to 3:38, and he finished about 18th in a stacked field doing that. So things weren't looking good for a defence of his IAAF World Cup 3000m title that he'd won 4 years earlier.

News reports filtered back from Europe that he was considering pulling out of the Oceania team for the World Cup and coming back early from his European tour because he was so jaded.

Somewhere, a month or so out from his World Cup, he had a change of heart. He decided he was going to "stand up" and defend his title, rather than going back to Australia with his tail between his legs. So the first thing he did was straight out of Arthur Lydiard's bag of tricks.

He jogged very slowly. For day after day, until he felt more like his normal self. Then he introduced some moderate uphill efforts on the parkland near his London base, without bursting his boiler. Then he did some longer anaerobic threshold runs, and relaxed and jogged a lot. His "snap" was returning very quickly, and the decision was made to definitely defend the 3000m title in Athens. A very late entry was world 5000m record holder and multiple world champion Kenenise Bekele of Ethiopia.

What would you do in the final days leading up to a race against one of the fastest finishers in world athletics? Especially if your form had been poor?

More speedwork was needed, right? If you're like 99% of modern athletes and coaches out there, that's exactly what you'd do.

And more speedwork was exactly what Mottram *didn't do*. On the Friday before the Sunday race, he went to a track and did several 200m strideouts at his current perceived 3000m pace. He took plenty of easy recovery.

If you can call this relaxed session "speedwork," then this was it. The times for the 200m strides? 30 seconds. A time schoolgirl athletes could do in training. But 30 seconds for 200m, repeated 15 times in a row, is 7:30 for 3000m.

He jogged easily the next day and fronted in Athens ready for action. He took off for the line well before the last lap, with Bekele right on his hammer, and in the last lap exploded away again to win by about 4 seconds in 7:32.19, a new Oceania record. His last lap was about 53 seconds. This was a stunning upset.

"I just ran well and he didn't. That happens in running sometimes" said Mottram later.

Kynan

Kynan had been training religiously with his club in suburban Melbourne for years but had made no real progress since his late teens and early 20s. He had once reached times as good as 1:51 for 800m and 8:50 for 3000m steeplechase and 3:50 for 1500m. In fact, despite training harder and harder, his running had come to a standstill and he was on the verge of giving up. He was a 31-year-old graduate chiropractor when he came to stay with me on a clinical residency.

We analysed Kynan's typical regimen and even in winter we found a club training culture that revolved around "speed training" several days a week. This would entail repetitions of 200m, 300m, and 400m, with short recoveries, all at hard fast paces. The repetitions would consist of sets of 2 x 200m, 2 x 300m, and 2 x 400m, and the paces would average around 26 seconds for 200m, 41s for 300m, and 58 seconds for 400m. Of course, the average speed for most of these was faster than his sustainable 800m speed, and had no relevance to the aerobic systems that winter training should be developing. His hard days were Tuesday, Thursday, and Saturday, which was either a race or a hard time trial over something like 1000m. The days between the hard sessions were devoted to short recovery jogs during the week, or a longer run on Sunday of 1 hour 30 to 1 hour 40.

The bottom line was that when Kynan entered at my clinic, he appeared terribly unhealthy. His face was puffy and swollen, and his skin was stretched and tight. He was continually eating sweets, salted potato crisps, and strong coffee with several sugars. His urine was as dark as molasses. His last race had been a disaster: 10k road in over 36 minutes going as hard as he could. He used to be able to do about 31 minutes easily. He was exhausted from the moment he got up. His blood pressure was elevated.

His symptoms represented classical adrenal gland exhaustion. The puffy face, fluid retention, and frequent "hits" of sugar, salt, and caffeine were all signs that his endocrine system was highly stressed. Essentially, he was self-medicating to restore some semblance of normal function in his highly stressed system.

The adrenal glands sit on top of each kidney, and they are involved in multiple hormonal pathways that can regulate blood sodium and blood sugar; therefore, they regulate blood pressure and energy levels. The adrenals also produce adrenalin, a natural chemical that closely resembles heroin and morphine, and is used medically to bring people back from the dead, literally. In the cortex of the adrenal gland, the stress hormone cortisol is produced. This is closely related to the drug cortisone. The adrenals are nick named the "stress glands" or the "get up and go" glands. In this case, Kynan's "get up and go" had long since "got up and gone." The constant high-level demands of training without aerobic restoration runs bombarded his endocrine system into submission, and the next step along the line would be early Type II diabetes and Cushing's syndrome, a disease of adrenal exhaustion.

The Outcome

We got Kynan to take large amounts of vitamin C and vitamin B5 (pantothenic acid) which are "stress vitamins." We got him to drink pure water only and eat healthy meals high in fresh vegetable and fruit content. He also had to throw his stopwatch away and spend his mornings jogging as slowly as possible in a local forest until he actually felt his strength returning. His residency was about 12 weeks and it took six weeks of slow jogging before Kynan felt that he was enjoying his running again. At first, 20 minutes of jogging wiped him out all day but eventually he found he could go for up to an hour and totally enjoy the experience. His aerobic systems were slowly returning to normal.

In six weeks, he lost over 7 kilograms in fluid retention alone, and started to look like an athlete again. He no longer craved chips, sweets, or coffee. He was able to run aerobically at speeds that were impossible two months earlier.

As his aerobic systems improved, Kynan naturally started to feel an urge to run faster. So I got him to run a "steady-state" time trial over a flat 8-kilometer course, which he covered easily in 29 minutes. This was equivalent to the pace of his last 10km road race.

He went back to two more weeks of very slow jogging in the forest, with some runs extending out to 90 minutes, and did another time trial over the same distance. This time it was a very respectable 26 minutes, done easily.

Eventually Kynan returned to enjoyable running and won a number of fun runs around Melbourne. "Compartment syndrome" injuries that he had developed during his "silly training" period prevented him from getting back to a high level in track racing, but he is happy and healthy now, and capable of getting well under 2 minutes over 800m as well as enjoying long runs.

Stephen

Stephen, 27, a former schoolboy champion, had not run anywhere near his potential since leaving school and going to university. The main problem was his enthusiasm. As a youngster, he had won most of his schoolboy 800m and 1500m races off natural talent, some good aerobic training, and a taste for a "big kick" in last laps.

As he moved into senior ranks, he moved into a pattern of intense weeks of training followed by leg soreness, illness, or outright injury. Some injuries became chronic, and to compensate for lost training time, Stephen would train even harder. He had never learned to run easily on a daily basis, as his club training group tended to place a focus on fast track-based preparations.

When he came to me, he was also on the verge of giving away the sport. He had spent the previous years "playing" with sports as diverse as cricket, Australian Rules football, and karate. The football and karate training had kept him in reasonable physical condition, but there were also old heavy bruising injuries to the leg muscles, which compromised our approach later.

The approach with Stephen had to be very cautious. Although he had a ton of natural speed and copious natural endurance ability, these were the very things that could harm his progress. He was such a tough customer that he could "push" his training and not realize the early signs of fatigue. So we devised a very cautious training plan aimed at getting Stephen back near where he should be over a number of months.

He was under strict instructions to gradually build up his weekly mileage until he was able to handle 9 or 10 "slow" hours of running a week on parkland and trails. This he did, and he reported to me in April 2006 ready for a winter's training. In the meantime,

he had hopped into a heat of the state 800m championships in February and popped a 1:56 time off 150 kilometers a week in jogging. This race had not been planned for or advised, but it showed that he had some real potential.

Since Stephen had missed so much training time over the years, his real level of performance and experience was about the same as the junior athletes we had been training. He made the same basic mistakes, too. We had to make sure that Stephen went to great lengths not to push long runs too hard. With a couple of months of more aerobic base, including a weekly "strong aerobic" session around a hilly park trail, he recorded 31:13 for a 10km on the road. He had a couple of promising cross-country results, too.

The whole winter was geared to getting a decent aerobic base back into Stephen prior to exploring some of his potential on the track. Even that plan had to be revised at one stage when he'd been "pushing the envelope" with late nights of study and part-time work; he promptly caught a nasty flu that lingered for over 6 weeks during the major cross-country racing period and had him bed ridden. When he got back to running, he kept re-injuring a groin strain. I checked him out and found an imbalance in his low back that was aggravating his hip flexors: chiropractic adjustments and some muscle balancing work got Stephen over that hurdle, but it meant he had to stretch all major muscle groups on a daily basis and be super-careful in his approach.

With the scheduled winter races that could have prepared him for a winter peak wiped out, we were running out of options. He had a few weeks to prepare for his Australian National cross-country race, which he'd entered. The only viable option was for Stephen to jog very slowly week by week until his strength returned and do a couple of sessions approaching high aerobic race speeds in the weeks leading to his Nationals. His earlier aerobic background along with the restorative aerobic running did the trick, and Stephen ran the National cross-country titles strongly, finishing 22nd amidst many hardened competitors with much longer racing pedigrees. This was a good run and yet again demonstrated untapped potential.

With the summer racing season approaching, Stephen set himself some challenging goal times over 800m and 1500m. His main goal was to establish himself at state level over 1500m and get into the national 1500m championships.

We decided to continue an aerobic preparation for as long as possible into the summer track season before commencing race-specific anaerobic work. Stephen would need all the aerobic base he could get to be able to race well at the end of the summer.

We decided to pair Stephen up with a track training partner, Tony, 39. Tony was experienced and cautious, but still fast enough and fit enough to make track training tough for Stephen.

Stephen recorded his current PB of 3:51 in winning his heat of the Victorian state championships, easing up. The next day in the final he couldn't back up, most likely because his recent aerobic base was sufficient for only one PB in a weekend, not two. He needs several more years of aerobic running to reach his potential.

In the national championships, he missed out on the final by a couple of hundredths of a second, but placed himself well tactically before being swamped by men who'd recorded 1500m times under 3:40 that season. So all in all, he did well for someone who was about to give up the sport.

To cap his summer, he did a couple of weeks of easy aerobic work after his national 1500m attempt and won an Easter road mile in Bendigo with a big finish in front of a crowd of several thousand. This is a good start for his winter preparation, which will be focused on consistency, avoiding injury and illness, and accumulating miles in the legs before some faster sessions aimed at bringing his aerobic systems to maximal capacity for a winter cross-country peak.

Tony

Tony, 39, had recorded some excellent 400m and 800m times as a youngster, but had never progressed from there. After a winter of long running in his first senior year of competition, Tony did a lot of fast track training with a middle distance coach and recorded 48.6 for 400m and 1:49 for 800m. Thereafter, he did a blend of short aerobic runs, hill reps, track reps, and "long" runs of under 1 hour, which kept him at a high level, but never improving for the next 16 years. He never approached his PB times from his first serious season again. He had never run for more than one hour continuously, or more than 100 kilometers, in any one week in all that time.

We put Tony onto a whole-winter regimen of upping his aerobic volumes considerably. Because he was well-used to short fast runs, the lower intensity longer runs were no problem mechanically. It took Tony several weeks to get used to the different feeling of fatigue that long runs induced and also to get him used to slowing the pace. Eventually he managed to run 2 hours or more every Sunday in the hills and hold an

average volume of 150 kilometers a week. This was a huge change for Tony. He maintained his leg speed with regular sprint drills on Thursday nights before aerobic runs on parkland. Tony recorded a 32-minute 10k road time early in winter and ended up getting 12th in the state half-marathon championship on the road in awful conditions, just a couple of minutes behind the winner. Not bad for a jumped-up 800m runner pushing 40 years of age.

The first track race was to be a 1500m race at the Victorian Milers' Club. This race was merely to start the season and establish a frame of reference, so the only "quality" training that was done was early-season hill-work to prepare Stephen and Tony for later track work. Stephen found that the hill training made his legs very stiff and sore, even though we started with only a few short repetitions and nursed him along very gradually, with easy aerobic jogging days in-between hill sessions.

Tony, who was far older, didn't have anything like the problems Stephen did because he had an unbroken string of years of running under his belt. Tony did complain of feeling "washed out" after a few early low-key sessions though. This was typical of the excitatory effect of hill training on the central nervous system, even though slow bounding and springing seem so "easy" to do. In Stephen's case, we felt that the hill work was exposing old injury sites and scar tissue in his calf muscles to new trauma, so we stopped doing it and got him to do easy striding exercises on the flat during aerobic runs for several weeks.

The first race came and Stephen ran 3:59 feeling like a "tractor." The winner ran away in about 3:51, and there was nothing that either athlete could do to maintain contact at that stage. Tony ran 4:03, feeling like he was "flat out" the whole way!

As the summer progressed, we gave both athletes hard sessions based on realistic goal 1500m and 800m times on Tuesdays, and these were designed to fine-tune the preparations for Saturday racing. Aerobic Sunday runs approaching 2 hours were continued until January, when we reduced the volume of these runs to enable the runners to freshen their glycogen stores amply before commencing very fast work. Easy recovery runs of an hour or so continued every second day, and morning jogs on track session days continued.

Both athletes competed a number of times over 800m and 1500m. Even though Tony was able to push Stephen to the limit in some track training sessions, even "beating" him in some, he wasn't able to find the right race situation to churn out the times his sessions indicated he was capable of.

Tony would make basic mistakes like taking off too soon in an 800m to "get a time," rather than concentrating on going for a "win" in a slower time. In fact, because he was 39, he was starting to focus on Australian age-group times each time he ran, rather than simply racing to win.

Stephen recorded 1:52.9 for 800m that season, even though he was often shaded by Tony in training. Tony recorded 1:54.1 for 800m, his best time in over 8 years. In one tactical race, he split two much younger athletes who had recently recorded times around 1:51. 800m racing requires near-perfect conditions and pacing for a PB to be possible, and these don't always appear on cue in a track season.

Over 1500m, their natural difference in endurance showed up more. Stephen got his time down to a PB of 3:51, while Tony recorded 3:57, his fastest since he was 21.

Chris

In 1987, Chris Pilone had come back from the United States absolutely "fried" from a racing tour. He plunged back into a diet of hard sustained running that took him further "off the boil." By the end of 1987, his running had reached such a low ebb that he wasn't even listed in the top 30 New Zealand contenders for the up coming 1988 World Cross-Country championships to be run in Auckland. From memory, his flat-out 10,000m time had gone way over 31 minutes, which was merely his cruising speed a few years earlier when he had won Auckland titles over 10k track and 10 miles road.

We talked about things over the phone and decided to look at what Chris had been doing. What I saw straightaway was screamingly obvious, looking from outside the box. Too much hard "grinding" training of one type, without any let up. No leg speed running. No running approaching VO$_2$ max. Just sustained runs at or near anaerobic threshold. Then long sustained Sunday runs, which were also too fast. No easy recovery days. So he was a glycogen-depleted, tired, ratty distance runner who had no hope of getting down to his potential times in the near future if he kept going the way he was.

Chris is now a terrific coach, having coached Hamish Carter to Olympic Gold in the triathlon, as well as managing a large group of elite athletes. A lot of his understanding is based on having learned the "hard way." At that time, neither he nor I knew much, but we decided that we could "tweak" his program successfully by picking each other's brains.

The first thing I think we did was get him to jog very slowly twice a day over short distances on Monday, Wednesday, and Friday each week. Then we got him to drop his regular repeated "effort runs" straight up Auckland's steep conical Mt. Eden, where his

heart rate must have maxed out. Although the cardiovascular system was getting a workout, he was too tired to benefit, and the intensity would be surely depleting the glycogen he needed for fast race-specific pace running for shorter distances.

Then we replaced that hill session initially with sessions of 1000m intervals at around 29 minute 10k pace, which was within Chris's earlier scope and was a realistic target to get him onto the team. Chris found that his system didn't tolerate these intervals with equal recovery very well; looking back now they were a little too fast for his recovering state. You need good glycogen stores to be able to run 1000m intervals at potential 10,000m race pace or faster.

It was clear to me and Chris that he needed something to kickstart his system into a higher realm, so we dropped the interval distance right down to 400m at about 65-66s, with 200m float recovery in about 45 seconds. He would do about 8x 400m, and we called this a "VO$_2$ max" session at the time.

This work he could cope with better, and he recovered quickly. We would alternate a Tuesday session like that with a short leg speed session on Thursday (4-6 x 150m stride, 250m jog recovery), and then look for a race on Saturdays to get him back into racing shape. Eventually the Wednesday became a longer easy recovery run, but Mondays and Fridays were incredibly easy for Chris after his notorious overtraining episode: they were just short recovery jog days. Sundays were still a good long run, with no need to run hard.

Chris thrived off this change and pretty soon this translated into a rejuvenated athlete who decided before Christmas that he was going to make the New Zealand team in the February trials or die trying. My brother Colin and I were both building up his morale with each successive good track result, and like a lot of athletes, he just needed encouragement, a little shift in outlook, and a light at the end of the tunnel.

To cut a long story short, he pushed classy New Zealand 3:35 1500m runner Peter O'Donoghue over the whole last lap of the Auckland 5000m title, in humid conditions, with a thumping last lap around 60s, for a time around 14:11. Considering Chris' 1500m best at the time was 3:58, this was very promising.

Later he did the same in the New Zealand 5000m track titles, finishing second with a similar thumping last lap, pushing 3:37 runner Phil Clode the whole way and demolishing many finer prospects on the way through. He was a man on a mission.

In the interim, in the New Zealand cross-country trial, with 8 men to qualify, and with Rod Dixon guaranteed a spot, it was all on for Chris. He ran himself right out to qualify in 7th place.

By the time the world championships had arrived, his confidence and focus were 100%. Chris ran his guts out to finish as 2nd New Zealander home in about 73rd place, outkicking highly performing Australians Brad Camp and Pat Carroll in the final straight. The crowd went berserk. By this stage, he'd acquired a cult following in his quest, and legend has it that he didn't need to buy himself a beer for many months in Auckland.

But, as you'll soon see, our future successful Olympic triathlon coach still hadn't learned enough! **Like a good computer, he needed the information punched into him!**

Part 15
NZ Coach Chris Pilone on Easy Days and Overtraining

It's the simplest rule there is when it comes to any type of training.

Stress + Rest = Adaptation.

It's also probably the rule that is ignored the most as well. Stress without rest usually leads to poor performance, illness, or injury and, in some cases, all three.

In setting up any training program, I think the most important part is to define what an easy day is. An easy day allows the body to not only recover but also adapt to the previous stresses placed upon it. In simple terms, this means that in key training sessions you should be able to perform the same or slightly better than previously.

Have I overtrained? You bet I have, and I remember those occasions well! It was the late '80s or possibly 1990. My flatmate Ken Moloney, a very well performing 10km runner and I decided we would train for the Rotorua Marathon and perhaps another marathon later in the year. We launched into 100 plus miles per week, some of it done very hard. About this time Phil Clode shifted to Auckland and, along with several others, we had a pretty good training group.

At first we were running what we called our basic 15-mile loop in 1:32 to 1:35. We would do this loop every Tuesday and Thursday morning and run again at night. One Tuesday or Thursday morning Moloney and Colin Livingstone, who has contributed cartoons to this book, proceeded to carve out the "Basic 15" in 1:22. Colin later described it to me on the phone as an "aerobic cruise", but then proceeded not to run another step for three months!*

The "puncture rate" among some of our training partners was pretty high! Injury, illness or just being plain stuffed were the usual reasons. Our easy days or socalled easy days were 30 to 50 minutes in the morning and 60 to 70 minutes at night. The pace wasn't slow either. The hard days in some cases became horrific. For various reasons none of us seemed to have jobs! Phillip Clode's capacity to absorb hard training and emerge still talking became legend! Moloney at one stage became so annoyed with this habit, he didn't talk to Clode for about a week despite being on group runs with him on a regular basis.

Between three and four weeks before the Rotorua Marathon, Moloney and I ran 26 miles over a hilly course in close to 2:30. In those days, we ran for Takapuna Harriers, and the club with Moloney and me plus others thought we had a very good chance to win the teams' race. I think it was 4 or 5 runners to count.

In the Rotorua Marathon itself I was sitting in the lead pack quite comfortably at half-way but then proceeded to blow up and descended backwards through the field like a stone! I ended up running in the 2:40s and relied on a wellmeaning spectator to hand me jelly beans to give me enough energy to get to the finish. Moloney started a bit slower than me but was in the top 4 or 5 at 30km and quite close to the lead. He then blew in a similar fashion to me and was trying to get jelly beans off the same person as me!

As we both groveled to the finish, various Takapuna team members came past us. Despite being two of the better runners in New Zealand, we didn't even make the Takapuna counting team! Considering Moloney had a 28:19 10km PB and I had run 2:20 or 2:21 at the Rotorua Marathon twice previously, (Chris was a previous winner of this event) to say our results were disappointing was something of an understatement. My next marathon with similar training was also a disaster. I think I was a DNF.

BEWARE THE WORDS OF THE KISS OF DEATH:
"Bloody hell! You know how fast we've run?"

These were the words I uttered years earlier, about a month before the Fukuoka marathon. Colin Livingstone and I had just pounded out a Waiatarua circuit with two miles added in 2hrs 19 mins. We averaged 5m33s per mile over the whole course. My subsequent Fukuoka marathon was not memorable.

Looking back it was quite apparent that some of our training was too hard and that the recovery between some of the hard or long running was totally inadequate. We got caught up in the euphoria of some of the hard training we were doing and adequate recovery went out the window!

So what is an easy day?

To me it means a considerable reduction in both intensity and duration. *As far as I am concerned a long run, even if at quite a slow pace, is not an easy day!* For an elite runner doing between 70 and 90 miles per week an easy day could be maybe a jog of 30 minutes in the morning and possibly 20-40 min at night. **Intensity should be low.**

For those doing less, it could be that a short run of 20 to 40 min would be quite sufficient. In simple terms, an easy day should be a considerable reduction in both volume and intensity. In some cases, it may mean a day of complete rest. For the athletes I coach, I have either hard days or easy days. There is nothing in-between. A hard day could consist of long running or some type of effort session or perhaps speedwork. Generally I use a combination of the following hard and easy days.

1. Hard/Easy

2. Hard/Hard/Easy

Don't do speed work or effort work on successive days. In extreme cases, I will get a runner to use a heart rate monitor to make sure they run slow enough on easy days. So make those easy days really easy and you will go a lot better on your harder days and, in the long term, will probably perform better in races. Making your easy days very easy and having a good definition of what they are won't make for fancy mileage totals in the training log but the boost in your performance could be huge.

Footnote

Many years (quite a few actually) after the great Rotorua Marathon debacle I revisited the Rotorua Marathon. It could have been in 1996 or '97 and I would have been in my late 30s. I was jogging 30 to 40 min on my easy days. I had done some good long runs and once per week was doing a session of slow aerobic type hill reps, probably at lactate threshold intensity or a fraction easier. I couldn't tell you how many miles per week I was running (it wasn't a hell of a lot!) but I do know I ran 2:28 or 2:29 in the marathon quite comfortably. Age and experience had taught me a lot, and it was far less painful than the slow drawn out grovel to the finish line some years previously!

* Colin Livingstone maintains that a hilly 15-miler in 82 minutes was reasonably routine in his overtraining phase, but as he was also gainfully employed mowing lawns all week, it certainly affected his racing. It didn't stop him from running, though. As a true training monster, the running continued.

Part 16
More On Overtraining

Malcolm: His Intense Training Story

When I was running at national level in Australia in the 1980s, one of my training partners was Malcolm Norwood, an Australian junior champion who had smashed Robert de Castella's Australian U-20 3000m and 5000m records and had won everything going around. He'd run times as good as 1:50 for 800m through to 48 minutes for 10 miles, at 19 years of age. On the track, he'd run 13:43 for 5000m at 18. He was used to dominating his usual training group and would train very hard frequently. Often he could absorb the training, but sometimes in a big race situation he would be vulnerable.

When he changed his running to a far more aerobic program under Chris Wardlaw, his 5000m came down to around 13:29, and he later ran a 61 minute half marathon in the IAAF world championships. His marathon debut at the Twin Cities Marathon in October 1991 was victorious in a world-class 2:12.11. But he never ran anywhere near his ability in international championship track races on his earlier high-intensity program.

I believe Malcolm was "over-cooked" with his intense sessions, which were faster in chunks than most state level runners could run in a flat-out race. He could do sessions such as 3 x 1500m with 3 minutes recovery, averaging under 3:55, but there was no need for this type of intensity so often.

Despite his impressive sessions, or because of them, I have a distinct memory of lapping the poor guy in Australia's annual Zatopek 10,000m track race. He did one hard session too many, too close to the race, and had nothing left. When the glycogen tank is near-empty, the racing carburetor will sputter under pressure, and the athlete will have a curious fatigue that does nothing for confidence or race predictability. This is both a physiological and psychological thing, and has to be avoided at all costs.

This potentially world-champion athlete did similar yet faster sessions a couple of years later leading into the 1990 Auckland Commonwealth Games 10,000m final that I believe he was capable of running away with. Instead, he ran well below his best. In earlier years he'd run away at will from top-class fields to win New Zealand and Australian senior cross-country titles in dominating displays. He was also one of the very few Australian athletes to have beaten Steve Moneghetti over cross country in a state title. At the time, Moneghetti was consistently in the top six in the world cross-country championships.

Keith's Story: How I Thrived on Aerobic Running

Lydiard's long run rescue works for lots of people, especially if they have a good natural endowment of slow twitch fibers. Long running certainly never hindered me as a youngster, even though I was a bit too enthusiastic sometimes and paid the price.

Barry Magee, at the end of this book, recounts how he was instructed by Arthur Lydiard to run the Waiatarua hill circuit of 22 miles on three consecutive days, because he'd had a form slump at the end of a racing season. Shortly after, he experienced stunning form once again.

I was coached by Barry for several years before I left New Zealand. Once, when I was 20, I'd run poorly in the Auckland Road Championships over ten miles. My training partner, Chris Pilone, easily won the title in close to 49 minutes. I was totally out of sorts and finished 3 minutes back. I was lucky to get selected onto the Auckland team for the upcoming National Road Championships. I think I'd overdone a faster session a few weeks earlier and it left me in a hole. This was all from inexperience and not being in tune with my body.

I'd placed highly in several quality road races earlier in the season, and on one occasion broke a record at my club's annual 5-mile road race, recording 23:30 to smash the existing record by 90 seconds, easing up in the last half because I'd caught all the back markers. It felt fun. The previous record holder had been Commonwealth Games 10,000m finalist, Phil Watson, so my running was looking promising. My training was basically aerobic running morning and night, and plenty of it, with weekend races.

In physiology terms, it was all medium pace aerobic to sub-threshold aerobic work, with a Saturday threshold effort every week or two. A too-fast session of 200 strideouts upset the applecart.

After my failure in the Auckland championships, Barry instructed me to run two consecutive Waiatarua circuits the following weekend. This I did, with a steady 2 hour 24 minutes on the Saturday, followed by a 2 hour 23 minute effort on the Sunday.

The next week I hopped into a track race over 3000m. I jogged about 8 miles to the track for my race before running home. I ran 8:23 for 3000m pretty easily, with the next guy running over 9 minutes. Then I ran home the same way. I'd done no fast work recently whatsoever apart from the 200s a month earlier. The next day was another long run in the hills. About 40 miles for the weekend. At the time, I think my PB was 8:20, done in a track race with very good competition the summer before.

The next weekend was the New Zealand 10-mile (16k) road title on a hilly circuit in Whangarei, Northland. For some reason, I didn't get enough warm-up in. When doing decent mileage, I always responded very well to a long warm-up.

The gun went off, and I didn't feel like being there. I just put one foot in front of another, feeling sorry for myself as I was heading to another bad performance. At the halfway mark, an official yelled out that I was 33rd and my time was 26:33. That really annoyed me, and as I was going to bomb out anyway, I thought I might as well sprint for a few hundred meters to see if I could snap out of the doldrums.

This sudden change of gear probably jolted my system back into VO_2 max. I went past runner after runner over the next 8 kilometers, and pretty soon I was looming up on a group of top guys fighting it out for the finish. I just waltzed right past very good guys who I thought I had no business doing that to. One was new Auckland champion Chris Pilone, another was the extremely consistent Dave Sirl, a multiple New Zealand champion over track, cross country and road, and another was Bruce Jones, a former Australian cross-country champion.

I finished seventh in 49:31, about 45 seconds behind the winner, Kevin Ryan, who'd beaten Paul Ballinger (later a 2:10 winner of the Fukuoka marathon) and Tony Good from Canterbury. In those days, every man and his dog ran good amounts of strong mileage, and reputations meant nothing if you hadn't been putting the work in. From memory, the then-40-year-old Professor Roger Robinson, who has also contributed to this book, finished about 5th in 49:26, making him the fastest distance veteran in the world at the time.

New Zealand *Runner* magazine said that I was the "fastest man on the road in the last half," but if the halfway time was correct, my berserk negative split resulted in a hilly last 5 miles about 30 seconds faster than my recent PB, set on a flat course. It certainly felt that good.

Interestingly, the winner was trained by Magee, the second-placegetter by Arthur Lydiard, the 4th man, Max Cullum, was trained by Magee, and I was 7th, also trained by Magee!

What did Barry Magee do with me to turn my season back on? Chris Pilone says it was this simple: 1. Recovery week 2. Big Aerobic Volume stimulus weekend 3. Small VO_2 max stimulus (3000m track race) and Aerobic Stimulus (long run) 4. Aerobic Recovery Week.

I believe Barry Magee's rescue tactic of two consecutive long runs in two days kick-started my aerobic system to a higher level.

Unfortunately, two weeks later, while running, I injured my lower back jumping out of the way of a car that was spinning out of control on a wet night, and that was that. I stiffened up over several days and from there on descended into weeks of sciatic pain and respiratory infections. Having left my secure, creative job at Radio New Zealand to train "full time" before an anticipated US road racing tour, my position was precarious. Eventually I came back to running, but it was a long haul.

I repeated that tactic the next year to win the Wellington 10 mile road title, going away in the last 2 miles to win by a couple of hundred meters in a good time for a hilly course of 49.33. I was with a pack of four good runners before I burst away. That win was very satisfying, coming off about 8 weeks of solid steady mileage and nothing much before that. I'd had no decent training for 6 months, and I'd been told by one physician that I'd probably never be able to run decent mileage again.

That's when I discovered chiropractic care and its commonsense application to life and sport. Chiropractic care enabled me to get back to athletics with hope. A weekly or fortnightly check-up while piling on the miles saw me clear of major injury or illness for an 18-month period of very high-level training. But that's another story in itself. It certainly changed my life direction, enough to "swap running for a career" as my coach Barry put it.

When I started training again I moved cities, started another job with Radio New Zealand, then got 43rd in the Wellington cross-country championships, but 8 weeks of gradually increasing mileage in fantastic new running territory saw me retrieve most of my aerobic background as if I'd never been away from the sport. There is definitely a "body memory" that allows a trained athlete to quickly resume high aerobic training levels.

Three weeks after winning the Wellington 10 mile road title, in the national road championships, with more easy long miles in the tank, I came from a long way back at halfway to waltz through the field again to finish 4th. Cullum won on this occasion in a close finish with Ballinger. On that occasion, I was very surprised to be able to run away by about 7 seconds over the last 800m from Geoff Shaw, who was an extremely promising distance track runner at the time.

It showed me that Barry Magee's description of aerobic "strength-speed" was certainly true and well worth pursuing. It is a different type of strength where one can access nearly all of one's reserves at the business end of a race, and keep pulling more and more out of the engine. This type of strength is attainable by nearly anyone who wishes to put the work in.

Poor footwear choices had resulted in me "carrying" minor Achilles tendon and plantar foot problems, so my track preparation wasn't done on the track much, and I compensated by keeping my mileage up and hopping into weekend track races.

The ensuing track season saw me do the same sort of "negative split" on several occasions, coming from well back in the field on a hot December day to finish 2nd in a 5000m trial for the Pacific Conference Games to Rod Dixon, and later on in the season, to convincingly beat the surging Japanese front-runners in an international 3000m race in Wellington, before the Games. I never got selected for those Games, with the New Zealand selectors going for more established runners who failed to perform anyway.

The Japanese duo ended up each getting a medal in the Games, over 1500m and 5000m. That was my personal education about selection policies, and at that stage of my life, I concluded that it was probably even harder to get chucked off a New Zealand team than to make one. It furthered my decision to move to Australia to study, a decision fueled by youthful impatience.

While I kept up my steady mileage, on each occasion, when I launched for home, there was plenty of gas in the tank. I lapped every competitor except the 2nd placegetter in the Wellington 10000m track title for a windy 29:41 debut. The second placegetter Dave Hatfield was 58 seconds behind, and as he'd run 14:08 for 5000m earlier that season, the long easy miles I was still running obviously had no ill effects.

In one 3000m race, still racing off the steady mileage base, I kicked away from Rod Dixon and a top NZ field, with 300m remaining. The whole field had banked up with a slow penultimate lap of 68 seconds, and the lanky Dixon and equally lanky Peter Renner were hemmed in. Dixon sounded like he was working hard so I took off. Dixon took some time to respond, but when he did it was like the night train from Chicago thundering past. He certainly showed why he was an Olympic medalist. Renner and the others didn't get past; Paul O'Donoghue did; but it was certainly a surprise to be able to kick past athletes of that caliber without any true speed training.

It was only when I started to do hard track sessions after recovering from my foot and achilles tendon troubles, that my form became erratic. A course of antibiotics for a nasty boil made my training lethargic, so I compensated by trying to run my track sessions harder; another mistake for beginners. A scheduled steady mile time trial in 4:20 for the Wednesday before the National 5000m became a grinding solo 4:11, just enough to take the wind out of my sails for the Nationals, where I was a lackluster 5th. I still haven't explained that one to my coach.

So what is the conclusion here? Whether you're a freakish talent like Craig Mottram or John Walker, or a contender like me, well-planned and scheduled long steady running can be of immense benefit. Do it. Take easy aerobic recovery days afterwards to absorb it. But don't do it too fast. And do exactly what your coach says.

You Can Do Too Much of a Good Thing

The following winter, after a good summer, I embarked on an ambitious buildup program where eventually I was covering my aerobic long run distances many minutes faster than in the previous year.

I lived in the center of Wellington's city area. Whereas the year before I was covering my version of the "Makara" long run in 2 hrs 44 minutes, in winter of 1981 I whittled that time down to a constant-effort 2 hrs 29 over several weeks, and then for another 6 weeks kept repeating the dose each Sunday, hitting 2hrs 25 a couple of times with a hard last 2-3 miles. Apparently the regular Wellington "Makara" group, which comprised several national-level marathoners, was never going faster than 2hr 39m for a course that was probably a couple of miles shorter. The "Makara" had some very challenging climbs and descents, including one monstrous climb up the back of Mt. Kau Kau, and I never did get to measure my exact course, but it may well have been over 24 miles. I would end the afternoon sitting in a hot bath for a couple of hours, eating endless toast and marmalade. I had a toaster, a kettle, and all the goods set up beside the bath. Somehow I never got electrocuted.

My steady "fifteen miler," which I'd been plodding around in 1hr 44 the year before, when I had such good race results, came down to a fun and fast 1 hr 24, a couple of nights a week. This was *not* on the advice of my coach, Barry.

One would think that with a base like this my race results would've been stupendous. Wrong. "Erratic" would be a better way to put it.

I raced solidly in a couple of early winter cross-country races, then in one race all the training and racing came together for a stupendous unplanned-for "peak." I took off from the beginning in New Zealand's hilliest annual cross-country race, the "Vosseler Shield," expecting a very tough battle from previous winners Derek Froude and Roger Robinson. The recent 2005 World Mountain Running championships were run on the same hill.

According to newspaper clippings, I ran the second half faster than the first and won by 27 seconds. According to the way I remember feeling, I felt like vomiting and pulling out at halfway, then thought of Ron Clarke, who'd said he felt like pulling out at halfway in every one of his world records. The second lap was a breeze, and it was surprising to be able to run away from someone like Froude, who was 2nd in the New Zealand cross-country champs later that year and eventually became a two-time Olympic marathoner. It was all Froude could do that day to hold off Roger, who wouldn't lie down for anyone. From memory, Derek ran a 2hr 15 marathon that year and Roger a 2hr 18 debut for 3rd in the Vancouver marathon, as a veteran.

The effort of that race, on top of my hard mileage, meant that there wasn't much left in the tank for the serious cross-country races leading into the National

Championships. My subsequent racing was uninspired and lethargic, and perhaps with hindsight, the very fast downhill running did nothing for my legs over the subsequent weeks. Needless to say I was a participant, not a factor, in the National cross country that year, finishing 13th, while Froude finished an excellent second to Ballinger. He and his coach had a knack for balancing his program beautifully. Froude actually understood what his coach was trying to achieve, unlike me.

I retrieved some form by running easier mileage for the road season, running some strong road relay legs. I managed to defend my ten-mile road title on a very windy day in a shade over 50 minutes. Froude was ten seconds back at the finish. My reserves were still probably replenishing from the previous overtraining and needed another month or two to come back to a decent level.

Three weeks later in the National championships, I went out hard with the leaders, Shane Marshall and Paul Ballinger, for most of the first 5 miles. They went so fast that I was about 100 meters back in 23 minutes 40 seconds by halfway. I'd always found a steady start better but decided it was time to place myself in the middle of the action right from the start if I was serious about bagging a national title. Marshall won in 47 minutes 30 seconds, in a frantic finish from Ballinger, 2nd for the third time in a row.

Several runners snuck past me in the second half, including Froude, who ran a well-judged race to finish 3rd in about 48m 30s. This was hard to swallow, as I'd beaten him handily in a road relay leg and the provincial title in earlier weeks, but I had to admit his careful preparation and intelligent racing yielded dividends my wilder approach couldn't. In the last 800m, Brian Kennelly, a hard man, also went past me, and my characteristic finishing burst came to nothing. The tank was empty. So that year there were three good chances for national honors and three misses. Ouch. The next year I was off to Australia for 6 years of study and a lot more learning.

The learning is continuing as I coach.

In the years since I raced as a youngster, I have seen many cases where not-too-inspiring juniors just piled on the steady work, and several years later reached world-class. I can remember two juniors who finished well down in the field in the national junior 5000m in 1978, but within a few years were winning everything. One was Olympian Rex Wilson, who ran a 2hr 10 min marathon, and the other was Derek Froude, who made it to two Olympics as a 2hr 11 marathoner.

New Zealand athletics history is full of stories of solid, persevering athletes who eventually reached national or international level by doing this work. If they can do it, then perhaps you can too!

Keith's Classic Mistakes

Always look at the big picture of your life when you're training and racing. When you're very young, this is naturally quite hard to do, but it certainly is worth the effort. If necessary, grab an experienced "old hand" or club coach to talk things over with regularly. It doesn't matter if the older person knows "nothing" about athletics; what matters is whether they know a bit about "life."

In mid 1987, when I had finally completed my degree, I felt exhilarated that finally I could run again and pursue a high level of training without worrying about shuffling part-time jobs, tutorial loads, and endless exams. Unfortunately, a few months earlier, my father, a terrific guy, had been smashed up badly in a nasty car accident and suffered a major stroke. He was nearly 70.

He was hospitalized of course and part of my final year of study involved several frantic flights from Australia to New Zealand because he was expected to die at any stage. Being an old soldier, he didn't die as expected. One day I found him congested with pneumonia in both lungs, looking purple and grey, with multiple wires and tubes connected to hospital equipment. "Hi Dad, how's it going?" I said. Slowly, over minutes, he spluttered "Could be better, could be worse." And so he continued, gradually fighting his way back in a see-saw battle with numerous hospital infections over many months.

To add to my emotional layering, a girlfriend had just dumped me, too! Looking back on things now, this probably wasn't the time to attempt a "comeback" to athletics, but I was a man on a mission!

I chose the ostrich approach and ploughed myself into hard training. I'd been experimenting with a pattern of training that quite suited my physiology and circumstances, and it was based on moderate mileage (usually less than 60 miles or 100km a week) and hard fast cross-country intervals of 800m-2000m with short recoveries.

I adapted this regimen because as a student I found that the very long runs were using the same glycogen fuel that my brain needed to be able to study well! Long runs of about 15 miles at a good clip interspersed with regular cross-country intervals or tempo runs kept me in the game quite nicely though.

A few years earlier, on this regimen, I'd placed 6th in the Australian cross-country titles, won state medals over 5000m and 10000m, and was always a factor in any race. It worked because I'd had a massive mileage base from earlier years. However, it was probably 6 years since I'd done regular high-mileage training and my base was beginning to diminish.

My twin brother, who I was now coaching, also thrived on this regimen for a short while, as previously he'd been doing compulsive mega-mileage over bush tracks in Auckland's Waitakere ranges where he lived. When he cut back his miles and sharpened, he started to be consistent for the first time in his life and ran a number of good races, despite a big weekly workload mowing lawns all around Auckland.

So on my temporary return to New Zealand, we found ourselves training together regularly for the first time in years, but with the emotional overflow from the struggles of our old Dad, we hammered each other and our training buddies. We'd have been so much better off just putting in steady "bread and butter" aerobic runs in the many scenic areas around Auckland and "smelling the roses," but adrenalin begets adrenalin, no matter the cause, and hard fast cross-country intervals can give a "rush" that is addictive.

One Thursday session was spent at Cornwall Park, where we did sustained hard efforts around the hilly perimeter, leaving our training partners well behind. We felt inexhaustible that day. The other guys were experienced internationals and wisely just let us go. The next day I knew I had done a fraction too much and felt strangely "empty." A few days later, on the Sunday, we took off like scalded cats in the first kilometer of a local 10k road race, and unsurprisingly ran out of steam to finish in 2nd and 4th. The winner, a solid performer, just had to run steadily to pick up the pieces. The winning time was well within our compass a few days earlier, so that was an opportunity that was blown by compulsive training.

The rest of that winter season was an erratic mix of good and bad results for me, involving bad stitches in major cross-country races, fastest lap times in road and cross-country relays, and a nasty flu right at the time of the Australian cross-country championships. "Stress" was obviously a major player, and with no planned coping strategy I was forced to "rest," even if it took the flu to do that. A later bout of chronic achilles tendonitis was predictable too, in that it forced me to stop "pushing" myself.

So "headspace and tactics" expand into the realm of everything else you choose to do. Nothing is separate from your training and racing. All have to be taken into account.

More Crazy Training Stories

Just to prove that I had learned nothing, three years earlier I had run a session of 800m intervals on a Thursday, three days before a Sunday 10km road race. My training partner that day was former Australian Junior 5000m champion Jeff Chambers, and we pushed each other hard, with neither of us willing to ease the effort. We ended up running four 800m intervals with 800m jog recovery in an average of 2:02, with my last one being 2:00. This was totally unnecessary and way too fast to have relevance to winter race distances at our level of development. However, the session was a "blast," and we were very pleased with ourselves.

On the following Sunday, in a 10km road race in Brisbane, I was still so full of adrenalin that I "cruised" the first mile in about 4:20, leaving a class field 100m behind, then died a slow and inevitable death to eventually finish 5th. If we do too many hard short sessions, realistic race pace at longer distances like 10km will feel like a Sunday stroll, so the temptation is to go out at a pace that feels "fine" but is unsustainable.

On that occasion, I had another race the following week over 10km on the road. This was part of a national circuit of road races sponsored by the Budget Rental Car firm. Having just run an embarrassingly bad race through stupidity and poor preparation, I duly jogged all week for about an hour a day until my strength came back, then went down to Hobart, Tasmania, for the "grand final" of the series.

This race was over a road circuit around Hobart's Domain, and the terrain closely resembled the sort of hills I was used to in New Zealand.

There was a team from the Institute of Sport in Canberra, who'd won their leg of the series. They were confident of knocking off our all-conquering Glenhuntly road team that had cleaned up successive legs in Melbourne, Perth, Sydney and Brisbane.

The too-hard and too-fast 800m interval session combined successfully with the tired Sunday 10km road race and 5 days of easy recovery jogging to bring me up for a "good day at the office" and I surged away from Gary Briggs, a national steeplechase and cross-country champion, on an uphill section to win going away by over 30 seconds from Gary and another AIS athlete, David Forbes. To top the day, our team won overall anyhow. I felt so good after relative rest that when Gary decided to put in a hard surge uphill, I went with him and kept on going.

However, the erratic nature of these performances was entirely unnecessary, and with a more intelligent and controlled approach, and with the benefit of hindsight, we now have a rational and predictable system for bringing athletes up for a good race performance within a Lydiard context. It's not rocket science. Just don't do hard sessions too close to races, and jog easily in the lead-up days.

"I Feel Like I Could Have Done it Again!"

An extremely experienced coach contacted me recently about his (female) athlete who had reached top regional level on the track over 1500m and 3000m last summer. His athlete had done a full winter's aerobic preparation, with some good winter races. Despite a good block of early season hill work and VO$_2$ max work (longer intervals with short or equal recovery), and some promising early-season results, she wasn't able to tap into her high-output glycolytic anaerobic stores in races.

She described the feeling as "I felt as if I couldn't get at my energy reserves," and "I felt as if I could've done it again, straight away." The athlete is a hard-working girl who has a good head for racing, so she was quite disheartened to "go off the boil" coming into National Championships.

A possible answer here is that some athletes just don't have a very big glycolytic/ anaerobic "tank". So we have to tread carefully when prescribing for these athletes. They can be very fast over 100m, showing a good endowment of IIB fast twitch fibers, and they can be very competitive aerobically, showing a good endowment of Type I slow twitch fibers. They can have a high oxygen uptake, and the heart of a champion racehorse, but they can't nail those glycolytic reps and come back smiling. There seems to be a deficiency of trainable IIA (glycolytic/oxidative) muscle fiber and so the lactate tolerance system can be overloaded very easily.

This DOESN'T mean that an athlete with this challenge can't compete at the very top level: it just means that she has to control training efforts well and hoard the lactate tolerance "reservoir" until race day. If the reservoir is depleted, it can't be accessed, can it?

If she's one of these, then she really shouldn't be doing sets of fast 800m-pace glycolytic/lactate tolerance reps (i.e.: 300s/ 400s/500s @ race-pace). Try two or three sets of threshold-pace steady state lapping (i.e.: 1200m) before 2-3 reps with good recovery over 150-200m @ 800 pace. Just dip into the high-power output lactic tank a tiny bit without killing it. That has been shown to solve this particular problem with an international level female 800m athlete who is similarly challenged but can 'kick' with the best of them.

One tip for athletes like this is to make sure that each week or training cycle in track season includes scheduled steady efforts of 2-5 km on the track at higher aerobic levels or even at anaerobic threshold, as well as paying attention to VO$_2$ max. It pays to look back at training diaries to see how athletes respond to their sessions. You may have to fiddle around a little bit to get it right.

One of our good male athletes, Daniel, had run 50s for 400m and 1:52 for 800, and 3:45 for 1500m before Christmas off, VO_2 type training on Tuesdays, then went off the boil in the new year when he started bringing in glycolytic reps. So despite his speed potential, his system just seemed to rebel with the fast hard reps at 800 and 1500 pace. He went back to his pre-Christmas form when we steadied him off with Tuesday sessions starting with leg-speed drills, then adding 4-6 laps of steady running at his threshold pace (about 3:15 per km), then 3-4 x 800 or 1000 at VO_2 pace (for him, about 2:50 per km, or 2:20 per 800m). Anything like fast 300s or 400s or 500s killed him, so we didn't do them!

Nic Bideau's Comments

(Nic's elite squad includes world-beating Australians Craig Mottram and Benita Johnson, and England's Mo Farah, now the owner of a 13m 09s 5000m time)

I had this kid come to me last year, age 20, who'd run 49s for 400m and 1m 52s for 800m but a year out of school his natural aerobic fitness had declined while his size had increased. He was struggling to break 2 min for 800m and told me it was because he lacked speed – despite having done a load of speedwork and no running beyond half an hour in between.

He came down the track one Tuesday and tried 2x1mile with a 15 min 5k runner I have – he did the first one in 5min, jogged a lap and then could only do 5.30 for the 2nd one. The 5k kid did his 3rd rep in 5 min and then proceeded to do some 4x300m in about 47 secs with 100 jog. I got the 800m boy to join in for those, and he blasted the 5k kid in running 43 secs or better.

He was pretty happy with himself at that point so I suggested he try a 1500m race that Saturday against the 5k kid – suggested it be a bit like the hare and the tortoise. He assured me he'd thrash the 5k kid in a 1500m race and off he went.

I rang him after the race and asked who won, tortoise or hare. Embarrassed – and no surprise to you – he told me the tortoise beat him 4.05 to 4.10.

It was enough to convince him to try my way for a couple more months, which got his 1500m down to 4.00 and he's now persisting with an aerobic fitness program during the winter. I don't know if he'll run what he thinks he's worth but I'm damn sure he'll run faster over 800m or 1500m than he would had he stuck to his bulk speedwork method.

Just another story to pass on.

We have coaches in Australia who tend to be able to convince athletes that speed is the be all and end all when anyone should be able to see that as the events we're dealing with are mostly dependent on aerobic efficiency, then aerobic development is the key area we should be focusing on.

But strangely enough they reason that by improving their ability over 400m by 1 sec, they will improve their 5k by 30 secs without considering that by doing all the work to get a faster 400m, they are abandoning the key element of fitness required for 5k running and, even worse, tearing their aerobic efficiency down with a load of anaerobic work.

Part 17
Getting Your "Headspace" Right

Setting Achievable Goals

BHAGOs: Big Hairy Goals and Objectives

"Ah, but a man's reach should exceed his grasp, or what's a heaven for?"
Robert Browning

BHAGOs are essential in our running. They tantalize us and give us a glimpse of possibilities. They get us out the door in the morning and keep us on track. Goals should be achievable but challenging, according to our level of ability and development.

I didn't start out as particularly athletic or fast. When I started running at high school, my original aim was to make the school athletic team and cross-country team. Eventually my horizon kept on expanding, with racing and training, until it dawned on me that maybe I was pretty good and with some training I could be a force at national senior level.

In training, I would often imagine myself running away from rivals in big races. I won more imaginary medals than anyone I knew. I think a lot of aspiring runners do this. It worked for me and made my long runs a lot of fun. I'd particularly push the gas pedal up big hills, thinking that every hill I pushed up was one my opponents weren't. The science of goal-setting and written specific goals wasn't known to me as a kid.

Gradually I started to accumulate good results, and once I'd won some senior titles, the next aim was to win a national championship or make a national team. I came close, but just when it looked like I could make it to that next level; I chose to move countries to study chiropractic. That in itself was a choice, although I have never regretted it.

I never did work out whether my sheer enthusiasm for running and prolific training "made" me good enough to win races, or whether I did in fact have any outstanding ability. What I do know is that the fitter I got, the bigger my belief, and the more training I did in all conditions, the tougher I got. The recipe is pretty simple.

Smart Goals

Goals should be:
SPECIFIC
MEASURABLE
ACHIEVABLE
REALISTIC
TIME-FRAMED

When I was running, I had no idea about the power of setting specific measurable goals. Because I wasn't setting specific measurable goals, I wasn't hitting anything in particular, either. I was living and training for the moment, really, with a hope that one day I may "crack" a big race wide open. It got me up to a certain level, but perhaps if I'd set very specific written goals with time-frames, I may have done better.

So how do we set goals in athletics? For a start, it's a good idea to "chunk things up."

If you feel you have the ability to eventually run under 4 minutes for the mile, then you'll have to understand what this really entails. As you will see elsewhere in this book, this will require a 10,000m capability approaching 29 minutes, and a 400m speed close to 50 seconds flat, with an 800m around 1:50. If you haven't got anywhere near these times yet, but feel that you have the ability and the dedication to eventually get there, then you have decided that the goal is *achievable*, but perhaps for now it isn't *realistic*.

Some extraordinary athletes have broken 4 minutes for the mile with slower short distance times than this, but they compensated with world-class endurance.

Murray Halberg ran a 3:57 mile with a best listed 440 yards of only 52.5 seconds, and an 880 yards of around 1:52, but then he was world record-holder and Olympic champion over 5000m and could run 10,000m in 28:30 on a wet grass track, and had a last lap kick that was only a second or so slower than his 400m PB.

Other athletes can get there with a very highly developed anaerobic capacity, which seems to compensate for a lack of aerobic ability. But these cases are rare, and you'll know pretty quickly if you have limitations aerobically or anaerobically.

If you are running 50 kilometers a week and can't break 32 minutes for a 10000m, then unless you revise your training you are unlikely to achieve a sub-4 minute mile. You won't have the aerobic capacity to support the anaerobic demands of training or racing. You may have to look at doubling your aerobic volumes over time, for several years, and you will have to work at your different aerobic training zones methodically to push the anaerobic threshold up, and then work on your VO_2 max levels.

You can also make the mistake of penning in all the hard sessions required to eventually reach the set goal, but not pen in the *easy* days that will allow you to recover and progress.

So, have a long-term plan that is achievable for your ability, and gets you excited with a big, hairy, audacious goal, but chunk it up into short-term realistic steps.

Specific Goals

Make short-term and long-term goals specific that are just demanding enough to require significant training effort to get there. A couple of years ago, we had a 16-year-old athlete who wished to get to the IAAF World Youth Championships. He'd won Australian Schools titles in his age group over 1500m but hadn't achieved the qualifying time of 3:56.0 for 1500m.

I knew from experience that if we have a qualifying time to aim for that is achievable but not demanding, then our subconscious won't get excited, and we will probably not quite achieve the qualifying time either.

So we set our athlete a BHAGO: to ensure he got his times and got selected without quibbles, it was necessary to go way past the qualifying times and demolish them. We set him a target of 3:50 for 1500m, which was ambitious for a 16-year-old. Our 800m and 1500m pace repetitions were tuned to that pace, which we felt was achievable, and the end result was that the youngster achieved 3:52.5 for 1500m, getting third in a senior men's state title race, with a scrappy last 800m in 2:00.

He got to the championships, held in Morocco, and managed a 3:54 run in 50 degree stadium heat to just miss the final.

If his goals and training hadn't specific and exciting, he might not have gotten the time. The same principle applies to anyone trying to make a national team. Don't just settle for the qualifying time, or B-qualifier. Go "for broke," and train for a time that is so good you can't be ignored. In doing this, you will have to chunk up the endurance requirements and anaerobic requirements to achieving training goals within set time frames along the way.

Measurable Goals

Keep an accurate diary and "chunk up" your training requirements.

For our hypothetical sub-4 minute miler, then, he needs a specific time to aim at that will ensure a sub-4 time should he "lag" behind his goal by a small percentage. We never do quite get our goal times, usually; this often requires perfect conditions and pacing, so we have to do our best with what we're given.

Perhaps a goal time of 3:56 for a mile will ensure that the athlete who meets the training requirements for this time, in a decent race, will get his sub-4 mile.

So in setting goals for training for a sub-4 minute mile, it becomes apparent that at some stage the athlete should be able to run 8 x 400m in 59.0s, relaxed, with ample recovery, weeks before his first serious race, and perhaps 4 x 400m in 54.5s with ample recovery. The 8 x 400m times would be the required specific times to achieve the mile, but we would also need to achieve the faster and shorter 400m session to achieve the 800m time that would be necessary to deliver a 3:56 mile.

When we also think about the underlying VO_2 max system beneath the glycolytic system on the training pyramid, then it becomes apparent that before we get to this race-specific phase of training, the VO_2 max intervals should be at a consistently repeatable level that will be compatible with a 3:56.0 mile. For Peter Snell years ago, this turned out to be 6-8 x 800m intervals in 2:10, but for our athlete it may be 4 x 1000m in 2:40: the effect will be very similar if the proper aerobic conditioning is done. Then we have to plan a specific session somewhere in the training plan that will prop up the anaerobic threshold system, and below this level, the various levels of the aerobic system.

Achievable Goals

These are your longer-term goals that can be "chunked up" into achievable and realistic training and racing goals.

For a 16-year-old with decent leg speed and endurance, who has run a 4 minute 1500m, then certainly a 3:40 1500m in 5 years may be achievable.

This needs to be chunked up into a 5-year plan that concentrates on the endurance aspect foremost each year, with interim goal race times and training times to be achieved each year on the way to the goal.

Perhaps an achievable goal over 5 years would be a 4 second per year decrease in race times, with the 1500m race pace repetitions over 400m coming down a second each year to achieve this target, and the aerobic volume work increasing each winter and spring so that eventually in 5 years, the athlete is averaging around 150 kilometers a week or more in his endurance buildup.

Realistic Goals

This needs to be looked at in a holistic sense. It's no good aiming at very high quality times if the athlete is working as a veterinarian in an outback station, even if he is phenomenally gifted and can put in the training. The part that is missing from the outback picture is a running culture with training partners achieving target times that will encourage the athlete to excel, as well as everything else!

The athlete needs access to quality training partners and races on a regular basis to be likely to achieve his goals. If he doesn't have this culture around him, then he has just placed an obstacle in his own path that he doesn't need.

Realistic goals are what we can do with our current aerobic base and experience, and therefore have to be based on "hard data." It's no good aiming for a 1:52 800m time if you can run 29 minutes for 10000m, but haven't been doing the progressive layers of VO_2 max training and glycolytic race pace training.

Your aerobic endurance will be very good, but your anaerobic buffering will be lousy, so you may run a good first lap with a stinker of a second lap. You would be better to aim at a time that is realistic to your current training history and progress from there.

Time Frames

It is no good aiming at a 3:56 mile if there is no target date attached to it. The target date is vital. Without it our human nature can allow our procrastination genes to switch on, and then we have an achievable "gonna do" goal that never materializes.

So time-frame your goal time or achievement to keep the urgency there.

A time-framed goal may look like this in your diary: make it present tense so that your subconscious reads it like an established fact.

Johnno's Goals for 2008 season.

I have run 1:51.0 for 800m and 3:45.0 for 1500m, before April 1 2009.

I average 150 km/ week in steady aerobic volume training between September and November to achieve this (8 weeks' training average), and I progressively build to this during July and August while making sure I keep healthy. I maintain one 2-hour hilly run a week all through my endurance phase and into my later phases until just before my most important competitions.

To achieve my 800m time in January or February, I am fast enough to run 600m in 82 seconds by December 1st, 2008, and I am also strong enough to run 4 x 400m in 55 seconds average, with walk/jog recovery.

I am also fit enough to do my 4 x 1000m VO_2 max session in 2:40 average, with equal jog recovery, by November 14th 2008, when I start my specific 1500m pace glycolytic repetitions.

I have broken 31 minutes for 10km on the road before October 30th, during my endurance training.

…That gives you an idea! See how many parts of the training pyramid you can get specific about, and chunk it! Make a scan of the goal-sheet and place it onto a small laminated business card that you can see every time you open your wallet. Or place the goal-card on the bathroom mirror or the dashboard of your car. You get the idea!

Confidence

All the correct training in the world is of no use if the athlete has no confidence. Confidence in racing comes from knowing that you have prepared yourself as well as you can, and also from having a good understanding of your own capabilities tactically.

Successful Olympic coach Chris Pilone says "I'm not a great believer in sports psychology. At the highest level, the training program is everything. It has to be the right training, and it has to be the right timing. We got both right for Athens, as you can see by the beautiful running rhythm Carter maintained all the way to the tape.

"A year out from the Olympics or the world champs, there are 30 to 40 people who can win. Some don't get selected. Some get sick or injured. Some don't time their training right and some do inappropriate training. A week out from the race there may be six contenders. Then some don't handle the pressure. If you survive that process of elimination, you're right in the hunt. Get those basics right and sometimes you can achieve an unbelievable result."

All the confidence in the world is of no use if the athlete has no tactical experience or common sense, either.

As someone who could train with and occasionally beat good internationals, I made a series of basic mistakes that prevented me from getting to the level I thought I was capable of getting to. A lot of talented people fall by the wayside in this game and perhaps a lot of it is preventable.

Correct "headspace" is something we learn over time, generally. Some people have a shrewd tactical capability from day one, but most of us have to learn the hard way. But rather than learn the hard way, it's a great idea to pick the brains of older wiser racing partners and coaches, and learn from their hard-earned knowledge.

Belief

"Belief" comes from the Middle English phrase "be in Love With." Most very good runners *love* to run. It is extremely hard to reach the top unless there is an inborn love of running and training.

More to the point, to reach a very big goal, there has to be a belief, or love of an outcome, that is way bigger than any obstacles on the way.

Obstacles are what you see when you take your eyes off the goal.

Lorraine Moller, one of history's "winningest" all-time marathoners, says that an athlete's belief systems have to be taken into account when planning a training program. "The belief system determines everything. So if an athlete has grown up with a particular type of program that he or she believes is crucial, maybe it's not a good idea to mess with that structure too much – it might be better to accommodate that work into a specific phase so that the athlete's belief systems are reinforced."

No Expectations – No Limitations
by Colin Livingstone

The Happy Science of Having a Go

Racing and running liberate you: where there are No Expectations – there are No Limitations. If you expect a certain result, you may be limiting yourself from a better one!

If you have to aim at all, aim well and aim high. An average expectation or goal excites no-one. Only mediocre performers are always at their best.

The trick is to aim at something that *excites you!* This exciting goal will forge adrenalin into your body and give you a reason to train hard.

Every race should be a journey of discovery. Intelligent training maximises potential and minimises risk. It is great to have goals, but the world will not end if you miss them. Accept the situation and come back fighting.
All things come from training.

Training removes you from the common man or woman.

Racing brings you into the seasoned world of uncommon people ...*Competitors*

The most important thing is to have a go; the real gold is found in personal achievement and improvement over many years.

For the common man to understand the athlete is like a battery hen trying to comprehend the soaring of an eagle.

Being an athlete brings you into the world of the "champion thinker." When you run the streets in pouring rain and wind, there will be many who stare at you in dull comprehension through hooded lids, but just remember no matter what level you're at, you're different, and you're having a go!

Too many athletes live with expectation!
Don't accept that someone is unbeatable – accept that you can improve an increment

at a time. Obviously, if your best 1500 is 3.50 and you are racing a 3.29 man, then the odds are that you will be beaten. Don't be mad and boldly take the first lap in 56 seconds following the runner be smart and hit the lap at your known comfort zone, a 61 or 62. Leave all your running to the last two laps, let your adrenalin and intelligent training carry you to 3.45. You might not win, but you've got a PB. The 3.29 guy might be 4% off form with 3.37, and you are in the same finishing straight. He's still hard to catch, yet looking mortal. If you can still see him in the finishing straight, he's beatable.

You cannot control the talent or preparation of your adversaries. You accept that there will be a fight, and you will be in it. You can only prepare yourself to be in the right condition at the right time. You can only maximize and deliver your own potential. Never be concerned with the abilities or reputations of others. Never bow to a reputation. Respect it if you must but always test it. Never accept you have reached your limits – push them – recover – push them again.

Expect the unexpected, rewrite the script, or rip it up.

If there is a script you don't like, rip it up. Many people go through life expecting others to play character roles in their scripts – they want control in races, in business, in life. They do not like the idea that there are many unwilling to comply who are willing and able to upset their apple cart. They expect a certain reaction from a certain line. They cannot handle loose cannons, the unexpected, an ad lib improvisation or spontaneity.

When someone thinks they have you all figured out, they are at their most vulnerable.

We've all seen a race turned on its head by a game competitor who snapped at the heels of an over-confident superstar. We've seen the all-powerful politician deftly cover his tracks and squirm out of tight corners, only to be downed by an honest Joe. We've seen the school bully wiped out by the nice kid with the braces and spectacles, the durable customer providing un-expected resistance – the person who was pushed too far.

The ultimate example of keeping one's focus and doing all one can do came at the 2002 Winter Olympics in

Salt Lake City. Steven Bradbury, an Australian in the 1000m short track speed skating event, negotiated an amazing set of circumstances to emerge with one of the most unexpected gold medals in Olympic history.

A hard trainer who had never featured in the very top echelons of this event, nevertheless set about his task calmly in each qualifying round. In the quarter finals, he thought he was eliminated by finishing 3rd, but a finisher ahead of him was disqualified. And so it went on in similar vein to the final, where he "ran" his own race and was 2nd last with a lap to go. Then the whole pack of superstars went down, and Bradbury stayed out of trouble to glide by for gold.

The trick is to back yourself to the hilt, and put yourself in a position where you can get such luck: you hang in through the desperate patch in each race until it is second nature. Then maybe preparation will meet opportunity and you can "get lucky."

> *"I will prepare myself, and some day my time will come."*
>
> Abraham Lincoln

You can only prepare yourself as well as possible, and beyond that it really doesn't matter much in the big scheme of things. Australian Olympic swimmer and world breaststroke record holder Liesel Jones lived under the crushing weight of personal and public expectation since she burst onto the world scene with Olympic silver at 14. She was becoming renowned as someone who was destined only for minor medals at world championship level before she was out of her teens.

> *"If I can't be happy without an Olympic Gold medal, then I sure as hell can't be happy with one!"*
>
> World record holder & world champion swimmer Liesl Jones

She was desperately unhappy, and then one day she had enormous revelation. She realized, "If I can't be happy without an Olympic Gold medal, then I sure as hell can't be happy with one!" Since that revelation, Liesl has focused only on her own preparation and racing, enjoyed her life, and she has been successful in very high-pressure world championship racing where expectations were enormous.

And remember, as the late, great John Davies said:

"You decide who you are, no one else!"

Attitude Determines Altitude

The difference between very great champions and lesser runners very often is not physical at all. It's attitudinal. From all accounts, Lydiard was a hard taskmaster who expected nothing but the best in effort from his charges.

His training group was a mix of champions and sloggers, but all of them trained hard and had high expectations. Lydiard-trained runners were taught to slug it out and do whatever it took in a race to get a best-possible placing. If a win wasn't possible, then one would slug it out for second, or third, or 40th, or whatever. In that way, if one was having a "bad day at the office," at least the attitude was right. If we learn to fight regardless of our "day at the office" then when we are in a good position we will be tough to beat.

The same approach is used by the modern-day training group of Nic Bideau. His athletes all adhere to a very positive "can-do" group ethos. Bideau has created a support structure within the group that includes former 2:10 marathoner Garry Henry, as adviser, masseur, and confidant, and Bideau's partner, Sonia O'Sullivan, a former world champion and Olympic silver medalist. Success breeds success in this group.

Coach Bideau's Thoughts

"The training is only one key element responsible for the success of, among others, our two leading Australian distance runners, Craig Mottram and Benita Johnson. But I would add that just as relevant is (a) the environment they train in, (b) the planning undertaken (including their competition program) and (c) the belief I have in them to run as well as they have.

Getting fit in training is certainly critical, but I have certainly seen cases where, despite being incredibly fit, a lack of confidence and belief in one's ability to compete well has cost an athlete in important races. The right training helps to build these elements but the structure of the training groups they exist in and the very carefully planned racing program they follow certainly enhances this confidence to take the athletes to a very high level."

Part 18
Developing Your Winning Strategies

Know When to Run

Kenny Rogers has a famous song called "The Gambler." The chorus goes as follows: "You gotta know when to hold 'em, know when to fold 'em, know when to walk away, know when to run."

On this subject, as far as middle distance racing goes, there is one huge error I see all the time in middle distance racing. It relates to the confidence of an athlete to *hold back* from kicking until the very last possible moment. If that sounds strange, bear with me.

In male 800m racing at an elite or national level, the speed reached averages 28 km/hour or faster. To the athlete leading such a race, this represents a frontal wind resistance of the same speed. So why would anyone take the lead at such a speed for any length of time unless there was no other option? If two equally talented athletes have to run side by side on treadmills, and one has to run with a big propeller blowing air back at him at this speed, then which one will wilt earlier? A big early move is unnecessary and can "spike" acidosis in the legs making a final sprint impossible. It is only necessary to be ahead at the finish line, if possible.

90% or more of 800m races are not won by the person leading at halfway.

So tuck in out of trouble and delay any significant move until the last possible moment, and even a "slow kicker" can surprise.

TRAIN TACTICALLY

This last track season we had a squad of three very evenly matched runners over 1500m. Daniel and Matthew both got their best times down to about 3:45, and Stephen got his down to 3:48. However, each one of them "missed the jump" in tactical races at one stage of the season, which cost them much faster times. This was all due to tactical inexperience.

In this year's state title race for 1500m, Daniel was with a pack of well-performed 1500m runners with two laps to go. A good distance runner, not known for his 1500m ability, ambushed the pack and took off as fast as he could go. Daniel let the distance runner go; wisely thinking that he'd made his break far too early and would get run down in the last lap. However, what he didn't plan on was that the rest of the pack immediately latched on to the distance runner: Daniel "missed the jump." His psychic and physical "connection" to the leaders was gone right there and then.

If he'd gone with the "jump," steadily, he could have tailed the front-runners and had a fighting chance in the straight. As it was, he clearly beat the distance runner but mucked up his defence of the state title from 2007. Ouch!!!

With only a few weeks to the Australian 1500m Championships, we had to take drastic action. So we devised a fun and hard track session where about 6 runners joined in the pack on each hard effort, and on each effort one of them was under secret instructions to burst away from the pack or sprint past from behind. They practiced getting out of the "boxed-in" position, going with the "jump" smoothly and using tiring runners to get up into the position they needed to be in.

We have now decided to add this type of workout regularly to our general anaerobic work because it gets the tactical training, conditioning and race-specific work done in one session!

Georgie's Smart Race

A good coach and athlete combination will look at every possible factor to get the best out of a situation. Recently I was given a DVD of an Australian Secondary School championship race to watch by coach Neil MacDonald from Geelong, Victoria. The race was for Under-15 Girls, and it was an absolute classic study in the use of tactics. The coach's athlete, 14-year-old Georgie, had a best 400m time of over 60 seconds and was up against 6 girls from interstate with faster 400m times, two of whom were capable of 57 seconds or better. Her best 800m time was close to the others' because she had good endurance, however on paper it looked to be a hopeless cause in a last lap finish.

The day was breezy, with a constant headwind along the back straight. Georgie's instructions were to get into a good position early and tuck in behind into the wind on both laps and only to make her significant move in the straight with the wind behind her. She did this to the letter, and her "kick" in the straight was sufficient to earn her a bronze medal in a PB, within a second of gold. If Georgie continues enjoying her sport and training and racing with her "head" then she has a bright future despite her perceived lack of 400m speed. 400m speed can always be improved with technique and training, but the ability to be cool under pressure and "execute" a race plan is much rarer than a fast 400m time.

It is very rare indeed to have a day when conditions are perfect for a "time," so I tell all my athletes to go for a tactical "win," or place rather than a time, wherever possible. One day the right conditions and competition will turn up, and the athlete who has learned how to "win" tactically in less than perfect conditions will be hard to beat in perfect conditions.

Never Look Back!!

Another point comes to mind. *Never* turn around in a track race to check on opposition, especially in a final sprint. Maybe earlier on it's OK but certainly not in the last lap. It's like igniting petrol for a determined competitor close by. Not only does the act of turning the head physically slow the stride rate a tiny amount, but it betrays lack of concentration on the important job at hand.

One year I found myself dropped with a kilometer to go in a state 5000m championship. Three guys took off as a group with a planned surge three laps out, and it was all I could do to hold on for dear life. So I just kept plugging away, even though the trio was well clear and appeared destined to scoop all the medals. It's never over till the fat lady sings for a Lydiard runner.

One lap went by, then two, and still they were well clear. The last lap bell rang, and I picked up for a last effort. The athlete who had initiated the big break, the 22-year-old Steve Moneghetti, had fallen back marginally from the front two, who were locked in a private battle for first.

He turned around over his left shoulder to check on me as we went into the last 200 meters. He was at least 20 meters clear of me. I was up on my toes in a headlong sprint before he knew it and snatched a bronze where before it looked futile. I put two seconds into him in the straight.

As far as I was concerned with 300m to go, I was probably going to miss a planned place, but the look over the shoulder was an open invitation. The last lap took about 57 seconds, and I ended up with a PB. Steve was also passed in the straight by another guy who took the opportunity. He made that mistake again in the same position heading into the last 200m of the Commonwealth 10,000m track final the next year in Edinburgh. It cost him a major medal that time, and I doubt whether he has ever done it again since in a race.

Respect

Another absolute No-No is this: *Never* take off too soon in a track race just because you feel good and your opponent appears vulnerable. The "rush of blood to the head" will eventually be matched by an exit of blood from your legs as you inevitably get mowed down in the straight. I've seen this particular error cost good athletes certain wins, many times – even in major events.

One of our "young guns" decided to do this in a schoolboy 800m race that had a slow first lap. He "jumped" the field 400m out because on paper he was several seconds faster than all of them over that distance. However, one tough customer was having a great day, and stuck to him like glue, then demolished him in the final meters. The winner was a better 400m runner that day and, being a good underdog, snatched his chance.

I made the same error one day in a 3000m event in Auckland in early 1984. I had been working myself back into some semblance of running form by a mix of track races and light mileage, after several months of very light training while I concentrated on my degree back in Melbourne.

A visiting Australian marathoner, Steve Poulton, had hopped into the race, and I "sat" on him for a number of laps as we left the field behind. He was a nuggety sort of guy, with a short choppy marathoner's stride, and I made an assumption that he was probably not a class track runner. I felt good and sensed he was working very hard, so for some stupid reason I took off about 450m out for a big last lap.

Aussie marathoners don't hand races over on a platter, so he did what any guy would do. He hung on and promptly did me like a dog's dinner over the final 250m, despite his lack of track grace.

There was absolutely no need for me to go when I did; I could certainly have bided my time and possibly the result would have been different.

Play Your Best Card

Lesson learned, I then jogged easily for a week and did a few light strides before an "International" 3000m I'd been invited to fill the numbers in. In this race, I stayed out of trouble and made absolutely sure that I didn't squander my resources until the last possible moment. One of the British guys in the race, Colin Reitz, had won bronze in the World Championships 3000m steeple the year before and had a 7:44 3000m time on the board, so he was the likely form runner.

The race became procession-like for about 6 laps as various athletes took their turns at leading. I had no real cards to play except that my leg speed seemed to be coming along nicely. Predictably, Reitz launched a big move 450m out, and although instinct made me want to "go" with a pack of four, I held to my race plan and staved off for as long as I could bear. This was hard, and I was cajoling myself as I watched the leaders stretch away.

One runner fell back slightly from the pack going into the last 200m, and I keyed off him. The last 200m took me a respectable 27 seconds, with a nice little kick in the straight, and I finished 4th, within 5 seconds of Reitz. By being conservative and hoarding my resources until the last moment, I'd bluffed my way to a reasonable result.

The only time it is advisable for an athlete to "take off" more than a lap out is when he or she has had a recent run of excellent predictable form, coming off a very good mileage base, and if he or she suspects that someone in the field may be capable of pulling off an upset with a short sprint. Then it's a matter of playing your cards and doing whatever it takes to make it work. There's always a risk no matter what you do, but racing well is a matter of risk-minimization.

One would think I would have learned from my 3000m results and filed it away for future use. However, within a few months, I was back to doing silly impulsive things in training and racing. Why athletes do this, I don't know. When we're younger we think our racing career will last forever. It won't if we keep doing silly things. Our chronic injuries may last forever though.

Snatching Defeat from the Jaws of Victory

The best description I've heard of this unthinking self-sabotage is "snatching defeat from the jaws of victory." Don't do it! Use your brains.

One of our athletes, young Navin Arunasalam, managed to find his own unique way to miss a state title, without any input from us at all! As a 16-year-old, he'd run a blinder in his heats of the U-18 state 800m, winning in a PB of 1:53.29. He was "pumped" after this terrific run. His father was at work and as the night was very young, and it was a summer Saturday in Melbourne, Navin and his brother Reuben decided to walk down to the riverside cafes of Southbank and bask in his accomplishment. He certainly had the conditioning to repeat his time the next day.

They walked and they walked, and got hungry, and it was 10 pm before Navin caught up with his family and had a meal. No real cool-down, no rub-down or spa, just walking on concrete.

The next day in his final, Navin accelerated away from his rivals with 300m to go...from off the back of the pack, and ended up with about 1:58. He'll never do that again!

One Story for the Road....

While I write this, I recall a particular run done by John Meagher and Brad Camp, years ago, in the weeks before Australia's annual Zatopek 10,000m classic. Brad, a 2:10 marathoner and near-record City to Surf winner, was looking to get a good 10,000m time on the board before returning to the marathon. John, with a 2:16 debut marathon time to his credit, was looking at getting his time down to around 2:13, which seemed a realistic goal.

They both hammered each other around a favorite very hilly course of 18 miles. From memory, they took a good 13 minutes off the best time recorded around the course. The result? I think Brad got injured before his race, and John ran over 33 minutes for 10,000m, slower than his marathon pace.

Part 19
Training for Longer Distances

5000m & 10000m Training

Whether an athlete specializes over 800m or marathon, the base endurance period will be virtually identical on the Lydiard system.

The purpose of the aerobic base for the middle distance runner is to INCREASE HIS CAPACITY TO DO MORE ANAEROBIC VOLUME, LATER, WITH FASTER RECOVERY.

The purpose of base conditioning for a marathoner is to INCREASE HIS CAPACITY TO DO MORE AEROBIC VOLUME AT HIGHER SPEEDS, WITH FASTER RECOVERY, and INCREASE UTILIZATION OF FATTY ACIDS, while CONSERVING GLYCOGEN STORES.

I have been asked often about the difference in final preparations for 5000m and 10000m to middle distance events. The 10000m, despite being twice the distance of the 5000m, is run at a speed only 4.3% slower.

Both of these events are predominantly aerobic, and have very similar energy system demands to each other, which is why there have been several Olympians over the years who have managed the "double" at one Olympics.

For these far more aerobic events, it is important that you stress the VO_2 work about once a week, and balance it out with some good leg-speed work and some sub-threshold running, and the other sessions would be all easier aerobic runs, of varying lengths.

Sub-threshold runs are extremely useful for building up aerobic capacity without tearing your glycogen stores down too much. You could include a sub-threshold ('3/4 effort' run somewhere each week in your training).

As you get naturally fitter, faster, and stronger, to really maximise your times it would be useful to regularly race 800m and 1500m distances on the track as well, but you could do this very well with just VO_2 max intervals on Tuesdays, leg-speed runs on Thursdays, and 800/1500 races on Saturdays.

These hints are useful for you as you attempt 5000 and 10000m distances. Hopefully you'll know all your heart rate training zones so you can control your efforts on your harder aerobic effort days.

1) Long EASY runs are maintained in-season, throughout early races, until about 2 weeks before THE major competition/peak race.

2) These long runs may be far more relaxed and quite a bit slower than during your base phase (i.e.: they can be 1 min/km slower and you will still get the aerobic/slow twitch Type I fiber stimulus you need).

   This is important because your more intense sessions during the week will tend to deplete your valuable glycogen stores, which we need for fast racing, and we want the aerobic running as easy, active recovery. Go for easy running time rather than distance.

3) One weekly session of VO_2 max type intervals, and one steady sub-threshold run (i.e.: 45min-60min S.T. inserted into an 80 minute run, when not racing).

4) Do an easy morning jog (6-8k) on your interval days (this will 'warm you up' for an evening interval session, and keep an aerobic stimulus present).

5) You need very little glycolytic work (i.e.: 300m-400m repetitions @ 800m/1500m pace) for 5000/10000m – it can be too anaerobic to yield a benefit for essentially aerobic-dominant events. In fact if you overdo 1500m/800m-type workouts, you could find your aerobic enzyme levels drop to compensate a bit. However, something like 8 x 400m @ 5000m race-pace might be fine, with 200m jog recovery.

6) I'd only do ONE 1500-type glycolytic workout in a leadup to a 5000, about 7-10 days out from the race, with plenty of aerobic running before and after, and only once you have successfully completed several weeks of the VO_2 work, AND seem to be improving well on it.

If you dig yourself into a little hole and feel more tired than you feel you should in the next days, just jog for an hour or so each day until fully recovered. It's better to be fresh and recovered and miss a planned harder session than to race tired or to 'over-reach' in training.

The 10000m is raced at a pace halfway between your VO_2 max and your anaerobic threshold. The 5000m is run at 95% of your VO_2 max. So for most of your leadup, you could get away with a strong set of intervals @ 5000m pace, with equal or shorter recovery. As you get to the last two weeks, you could make the intervals a bit faster, at 3000m pace (100% VO_2 max pace). You might do one less interval to cope with the increased intensity and recover well. To make this training fun, you could do it around a parkland loop, or on trails.

Your training doesn't have to take place on the track. IT IS ESSENTIAL THAT YOU TRAIN AT YOUR OWN LEVEL IN ANY INTERVAL WORKOUT; a little bit too fast, and you might harm your recovery. You get stronger in your good recovery time.

What Not to Do!

One of the guys in our training squad couldn't get it through his thick skull that his incredible ability to churn out very hard and fast 400s or 1000s on the training track was the same reason why he couldn't or wouldn't improve. His racing results were up and down like a "yo-yo"! This guy was doing anaerobic work two or three times a week that would deliver a sub 3:35 1500 to anyone else who had put in the appropriate steady aerobic volume, but he was so near his absolute limits in training that his racing was awful. This of course affected his psychology. Why did he do it? He said, "I need to run fast in training so that I feel I can race these guys!"

As a young athlete you DON'T have the luxury of making big training mistakes. Time flies before you know it, and the promising wunderkind can become very ordinary after several seasons of poor results and injury niggles.

Big Hints

It is EXTREMELY IMPORTANT that you match up your VO_2 work closely to your realistic 5000m time. The safest way to get in a decent volume of work that will push up VO_2 is to do your 2-3 minute intervals at YOUR 5000m pace. By now you will realize that your 5000m pace is 95% of your VO_2 max pace (3000m pace), so just believe me and we'll move on!

How to Put It Together

Here's a sample early-season week for someone wishing to sneak under 14:00 for 5000m: remember, these workouts are useful ONLY IF YOU HAVE DEVELOPED THE AEROBIC CAPACITY and have performed at a convincing level that indicates you can "take the next step". So for the athlete ready to break 14:00, a realistic session that he should be able to complete convincingly would be 5 x 1000m/ near equal time recovery at 13:45 pace.

Make Monday-Wednesday-Friday your easier running days year-round. Wednesday can always comprise longer "bread and butter" aerobic running in the recovery zones, and Monday can be shorter to recover from Saturday and Sunday. Friday can be an "active jogging rest" day prior to a solid Saturday & Sunday.

Mon:	1 hour easy jog
Tue:	**am:** 8k easy
	pm: w/up 3k easy. 10 x 'rolling start' 60m leg-speed runs, with 1-2 laps easy jog recovery. INTERVALS: 4 x 1000m @ 5k race pace (appx), 2:45 rec (i.e.: 1 every six minutes- easy to set watch).
Wed:	70-90 minutes very easy running on parkland/river trails/etc.
Thu:	**am:** 8k easy
	pm: w/up 3k easy. 10 x 'rolling start' 60m leg-speed runs, with 1-2 laps easy jog recovery. Then 30 minutes light, fun fartlek on parkland, in racing shoes or track shoes. Work efforts and recoveries to suit; make sure that the surges aren't too long or hard – they should be relaxed and fun. Then 15 minutes warm-down, easy.

Fri: **pm:** 1 hour easy jog.

Sat: **am:** 8k easy jog

          pm: RACE, or 80 minutes incl 45-60 mins @ sub-threshold pace (for this person: about 3:15 per km). The 80mins would include the warm-up, with the progressive easing into sub-threshold, and the cooling-down.

Sun: Long easy run 2hrs + .

Later on, you'd keep the easier days much the same, but would 'tweak' a couple of other energy systems in just to keep them all trained. So you might do your Saturday session as above, but raise the tempo to nearer your threshold, for a shorter duration. In the last weeks you may drop the long run by half an hour to freshen for your biggest races, but if you run easily and appropriately the long runs should just add to the race day strength, not detract.

You might also do time-trials just to iron out psychological flat spots, on a track, for 5000m or 100000m. These trials should be constant laps, and may be over one minute slower than your best (5000m) and 3 minutes slower for 10k. The key for time trials is rhythm, constancy, no real variation in lap times, and to train your concentration.

Final Preparation Weeks for the Marathon

In a Nutshell...

The Lydiard base (or build-up) is perfect for most of a marathon preparation, except that during the last 4 weeks, on a strong running day, we'd replace the sub-threshold runs with threshold (for a couple of weeks) and then if that's been successful, we'd just polish up VO_2 with a couple of VO_2 max sessions too. You'd gradually taper your long run miles over the last two weeks – NOT suddenly. On your effort days, you'd NEVER NEED to do any higher intensity than the first part of VO_2 max training (5k pace) above. Because of the low intensity requirements, you'd hop off the training pyramid before the 800m/1500m pace zones. The faster 5k pace work brings an element of efficiency and speed reserve to your marathon without blowing the barn doors off.

In slightly more detail

The regular Lydiard buildup as outlined in the book is fine for most of a marathon preparation. In the last 4 weeks, on your selected weekly stronger running day, we'd smoothly transition up a cog and replace the strong, fun sub-threshold 1 hour (marathon-pace/75% MHR) runs with threshold runs (15k race pace/85% MHR) for a couple of consecutive weeks.

The rest of the week would be much the same as a regular base week.

DON'T do the threshold runs for an hour – that's too long for most people: to get the effect you're after without knocking yourself around too much, try something like 20 mins w/up: 20 mins A.T. tempo: 20 mins cool-down. If you're particularly strong and coping with much higher easy mileage for the bulk of your training, you could add another burst of tempo to the session. The only rule here is to think of efforts above threshold as a little innoculation of what you need. If these efforts have been successful, we'd then just polish up VO_2 max to get you nicely efficient. For instance, a couple of VO_2 max sessions at a maximum intensity of 95% VO_2 max (5k race pace) i.e.: for a 15 minute 5k runner, 5 x 1000m @ 3:00/3:00 jog recovery (1 every 6 mins), OR 6 x 800m @ 2:24/2:36 recovery (1 every 5 mins). No need for anything more intense than that. KEEP THINGS SIMPLE!

NEVER do more than two tough workouts in a week leading into a distance race, unless you really like gambling! Assuming a limited 12-week programme, the last two weeks you'd taper GRADUALLY, by firstly cutting your longer runs of the week to 80% of that achieved by week 10, and the next week back to 60%. i.e.: your 20-mile (32k) run would become 16 miles, then the next week 12 miles (19k), before your race. If you suddenly taper by dropping long runs, you COULD experience undue fatigue – it happens commonly. So keep an EASY aerobic undercurrent going right till race day.

You should be able to train every day at a level that you know is repeatable, ad nauseam. You'd be better off by far to drop the short fast harder efforts, and replace them with constant steady long efforts of around 75% of your heart rate reserve, but well below your anaerobic threshold (usually around 85% HRR), which is right about 15k road race pace for a good distance athlete.

'Tempo runs' or 'threshold runs' have been lionized in recent years, but I totally disagree with the regular use of this type of training in an aerobic buildup. Running at threshold for any period is a bit like like hopping into a road race, and will ensure twin outcomes: glycogen depletion, and residual muscular fatigue, each time it is done. You want to BUILD UP your aerobic system and fatty acid utilization to stave off glycogen depletion as long as possible in a marathon. So keep any of that sort of intensity down to a relatively short duration that won't wipe you out.

With correctly done sub-threshold running, you're measurably increasing your aerobic ceiling so that what was previously 'anaerobic' now becomes 'aerobic', but you're also leaving the true aerobic zones behind in doing it. YOU CAN STEADILY RAISE YOUR ANAEROBIC THRESHOLD MUCH MORE SAFELY WITH SUB-THRESHOLD RUNS.

These runs are much the same as your marathon race pace. Good 'Marathon Conditioning' is as much about regular hour long runs at marathon pace as it is about very long runs. People often think that Lydiard conditioning is only about long slow runs. It isn't. It's about an intelligent steady increment of aerobic pace over many weeks in the hour runs, and naturally progressing from long slow Sunday runs to long faster Sunday runs – ALL IN COMFORT, then taking the pressure off the long run pace the last few weeks.

Anaerobic Threshold sessions are only a good thing to do once a huge aerobic base has been built, in specific sessions, which are preceded and followed by AMPLE low-intensity recovery running. These sessions should be safely spaced maybe a week or so apart, to allow for ample recovery, and carbohydrate and protein replacement should commence immediately after the session is completed. The idea is to steadily transition into the higher intensities safely without unhappy surprises, and gradually push your anaerobic threshold up 'from below' with Lydiard's time-proven constant 1 hour "3/4 effort" runs, (roughly 75% of maximum heart rate by the Karvonen method). This is all well-covered in the book on Page 54. These runs may be done once or twice a week in your build-up. This sub-threshold running is "magic" according to Kiwi marathon great and Lydiard pupil Barry Magee, and can be considered a "cornerstone" of a good aerobic build-up. Kiwi greats John Walker, Dick Quax and Rod Dixon used these runs as cornerstones for their extensive aerobic preparations for very long European track seasons.

If you're training too hard and feel a bit ordinary, it's possibly because your system is running in a mildly acidic environment (BAD!). For the regular runner who wants to check this, urine dipsticks available from the chemist are probably useful to ascertain if your operating system is running in an alkali or acid environment. I find diluted red grape juice is a very good alkali (diluted to be slightly weaker than isotonic with regard to sugars – usually 3:1 is about right), as well as (very surprisingly to me!) tomato juice or V8 vegetable juice. The latter is a terrific post-training recovery drink. Red grape juice is a rich source of potassium and the powerful antioxidant resveratrol.

Ideally you'd have 14 weeks from a good injury-free fitness base to your marathon.

How to Safely Reach Your Target Volume

Often athletes who claim that they "can't do mileage" are really saying that they can't slow their training pace enough to easily cope with mileage. Once in the regular habit of running long slow distances, as the weeks go by, the running naturally gets faster and faster and faster, all still at aerobic speeds, with the perceived effort being largely unchanged, but with the stopwatch telling the truth.

You'll have to gradually increase your volume runs by no more than 10% running time per week, taking it really easy, until your long ones are at least 2hr 30-40, and you can do TWO mid-week ones about 1hr 30. One way of doing this that's very good is to jog or plod for 30-60 minutes as slow as possible before running your normal medium or long run circuit. What'll happen is you'll finish with quite a long run, but the sensation that you've only really run your regular course at an easy effort. Distance doesn't kill, but speed does. The first slow part has to be around 60% MHR (Karvonen) to achieve the low-end aerobic effect desired. This will just perfuse your running muscles with lovely oxygen-rich blood in a mildly alkali environment – a perfect warm-up for higher aerobic levels without depleting glycogen stores.

In your build-up you want to start running controlled 1 hour runs at sub-threshold HR on a set course, trying to chip a couple of seconds off each time. You'll find the first few weeks of volume training are quite tiring, however once those mitochondria kick in you'll be off and away. Any additional easy aerobic activity (jogging, cycling, swimming) will help your overall efficiency.

After taking a few weeks to steadily reach your goal levels, your typical training week could look more like this: about 9.5 hours of aerobic training in your key sessions. Over a few years, you'd increase your pace and volume quite naturally.

DAY	MAIN SESSION
Mon	1hr run, EASY
Tue	1hr 30m STEADY
Wed	Light fartlek 1 hour incl 6-10 short sprints
Thu	1 hr 30m STEADY
Fri	1 hour EASY
Sat	1 hour 3/4 effort marathon pace
Sun	2 hr 30m

Lydiard training for the marathon therefore would be essentially the common base training period for (ideally) 10 weeks, introducing only a touch of anaerobic threshold (maybe one specific session a week: i.e.: warm-up 5k, AT 6k, cool-down 5k) for two consecutive weeks, then transitioning to 2 or 3 tightly controlled, evenly paced VO_2 max sessions (i.e.: 5 x 1000m @ 5000m pace/ equal or shorter recovery) a good week or so apart in the last few weeks. These sessions, combined with a weekly light fartlek session that includes several short relaxed sprints with ample recovery, done throughout the base period and continued through to the eve of the goal race, would train the essential energy systems enough to get the ideal outcome.

Try to do very easy medium-length aerobic runs on the day before and after tougher sessions.

You should do no hard or extended long runs in the last couple of weeks generally, and no more than two VO$_2$ sessions in a week. Any more in a week and you're dicing with marathon death. Then a controlled taper for the last 2 weeks.

Tapering

Your taper should be gradual, and not sudden. It's an odd thing, but many people who suddenly ease up on volume aerobic training complain of feeling sleepy and fatigued on marathon day. So whatever volume you've reached in daily runs on set days by week 10, you want to reduce to 80% in Week 11, and then 60% in marathon week leading up to race day. With aerobic training, it's essential that a certain volume or aerobic undercurrent is kept up to maintain the necessary oxidative enzyme levels and mitochondria, i.e.: if your Sunday long run is 20 miles, this becomes 16 miles the next week, then the next week 12 miles. Pretty obviously, all other run lengths and times would be cut down by the same amount!

We don't do any glycolytic/lactate tolerance training anywhere near a marathon or during base training. Those sessions are very intense, flooding the running muscles with highly acidic metabolites that soon force the exercise to cease due to the localized neuromuscular junctions going on strike. While absolutely necessary for a middle distance athlete's final preparation, the acidosis created has the distinct possibility of harming aerobic enzyme levels, glycogen and fatty acid utilization, and mitochondrial function at the expense of your marathon potential. VO$_2$ max intervals are far longer and far less intense, (i.e.: 1000m intervals @ 5000m pace/ equal time recovery or shorter) and are much safer and more useful coming into your absolute final phase.

For a 15 min 5000m runner this could be something like 5 x 1000m on the road @ 3:00/3:00 active jog recovery, preferably on a non-cambered asphalt road surface. Really, your estimated 5000m race pace (95% of absolute VO$_2$ max pace) is the safest to develop VO$_2$ max without overdoing things. Anaerobic training is like playing with matches for a marathoner.

These controlled VO$_2$ interval sessions will top up the final anaerobic contribution to VO$_2$ max, and thereby increase efficiency at any of the aerobic, sub-threshold, or threshold speeds, but they've got to be sparingly introduced AFTER those lower systems have been trained.

It's an idea to have sufficiently trained each of the energy systems most related to your event in the preceding weeks to your goal race.

What's Going on in There?

The body will adapt to anything you consistently ask it to do. With prolonged high-aerobic efforts, the resting heart rate can drop markedly with the left ventricle becoming larger, and its muscular walls becoming thicker and more powerful. (This is effectively like training up a much more powerful pump).

Every high-pressure heart beat delivers far more blood, far further, into an ever-increasing network of low-pressure web-like capillaries. Because there are now so many very fine blood vessels developing into muscle beds that have been exposed to constant perfusion, the flow rate and pressure of the oxygen-rich blood is lowered exponentially, thereby allowing the red blood cells exponentially more time to deliver their payload to an ever-increasing surface area of working muscle cells.

More oxygen and fuel can be delivered to far more muscle cells, and the resultant metabolites can be flushed away back to the liver more quickly. Eventually very long runs become like a pleasant "walk in the park" where you can play tourist as you cover favourite courses. One can almost dissociate from one's body on long runs as it becomes a long, smooth ride. This is the type of fitness you want to take into the final weeks of a marathon preparation, at your own level.

The long running becomes continually easier because the muscles develop very fine networks of capillaries that can perfuse and deliver oxygen and fuel-rich blood "right to the doorstep" of the muscle cells. A network of finer and finer blood vessels courses throughout the working muscle over time. Oxygen and fuels are ideally delivered to an actively working muscle cell across its semi-permeable cell wall. Muscle cells that don't have any direct capillarization have to obtain their nutrients second-hand, or delve into anaerobic metabolism because they haven't received the necessary oxygen. An untrained muscle will generally have the usual major arteries, merging with finer arteriole beds, then merging further with a relatively small bed of even finer capillaries. Each capillary may have to be accessed and shared by several muscle cells initially, but biopsies of muscles that have been extensively trained aerobically show that the surface area of muscle cells experiencing direct capillarization can increase vastly.

An example from nature of what I am describing is the leg muscle of one of the most aerobically fit creatures on the planet – the kangaroo. This meat is almost "spongy" on first inspection, but if you look very closely you will see that it is traversed by many very fine capillaries; many more than in meats from relatively sedentary farm-raised livestock like beef cattle.

Initially in building your marathon base, you want to run long enough, about once a week, until you achieve the "tired heavy legs" stage (this represents glycogen depletion) and then run a few more miles like that, forcing your body to respond over time by utilising a higher ratio of fatty acids. Initially this "tired, heavy legs" response may kick in quite early if you're not used to decent long runs regularly. However, as you respond, it will be entirely possible to run for over 2hrs 30 at a good clip, without undue fatigue over the last few miles.

The thing NOT to do in training, especially on long runs over 2 hours, is to carbo-load with something like a power-bar or gu-gel. Many distance runners these days do that, and think it's great because they finish their training runs with that extra shot of 'juice' in the system, then wonder why they crash badly in the marathon. HOWEVER, at marathon race pace, it's all about conserving our limited glycogen stores and becoming very effective at utilizing our ample fatty acid stores.

If you want to go as far and as long as possible without hitting the wall, you must have THREE things going for you:

1. A trained ability to utilize a blend of ('unlimited') fatty acids and ('limited') carbohydrates for long periods at high aerobic levels, thereby conserving glycogen (high energy) stores for the business end of your race.

2. Sufficient hydration of the muscles to allow access to the stored glycogen. Glycogen is really an endless starchy chain of glucose molecules. It needs about twice its volume in accessible H_2O to be metabolized. So a marathoner who is ready to race will often be slightly heavier than normal.

3. The patience to start slightly slower than your intended race pace, so as to spare glycogen and come home full of running. The marathon doesn't 'start' till the 20 mile/32km mark, so go steadily till then.

The traditional "wall" that marathoners hit at around 20 miles represents the final unloading of glycogen stores from the type IIA fatigue-resistant (aerobic) fast twitch fibers as they are sequentially recruited while the slow twitch fibers have exhausted their work capacity.

HOWEVER, if one has trained the fatty acid system properly by many weeks of long runs to depletion, BY ALL MEANS use a carbohydrate gel in the last few kilometers of a race (but test it out in training at least once on one of your weekly long runs!).

Finally

We'll leave it at that for now. Hopefully you now understand more about the way Arthur Lydiard approached things and perhaps will be able to apply it to your own training or coaching.

We haven't talked about the psychology of racing, but I'll finish with a few words that Barry Magee spoke at Arthur Lydiard's funeral. Barry once said that he was more afraid of Lydiard than any potential rival. When there's a sure foundation and certainty, the human spirit will do the rest. So here, from Barry, is a taste of Lydiard's psychology: it's a great example for coaches and athletes.

From Barry Magee

What a life! What a man! On December 12, 2004, New Zealand lost one of our greatest treasures. Arthur Leslie Lydiard passed on to his higher reward. The world has lost a very caring and wonderful person. The world of sport and particularly running has lost someone far greater; it has lost a genius of coaching and motivation, the inspiration for thousands of athletes and millions of joggers. Personally, I have lost a friend and father figure.

What was it that made Lydiard different, that made him a maker of history? Often I wonder what this man possessed that from modest beginnings he could turn someone like me into an Olympic medalist and world-ranked athlete? It started in 1952, when I was 18. I had been running for three years with Wesley Harrier Club, guided by a sound and sensible club captain in Gil Edwards. I had enjoyed a successful season, but one day after winning a junior road race in Hamilton, Gil sat me down for a chat. "Barry," he said, "I think you have quite a lot of potential, and I am not sure if I am the one to develop it. But I know who can."

Gil introduced me to a small man with a hawk-like face who spoke in short, abrupt sentences while fixing me with a piercing stare. Gil told the man he thought I could develop well and asked whether he'd take over my training. Those piercing eyes looked right through me as he said, "Son, are you prepared to run 100 miles per week? If not, just tell me, because you would be wasting your time and mine."

I must have stuttered out the word yes, because the next morning I arrived at the home of Arthur Lydiard to get my first training schedule. Much has been written of Lydiard and his training methods. But like the man himself, what he gave me was straightforward. Two months of 100 miles a week which, while termed marathon conditioning, he made everyone do. After that came four weeks of resistance work that included a lot of hill springing with downhill striding and gradual implementations of reps, but still close to 100 miles a week. This was followed by 12 weeks where we mixed long runs with track training, time trials, reps, fartlek, sharpening sessions and races to arrive at a peak for the major goal. Eight years later, I won an Olympic bronze medal in the marathon.

This man changed my life. He spoke with such confidence and authority that I never doubted any word he said. He was a trailblazer, and today I still look back with amazement and admiration at how he totally changed the way the world approached running, sport and fitness. His training brought me an incredible confidence in my fitness and ability, and with his inspirational, motivational and believable manner, when Arthur Lydiard told me I could win a race, I knew I could.

I never doubted Lydiard's word. I remember in 1960 I received an invitation to run in Japan's prestigious Fukuoka International Marathon, an event that is often harder to win than the Olympics. Fukuoka was the first week in December, but I had already been away for six weeks at the Rome Olympics. December was the busiest time of the year for me as a grocer, and as a married man with two children to support, the last thing I needed was more time away. I thought it only fair to tell Arthur about my decision to decline the invitation, so I told my wife I'd be back in half an hour and drove around to Arthur's house. Two hours later I arrived back home to tell my wife that I was going to Japan!

I am not sure if I got a word in at Arthur's place that night. His opening sentence was, "Barry, you are going to be the first New Zealander to win an international marathon. You can do this for every marathon and distance runner in New Zealand. This is an opportunity that you cannot let pass. You go and win it." So I went, and I won!

This ability to make people believe in themselves helped me and others follow his arduous training regimes. I did whatever Arthur asked of me. Twice, at 19 and 20, I did a 30-mile run because Arthur said to. On another occasion, I ran from Mt. Roskill to Pokeno – 35 miles in four hours! Once he merely suggested I run the Auckland to Hamilton 80-mile relay on a two-man team, so I did.

As a coach he had incredible insight. After a national track championships one year, I was feeling weak, tired, and worn out from the summer of racing and training. I told Arthur how I felt and his immediate response was, "Barry, go and run three consecutive Waiataruas next week." Anyone who has followed the legend of Lydiard will know that the Waiatarua run is a very tough 22-mile course around the back blocks of Auckland. Usually we ran it once a week on a Sunday, but this time I did it three days in a row, and two weeks later I ran a tremendous road race in Tauranga as a revitalized runner. That was Arthur Lydiard.

He was a man of incredible insight and determination, but one who didn't suffer fools. He could be fiery and at times had a short fuse. One day while jogging home from cross country training around a muddy course in Owairaka, we ran past a fish and chip shop where a group of loud-mouthed teenagers took great delight in commenting sarcastically on the bedraggled appearance of the runners. This was reasonably common in the '60s, and normally we ignored it. But this time Lydiard suddenly turned and ran back to them, wiping a muddy running shoe several times across the face of one of them while letting the others know exactly what he thought of them.

Yes, Lydiard was fiery, but that fire changed the world. Yes, he made and nurtured Olympic medalists and world-record breakers, but the measure of this man could be seen in his willingness to help anyone of any ability achieve a quality of life they had never dreamed possible. He gave everybody the same time he would give Peter Snell, Murray Halberg, or me. He produced champions, but he was also the first to encourage people to run for health, fitness and fun.

Barry Magee and Colin Livingstone give Arthur the "Thumbs Up" (UK, 2006)

BIBLIOGRAPHY

The following titles have all been read and enjoyed by the author over the years and include some classic texts. As this book is just my particular contribution to the literature, I recommend that all coaches and athletes read as much as they can get hold of and not limit themselves purely to running books. I have learned a great deal by reading research and texts relating to strength conditioning, cycling, swimming, and multi-sports.

Perhaps the "encyclopedia" of all running books is the wonderful *Lore of Running* by Dr. Tim Noakes, which has a great deal of practical information and history. This stands alone in my opinion as a "classic" that should be on every coach's bookshelf, as a lovingly researched book that encompasses history, physiology, training methods, and far more.

If you can get hold of them, the classic Lydiard books co-authored by Garth Gilmour are well worth reading, especially *Run to the Top*, *A Clean Pair of Heels*, and *No Bugles, No Drums*. These last two with Sir Murray Halberg, 1960 Olympic 5000m champion, and Dr Peter Snell, three-time Olympic champion, will still inspire modern-day athletes to get out and run. *Kiwis Can Fly* by Ivan Agnew got a generation of schoolboys out running in 1976. In recent years, the late Ron Daws wrote *Running Your Best*, which was a terrific Lydiard book. The Herb Elliott and Percy Cerutty classics are great to read before a big race, and one wonders what these two men could have achieved in the modern era. The books on distance greats Paul Tergat, Haile Gebrselassie, and Ron Clarke are very inspiring and illuminating.

For a more complete understanding and sensible application of good physiological principles, the books by Pete Pfitzinger and Dr. Jack Daniels are excellent. I personally got a lot out of Dr. Dave Costill's small 1979 classic *A Scientific Approach to Distance Running*, as well as Dr. Peter Janssen's 1987 book *Training Lactate Pulse-Rate*.

In addition to the bibliography, I have included referenced research papers mentioned in specific parts of the book and some further resources.

Keith Livingstone

Title	Author	Publisher	Year
A Clean Pair Of Heels- The Murray Halberg Story	Gilmour, Garth	AH & AW Reed	1963
A Scientific Approach to Distance Running	Costill, David	TAFNEWS Press	1979
Advanced Marathoning	Pfitzinger/Douglas	Human Kinetics	2001
Alberto Salazar's Guide to Road Racing	Salazar, A; Lovett, Richar	McGraw Hill	2003
Arthur Lydiard Master Coach	Gilmour, Garth	Exile Publishing	2004
Athletics How to Become a Champion	Cerutty, Percy	Stanley Paul	1962
Computerized Training Programs	Gardner, J.B; Purdy, Gerry J.	TAFNEWS Press	1970
Daniels' Running Formula	Daniels, Jack, PhD	Human Kinetics	2005
Encyclopedia of Track and Field	Rizzoli Editori	Prentice Hall Press	1986
Everyone Is an Athlete	Maffetone, Phillip, Dr	David Barmore Prodns	1990
Exercise Physiology	Clarke, David H	Prentice Hall Press	1975
Fitness Cycling	Barry, D; Barry, M; Sovendal, S	Human Kinetics	2006
Franz Stampfl on Running	Stampfl, Franz	Herbert Jenkins	1960
Get Carter: The Hamish Carter Story	Taylor, Phil	Hodder Moa	2007
High-Performance Cycling	Jeukendrup, A E	Human Kinetics	2002
It's Not About the Bike	Lance Armstrong	Allen & Unwin	2000
John Walker Champion	Palenski, Ron	Moa Publications	1984
Kiwis Can Fly	Agnew, Ivan	Marketforce Auckland	1976
Lore Of Running	Noakes, Tim MD	Leisure Press	1991
Marathoning	Steffny,Manfred	World Publications, Inc	1979
Middle Distances	Jarver, Jess	TAFNEWS Press	1979
New Exercises for Runners	Runners' World Editors	World Publications, Inc	1978
New Views of Speed Training	Runners' World Editors	Runners' World	1971
No Bugles, No Drums	Snell, Peter; Gilmour, Garth	Minerva	1965
On the Wings of Mercury	Moller, Lorraine	Longacre	2007
Optimum Sports Nutrition	Colgan, Michael, Dr	Advanced Research	1993
Paul Tergat Running to the Limit	Wirz, Jürg	Meyer & Meyer Sport	2005
Peter Snell, From Olympian to Scientist	Snell, Peter; Gilmour, Garth	Penguin	2007
Precision Training	Ackland, Jon	Reed	1998
Ron Clarke Talks Track	Hendershot, John	TAFNEWS Press	1972
Run Like You Stole Something	Farrow, Damien; Kemp, Justin	Allen & Unwin	2003
Run Strong	Beck, Kevin	Human Kinetics	2005
Run the Lydiard Way	Lydiard, Arthur; Gilmour, Garth	Hodder and Stoughton	1978

Run to The Top	Lydiard, Arthur; Gilmour, Garth	AH & AW Reed	1963
Run To Win: Training Secrets of Kenyan Runners	Wirz, Jurg	Meyer & Meyer Sport	2006
Run With The Best	Benson, Tony; Ray, Irv	TAFNEWS Press	2001
Runners and Races: 1500m./Mile	Nelson, Cordner; Quercetani, R	TAFNEWS Press	1973
Running For Peak Performance	Shorter, Frank	DK Books	2005
Running Free	Coe, Sebastian; Miller, David	Sidgwick & Jackson	1981
Running to the Top	Clayton, Derek	Anderson World, Inc	1980
Running With The Legends	Sandrock, Michael	Human Kinetics	1996
Running Your Best	Daws, Ron	Stephen Green Press	1985
Schoolboy Athletics	Cerutty, Percy	Stanley Paul	1963
Scott Tinley's Winning Guide to Sports Endurance	Tinley, Scott	Kangaroo Press	1994
Serious Runner's Handbook	Osler, Tom	World Publications, Inc	1978
Strategies of The Champions	Peterson, Vicki	Pan Books	1988
Strength Training Anatomy	Delavier, F	Human Kinetics	2006
Strength Training-NSCA	Brown, Lee E.	Human Kinetics	2007
Tear Along The Dotted Line	Alcorn, Roger	Alcorn	1987
The Complete Runner	Runners' World Editors	Avon Books	1978
The Golden Mile	Elliott, H; Trengove, J	Cassell	1961
The Greatest: The Haile Gebrselassie Story	Denison, Jim	Breakaway Books	2004
The Marathon	Hopkins, John	Stanley Paul	1966
The New Aerobics	Cooper, Kenneth H.	Bantam Books	1976
The Runners' Essential Guide	Frank, Bob; Frecknall, Trevor	Today's Runner	1995
The Unforgiving Minute	Clarke, Ron: Trengrove, Alan	Pelham Books	1966
Train Tough	Webber, Jason	ABC Books	2005
Training Distance Runners	Martin, David E.; Coe, Peter	Leisure Press	1991
Training Lactate Pulse-Rate	Janssen, Peter	Polar Electro Oy	1987
Training Techniques for Cyclists	Hewitt, Ben	Rodale Inc	2005
Triathlon into the Nineties	Cedaro, Rod	Murray Child and Co	1993
Why Dick Fosbury Flopped	Farrow, Damien; Kemp, Justin	Allen & Unwin	2006

Index

ONLINE RESOURCES

ANY QUERIES?

- To purchase signed copies of this title or to contact the author with any detailed questions ...
  www...
- TO ... or ... range of Meyer & Meyer titles sh...n below. ... on overdue... to w... on a weekly b..., or part ther...

There ... 07. DEC 15. ... t will help you unde...

- 1 2 APR 2019

- 29 JUL 2019 ·g ·sults. For more n the USA:

- 2 AUG 2019 tion:

- chanics, and all ne advice.

-

Photo & Illustration Credits

Cover photos:	Neil MacDonald, fotolia
Cover design:	Sabine Groten
Other photos:	Colin Livingstone, Chester Livingstone, Diana Mills, Gavin Harris, Barry Magee, John Meagher, Sue Coloe, Tim Crosbie, Daniel Dineen, Keith Livingstone, Trevor Vincent, Tim Chamberlain, Barry Ross, Chris Pilone, Robbie Johnston
	Polar Electro GmbH (p. 28, 140, 142, 171, 193, 199)
Illustrations & Cartoons:	Colin Livingstone (dreamtree.co.uk),
	Keith Livingstone (graphs)